Dear Jermey !
Thank you for
this world a be
this place, brot
♡ *Daisy*

Juxtaposed

Finding Sanctuary on the Outside

Daisy Rain Martin

Dear Cherise,
Hope, Health, &
Happiness to you always!
I love you !
♡ *Daisy Rain*
Martin
Zeph 3:17

Christopher Matthews Publishing

www.christophermatthewspub.com
Bozeman, Montana

daisyrainmartin.com

Juxtaposed

Editors: Dr. Donna K. Wallace and Jeremy Soldevilla
Cover design: Armen Kojoyian
Cover photo: Tammy Williams, Charming Impressions Photography
Typeface: Garamond

ISBN: 978-0-9852431-2-8

Published by
CHRISTOPHER MATTHEWS PUBLISHING
http://christophermatthewspub.com
Bozeman, Montana

Printed in the United States of America

Dear Readers,

This book is the story of my life, my challenges and successes, and it includes various facts and anecdotes about the people who shaped me into the person I am today. No false statements of fact about any living or deceased individual have been knowingly or negligently cited herein. For facts I did not personally witness, I still carefully considered all reasonable grounds for believing the truth of all statements included.

Matters concerning the private lives of others were herein cited because they are of legitimate concern to the public, even if considered highly offensive to the individuals herein mentioned. Furthermore, certain names have been changed to protect the privacy of those involved, as I never intended to offend anyone.

The opinions expressed in this book do not reflect the views and opinions of any one of my employers, past, present or future. This book is a personal reflection on my own journey and the ideas expressed within these pages are mine alone.

Finally, this book is unsuitable for minors, especially my students. By reading it, the reader agrees that he or she is over the age of eighteen and that he or she will take necessary precautions to keep this book away from children's reach.

— Daisy Rain Martin

For Tabitha who now knows as she is fully known...

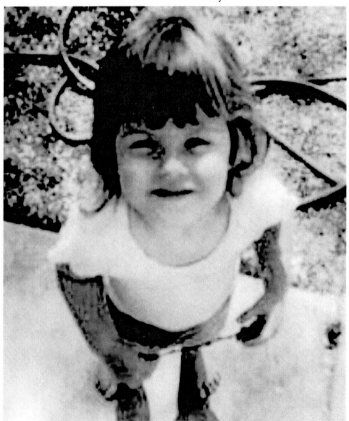

...I'm sorry for what I said.

Acknowledgments

With Soul-felt thanks…

Amidst all the laughter, all the heartache, I have not been alone on this journey, and there are several people I would like to thank:

Grandpa Ben and Grandma Polly, you were the sanity of my childhood, and will always be the brightest lights of my life. Thank you for teaching me what it is to love and how to be happy.

Grandma Jean, I am so grateful to you for all the bountiful love you lavished on us. The world is grateful for your gift of music, and I am thrilled to have been lucky enough to grow up in the wake of your legacy. Thank you for giving me a voice and for teaching me what it is to be ambitious and believe in myself.

Dad, (Donald Eugene Lofton) thank you for providing the answers to all my questions, for clarity, and for teaching me who I am and where I came from.

Randy and Pam Greer, you have always offered this wild child a safe place to land. You delighted in me and somehow convinced me that God did too. It changed my life. Thank you for teaching me that sanctuary can, indeed, be found on this earth.

Dean and Jenell Sanner, I have run to you in my darkest times, and you have always sheltered me. You've held my hand and my heart through the toughest decisions and the most devastating grief. Thank you for teaching me that joy surely comes in the morning.

Rob Lee, you provided a pivotal moment on my journey by showing kindness when all I had was rage, and my life was never the same after that. Thank you and Debi for continuing to show that same kindness to the world, and thank you for teaching me that God's grace trumps man's answers any day.

To the professors and faculty at Vanguard University, especially Noel Wilson, Dr. Phil Robinette, Dr. Vince Gil and Virgil and Donna Ziegler, you showed me for the first time, a Godliness that was untainted. You exposed the fraud and introduced me to the real Jesus. Thank you for teaching me to be still and know that He is God.

To the most supportive writers' group in the Northwest, the Ink Slingers of Bozeman, Montana, I thank you for allowing me to pop in and pop out. Your friendships, as well as your advice, your laughter and your stories are so very dear to me.

Jeremy Soldevilla, I am so grateful for your belief in me. There is no one else I would rather have traveling with me on this journey. Thank you for your guidance and profound patience. Thank you and Melissa for laughing at me in all the right places. If and when you jump off that ledge into the Great Unknown, let me know. I'm liable to follow.

To the Farless/Stevens clan, you helped heal me. I have always been yours even before the beginning of time, and you were mine. Thank you for embracing me as your own. I could not have landed in safer hands.

My Geoff, you are and always will be the joy of my whole life. You are my Heaven on earth. You have helped the most in my healing. Thank you for showing me such grace and for teaching me the infinite and effortless love of God.

Sean-Martin, you are a treasure. Lord knows it's not just any man who could be married to me. Having this family with you is a spring of Living Water that flows up from my soul. I have a life now that is beyond anything I could have ever imagined. Thank you for breathing life into some of my old theology and continually teaching me new and fresh ways to see God.

And, finally, my Donna K. Wallace. You, my sweet princess, are the best "baby daddy" I could have ever wanted for each of my books. You are not just my editor—you are my book architect, and this work would never have been completed without your talent, your wisdom, and your mad skills. You have played an integral role in my own spiritual formation, and I don't know who I would be without your fingerprints on my life. Thank you for teaching me to write well, to live well, and to love well.

Chapter 1

Vegas, Baby!

PEOPLE OFTEN SPEAK of their childhood memories in a way that seems attached to the place they are from. I have childhood memories. But I can't say that they're particularly attached to my friends and neighbors. I mean, the thought of growing up with one group of friends for my whole childhood and still being in touch with those people to this day is really something that I thought only happened on TV. That's the only "place" I ever saw it happen. In a city like Las Vegas, people move in and out all the time. I moved. Often. I certainly don't have these feelings of nostalgia that others have who are not from here.

You hear people say, "Remember when we all used to play stick ball in the alley behind the Piggly Wiggly?"

I don't say that.

Or, "Don't you miss those cinnamon rolls we used to get after school at Grandma Rosie's?" I don't say that either. I didn't climb any water towers. I can't remember the kids I hung out with in junior high or high school. And my grandmother did not live in a little cottage on a quiet hillside with ivy growing green and thick up the side of a brick, smoking chimney. Nope. Her kitchen did not smell of cinnamon or chocolate, so you wouldn't find my brother, sister, nor I scurrying in to see what kind of delicious goodies she had just taken out of the oven.

My maternal grandmother traveled the world and managed music groups. Now *that's* Vegas, baby! And like Lady Vegas, my jet-setting Grandma, Jean Bennett, never stops. She is the quintessential glamour girl who, in many ways, embodies Lady Vegas herself, and I'm proud to call her mine. She never sleeps. She is every brilliant, flashing light in the marquis, all the bells and whistles of the casinos, pouring out lavishly to her visitors, and always the consummate hostess.

In fact, you would say that my grandma is hot. Well into her 80s, she's spunky, ambitious, and always looking for the next big opportunity. Grandma Jean didn't have time for a husband and if there's ivy growing up the side of her house, she can't be bothered with it. Hell, the closest she gets to being bothered with foliage is when she tosses it for dinner. The woman eats salad. Lots of it. She drinks orange juice every day and lives on roughage. She reads biographies, loves the Clintons, and still insists on putting in a good eight hours of work a day. Most of all, she loves show business.

The glitz and the lights have always been my grandmother's Holy Grail, and her quest to drink from that chalice has lasted more than 80 years. She wanted to be famous, make a lot of money and sing on stages all over the world. Much of her youth was spent winning singing contests and auditioning for the lead roles in plays. The fame she garnered from her small Midwestern town, however, would never satiate her longing to be known the world wide, and her eyes were on Hollywood. Her father wouldn't even let her attend school an hour away, let alone chase her dreams to Southern California.

It didn't help matters that she pined for the glamorous life of her cousin— silver screen star, Lana Turner. Lana and Jean shared grandparents and spent time together on the Turner farm where Lana was known as Julia Jean. When Lana allegedly skipped school one day and was "discovered" at Schwab's (although our family's version of events always named the place as the Top Hot Café), my grandmother was inspired. She made the decision to skip her classes for the entire day at Joiner's Business College, in cahoots with her resourceful mother and completely unbeknownst to her overprotective father. She took the bus and applied for a job with the Red Cross, about thirty miles away from her home.

A huge army base was being built, and she wanted to spread her wings in a place that didn't stifle, didn't confine. Her charm garnered the job she'd come for, but she had her eye on something else. She inquired at the base as to whether or not they would need entertainment for any upcoming events they might be having. In fact, there was a soldier whose birthday it was, and they were looking for someone to entertain for that party. My grandmother was thrilled to be on any stage for any audience for any reason. That soldier was smitten with his lady singer, so he decided to become my grandfather.

After the war, the couple moved to Hollywood with their daughter, my mother, so that my grandmother could pursue her singing career. Advised that she needed to "pound the pavement," she began on one end of Sunset Boulevard and didn't stop knocking on doors until she got very near the end. It seemed no one wanted her to sing—they only wanted to know what she had to wear and whether or not she had musical arrangements. Finally, she stopped into an office where she recited once again her worn and weary shtick—*is there anyone who will listen to me sing?*

She was told, "There's a guy in the back office who handles some acts. Go see him."

"Hello?" she called out after peeking through the door. A very flustered gentleman popped out from behind a filing cabinet. That very flustered gentleman was all by himself in that tiny space with papers and lead sheets and clutter. She found that he would, indeed, listen to her sing, and he found out that she had, indeed, been to business school. Jean got him organized, and the flustered gentleman paved the way for her career in show business. Kismet.

The gentleman turned out to be none other than one of the industry's top songwriters. I'll call him "Sam." He managed, produced, wrote and arranged music for the top groups of the fifties and sixties. He worked with Ike and Tina Turner, Duke Ellington, Glenn Miller and Ella Fitzgerald.

The Platters' first hit, *Only You*, became a hit in part because of my grandmother. Not long after she'd started working with the songwriter, she came across the lead sheet to the song. She pulled it out of a dusty box on a dusty shelf in his dusty garage. She looked the music over and thought the words were compelling enough to bring it in to where he was working.

It was a song Sam had written originally for the Ink Spots. He had never pitched it to them and had forgotten all about it until my grandmother shook it out and held it under his nose.

From 1955 onward and upward, my grandmother's life was the whirlwind into which I was born. Although she never quite acquired the fame she sought as a young singer herself, she saw to it that many talented musicians made their way to worldwide fame. She made other people's dreams come true and stood backstage instead of actually being *on* the stage. I have asked her if she has any regrets regarding her life, and, without a thought, she says, "Heavens, no! I've lived a great life! I wouldn't change a thing!"

Grandma Jean and Sam simultaneously ran offices in Los Angeles, Chicago and New York. In 1964, however, she closed up shop in America's traditional hotspots and set up her home office in what was quickly becoming America's up and coming hotspot: Las Vegas. It was *the* place to be.

Not to mention, she got a killer deal on the house.

The house where I spent most of my childhood was a huge, ranch-style spread, which sat regally on a full acre in one of the classiest sections of town. The sunshine twinkled on the dazzling, glittered-white brick exterior in stark contrast to the red, Spanish-tiled roof. The peanut-shaped swimming pool sparkled perpetually. The lawn was manicured exquisitely. The trees were always trimmed, the flowers poured out of their beds three out of four seasons. The property and all the vehicles were immaculately maintained.

And what dream team executed all of this? How many people did my grandmother employ to maintain this gorgeous property? Just one—my grandfather—her ex-husband. Their marriage didn't survive my grandmother's pursuit of fame or her indelicate relationship with Sam, but, thankfully, their friendship astonishingly did. It may seem strange to some that my grandmother employed her ex-husband to be her tour manager, groundskeeper, mechanic, carpenter and handyman, but that's exactly what she did. But I can even one-up that one: My grandfather's wife, Polly, kept the books. Yes, as crazy as it sounds, my grandmother's ex-husband's wife handled her money. A recipe for disaster in other people's families, however, it was perfectly normal in mine. We kids didn't think twice about my grandfather's two wives under the same roof.

They all got along famously.

My Grandma Polly was, in many ways, the polar opposite of my Grandma Jean. Jean had a rock-star personality and was bigger than life. She was not domestic in any sense of the word and would just as soon rack up as many frequent-flyer miles as she could and rub elbows with celebrities in some exotic new place she'd never been. Polly was humble and sweet, nurturing and unassuming, and apologized for every dish she put in front of us.

"This is such a mistake!" she lamented, asking forgiveness for every crumb. Maybe it was her cooking that she confessed behind the curtain at her Greek Orthodox Church. Lord knows she never committed any other sin in her sweet and innocent life. She would cry, "Such a shame, this meal! These cookies are an atrocity! You don't even have to eat this—I'd understand if you didn't!" Of course, what she was really looking for was for us to lavish her with laud and praise for her every effort. And we did. I guess that's how it was done in her home country. Her self-deprecation was every bit a part of her DNA as her sweetness and her humor.

Thus were spent our summers and weekends and holidays. Between Grandma Jean providing this Cornucopia, this horn of plenty which bankrolled everything—with Grandpa Ben and Grandma Polly doing all the legwork, this triad gave us the kind of childhood that anyone would be jealous of. They truly illuminated our lives with their resplendent radiance.

Still the shadows fell.

There was little any one of the three of them could do to exorcise the scary juju that seemed to hover over the house itself that sometimes had me looking over my shoulders. Something amiss seemed to float through the many rooms that could not be identified or explained. I'm not going to say that the place is outright haunted, *per se*. I've never seen an actual apparition or anything, but that house has always had some very unsettling mojo attached to it. It's as if a particular darkness looms, hovers, settles… moves.

Follows.

So, although I have fond memories of spending the bulk of my childhood on that property, I was also slightly disconcerted at times when I was there. I find it twisted and freaky that the setting for every nightmare I've ever had in all of my years on this earth has been that house. That's not to say I was always sleeping at my grandmother's house whenever I had a bad dream. I mean that whenever or wherever I've had a nightmare, that house is *always* where I am in my dream. Without exception. When I dreamed that my little brother caught on fire, he was standing in my grandmother's kitchen. When I dreamed that killer bees were covering the house and swarming in to sting me, I was standing in her living room looking out into her front yard seeing the blasted creatures filling up the gargantuan front window. I dreamed once that the Devil flew out at me from her fireplace. I can't remember having a nightmare where I was any place other than that house.

My Grandma Jean, however, thinks I'm nuts, which doesn't surprise me. She just laughs and waves off my reluctance to sleep in her master bedroom or my preference to sit by the pool instead of at the kitchen table. What does she know about it? She never sleeps anyway and doesn't have time to sit by the pool or anywhere else for that matter.

She loves that house and will never, ever leave it.

"I got the deal of the century on this house!" she defends herself.

Yes, Grandma. Let's chew on that for a while! Why do you think that was?

The woman who owned the house before her was also a pretty savvy businesswoman, although not in quite the same enchanting way as my grandmother, and gave the home a different brand of notoriety from the kind my grandmother brought to it. The previous owner had a certain business arrangement with a doctor who performed abortions—an illegal procedure back in those days. For every referral she sent him, she received a kickback. Girls who found themselves in the predicament of an unintended pregnancy stayed there in the house while they waited for, received and recovered from illegal abortions. The house has six rooms where girls could be double-bunked, as well as a huge living room, three bathrooms, a monstrous kitchen and an enclosed back porch that runs the length of the entire house. Beyond that, a gargantuan stone porch extended into a gorgeous back yard, pooled and treed and spacious.

The place was palatial.

The woman shared all this with her live-in boyfriend. They seemed to have the world by the tail. The allure of the Vegas nightlife beckoned the young lady to try her luck down on the Strip—without him. Her lover began to suspect she was having an affair, so he followed her one night through the glimmering lights to the Frontier Hotel. There he was easily lost in the crowd of gamblers and partiers playing slots, throwing dice and tossing back drinks. The haze of smoke loomed as he stood in the shadows of the casino floor and witnessed, indeed, her lascivious rendezvous first hand. Seeing all he needed, he returned to her lavish home and shot himself in the head.

When she arrived back at the house in the early morning hours, she tiptoed into their master bedroom. Instead of finding her jilted lover sleeping peacefully and obliviously in their bed, she found him sprawled out in a twisted mess— brains and blood spattered everywhere, a gun hanging sickeningly from what was left of his mouth.

At least, this is the version as told by the neighbors and handed down to us by my grandmother in typical Vegas oral tradition. I'm sure the story got better every time it was told. The real estate agent had her own spin on the incident. She claimed that the gentleman of the house had had a terrible "accident" in the back yard. However, no one can convince me that this guy didn't off himself in the master bedroom. All anybody has to do is stand in there. Even 40-plus years later, a person can still feel the butterfly effect of that man's ultimate payback.

How many Christmas Eves did I spend in my grandmother's king-sized bed in that master bedroom with my aunt and my sister looking up at this old painting my grandmother had of a Spanish *señorita* holding her baby tightly to her chest? In the picture, the child looked teary-eyed and apprehensively up at her mother. She seemed afraid. It made *me* afraid! The expression on the woman's face convinced me that we both needed to be! The woman didn't return her daughter's anxious gaze. Instead, her slant was downcast and dark. She *knew* something. She knew her baby was in danger—perhaps she was the danger! I hated that picture, and I hate it to this day. But could I stop looking at it? I couldn't take my eyes off of it! I thought if I turned around and looked back, the baby would be gone, and the Spanish *señorita* would be staring back at *me* with a smirk of sick satisfaction on her face.

That blasted picture was the first thing Sam bought Grandma Jean when she first bought the house. Then he proceeded to furnish the whole monstrosity. The piece had originally hung on the mantel over the fireplace. He thought the woman looked just like my grandmother, and the baby looked like their love-child—my aunt. Now that I think about it, the *señorita does* bear a strong resemblance. Back then I only wished they'd have left it in the living room where they put it in the first place.

That was before I even *knew* about the guy with the gun and the cheating girlfriend and the paneling and what lies beneath…

For the real estate agent, trying to pawn that house off on somebody was like trying to get rid of a bad rash in a most unfortunate location.

My grandmother walked into that agent's life and gave that woman her own personal miracle. Jean Bennett didn't scare easily. Pissed off ghosts of discarded lovers didn't faze her in the least.

This, however, was not the tragedy that made the former owner vacate the house. The woman in cahoots with the doctor simply put that paneling up in her bedroom and went on with business as usual.

The phone rang one sunny afternoon, and the panicked voice on the other end warned, "The cops just raided the office, busted the doctor, and he busted you out! They're on their way to your house! Get out now!"

She and the girls in her care, who were living there in whatever condition they were in, gathered what belongings they could and fled the property in that very moment, leaving the house in shambles. What they abandoned was left to the elements.

As the real estate agent walked through the house with my grandmother, it was glaringly evident that its large group of occupants left abruptly. A pot roast with veggies was discovered rotting in the oven. Thankfully, someone had had the foresight to turn the oven off as they went tearing out the door the way hands fly out of a cookie jar when Mom comes home. The table was set for nine or ten people with plates, glasses, silverware and paper napkins. A Monopoly game had been turned up on the floor. Money scattered. Little green houses and red hotels poked up in the carpet in a five-foot radius. Clothes were still in drawers. Furniture in every room. Make-up and pill bottles in medicine cabinets. Refrigerator and cupboards fully stocked. The pool was filthy, the yard overgrown and the stank (this is a real word in our house) from the rotten roast dinner permeated throughout the entire house.

"I'll take it!" my grandmother proudly proclaimed.

Of course she did. Dirt cheap. She could easily hire someone to come in and clean it up before she stepped one foot back inside of it. She would make all the renovations she wanted, and she did. As aforementioned, Sam bought every stick of furniture in the whole place and even had an office built in the back yard where business could be done.

The paneling that covers the blood-brain splatter in the master bedroom, however, remains to this day. I don't think anybody ever attempted to take it down.

I listen to celebrities in interviews say that their own children really don't have a clue that their parents are famous. We had no clue either, really. Perhaps because my grandmother's name was only well-known within the music industry itself and not so much to the general public, we didn't really grasp the enormity of her endeavors. We took the family business in stride. Didn't every house on the block have gold records on the walls and little golden statues on the shelves? Wasn't everyone's house filled with singing? Jam sessions? Parties? It was fun when we got older to go to the shows and even be invited on stage to sing in some Vegas lounge with her entertainers. It was just a good time for us, and we took the fun for granted. Didn't everybody have a jet-setting grandma? Didn't everyone answer the phones for the family business at some time or other? And wasn't Dick Clark or Little Richard occasionally the voice on the other end?

Well, why not?

Going back and discovering the sheer magnitude of my grandmother's accomplishments make me love and appreciate her more than ever. She's definitely built a legacy, and she's drunk deeply from the chalice she pursued with complete, and sometimes reckless, abandon. Abundance poured out of that vessel. It was a bounty of prosperity and completely juxtaposed from our own house across town.

The house I lived in with my parents, my sister and my brother when we weren't at my grandmother's was small and messy, clutter in every crook and corner of it. The cupboards were hardly overflowing with food. We could usually find peanut butter and bread, but we didn't get too fancy. A different sort of darkness loomed there. We much preferred being at Grandma's house, despite the scary juju, where there were bananas and cookies and Fruit Loops and a swimming pool and barbeques and music and fun.

My party-like-a-rock star grandma could throw some spectacular shindigs. On that single acre, she hosted huge barbeques and swim parties that rivaled any Hollywood bash. We kids pounded the chicken legs and ribs that my grandfather slaved over with a Pabst Blue Ribbon in one hand and a big metal spatula in the other. We were too busy jumping in the pool to notice the names walking around from the industry: radio deejays, producers, singers, songwriters, agents… And who were these people to us, anyway? Generic figures in polyester suits with Benson and Hedges 100's between their fingers and multicolored sunglasses on their faces. Afros, bellbottoms, and sideburns straight out of *The Mod Squad*. They were friends of my grandmother's. She had a million of them. The buzz they made affected us about as much as the cicadas on the giant oak trees hovering over the yard, shading the whole retro lot of us.

Grandma Jean spared no expense with family holidays as well. Every holiday of my entire childhood happened at her house. Grandpa Ben and Grandma Polly took care of all the cooking and cleaning, hosting as if the house were theirs. And, truth be told, the house was pretty well theirs too. Grandma Jean bought all the turkeys and hams and the fixings; she bought the Easter clothes and the Easter eggs and the Easter candy; she bankrolled everything from Thanksgiving, Christmas and Easter to Groundhog Day, Kwanza and International Talk Like A Pirate Day. Grandpa Ben and Grandma Polly would roast the meats, bake the pies, hide the eggs, wrap the presents— whatever else needed to be done to provide some semblance of normalcy to the children in the house. Sometimes Sam was there with us, and sometimes he was with his own family.

Grandma's love-child, my aunt, was always fun to be with, especially on the holidays. She was like a big sister to me. When we played with dolls, though, I never got to have the tall beautiful blonde doll in the wedding dress. I always had to play with the little fat baby doll in the diaper. It's somewhat satisfying to finally get that in print, I'm not gonna lie. But she did come up with the best ideas to entertain us all. She suggested one Christmas Eve that we dress up my little brother, Jimmy, as Santa Claus, and she, my sister and I would be his elves. She put a big red shirt on him, which she stuffed with a pillow, got him a Santa hat, and made a white beard for him by gluing cotton balls together and taping it to his chin. He was adorable. She put us girls in leotards, tights and scarves—showgirl elves working the swing shift for Santa. Jimmy was so little he couldn't yet read the names on the packages, so we elves had to tell him which presents went to whom. He held his belly and "ho, ho, ho'd" all night. Christmas Eve would always end with us kids sharing the bed in my grandmother's scary-ass bedroom while Grandpa and Grandma Polly went home, promising to come back the next day and fix Christmas dinner.

Thankfully, because of the magic of Christmas, we always survived those long nights and the terrifying Spanish *señorita* in the picture.

Our cousins from San Diego loved to visit us in the summer. My uncle and aunt would bring their four children—until the stork came again and they had five—and we would swim the days away. Some of my earliest memories: falling off a merry-go-round at the park and my two oldest cousins almost getting into a fight with the boy who was spinning it too fast; my cousins convincing me to eat an artificial grape from the "fruit basket" off the kitchen table; accidentally stepping on my cousin Matt while he was sleeping on the floor and getting sent to my room. Totally not fair. He doesn't even remember it, and it wasn't like I stepped on his head or anything, which was a good thing because he truly was the cutest baby God ever made.

The nine of us were like brothers and sisters. We played and swam and ate together. We laughed. We built forts in the living room and slept in them. We went places. We had a great time. I had the best grandparents. I had the best sisters and brothers.

It was parents I never had.

I wished so many times that my aunt and uncle would take us to their house and raise us with all their kids. My aunt, in particular, spoke so sweetly to her children. Her eyes would light up whenever she saw them. It made me wistful. My uncle was funny and smart, and he was good with money. He provided for his family and was never unemployed the way my mother's husband often was. He exuded goodness, and his children were completely safe with him.

I wished they were our parents.

After all, my aunt and uncle only had one girl of their five children, so I was pretty sure that they'd have taken me and my sister home with them if they could. And my little brother Jimmy too—he was every bit as cute as Matthew was. Matt had almost white blond, straight hair and big blue eyes with the tiniest button nose that fit his sweet face. Jimmy was his opposite. He had dark, curly hair, almost black, with eyes the color of coffee. He looked very much like my sister, Tabitha; they were both angelic. Tabitha's chocolate brown curls dangled down around her chubby cheeks, and she had mocha eyes too. I looked more like Matt. In fact, one day I realized that I didn't look like anyone in my own family. My hair was light. My eyes were blue. I got burned to a crisp in the summer whereas my sister and brother looked like Paiute American Indians in just one afternoon in the pool. My parents' features were very dark too, which made me wonder if the stork hadn't dropped me off at the wrong house. When I asked my mother why that was, she told me I took after my Grandma Jean, which was a-okay with me.

Like cream cheese frosting, we ate up the much-needed, healthy affection that my aunt and uncle and grandparents lavished upon us, but our uncle was especially taken with Tabitha. She was sassy enough to banter back and forth with him, and she was a constant source of great amusement for him. He took to calling her "Ding-a-ling" in his gentle, teasing way. One day she put her hands on her hips and announced to everyone, "I'm *not* a ding-a-ling!"

"You're not?" He put his hand to his chest in feigned shock.

"No!"

"What are you then?"

"I'm a *sugar* ding-a-ling!"

Never again did he call her anything else.

❧   ❧   ❧

Showgirls, Sunday School and One Impressionable Little Girl

Mostly because of liquor laws, I was not allowed to hang out in casinos as a child, but that didn't mean I didn't walk through them to get to the buffet or the pirates or the shark tank. When I close my eyes I hear the "*ding-ding-ding-ding*" of the slots paying out, the rattle of the coins falling into the metal trays below, the "*Yes! Yes! Yes!*" of a winner whose machine just rolled up three sets of aligned cherries interrupting the buzzing drone of the crowd. Beautiful women wearing smiles, short skirts, high heels, and trays balancing highball glasses with straws, tall glasses with umbrellas and short skinny glasses filled to the rim. Another lovely lady wearing all black, sporting pads of paper and long black crayons ambling through the smoky haze and the confounding maze of the casino floor calling out, "*Keno! Keno!*" You might think this is a lot to take in for a six-year-old girl, but these were the sights and sounds of my hometown. And what was a six-year-old girl doing in the middle of a casino, you may ask? She was with her grandmother, that's what! And we were probably on our way to get something to eat.

On very lucky days—and Lady Luck is so often generous—I would stop and stare, awestruck, at the Amazon goddesses who glided across the casino floor. The showgirls, their slender and statuesque bodies barely covered in rhinestones and g-strings. They were every bit of seven feet tall from the top of their hot pink feather boa'd headpieces, their long bare torsos, sharp-angled hips, fishnet-clad legs, and right on down to their 4-inch stiletto pumps. I'm pretty sure I was born with the knowledge that they showed their boobies for the late show.

I loved them.

Whenever the showgirls would walk through one of the properties, I would invariably stop cold in my tracks and stare, mouth agape, in complete and utter adoration and watch them as they floated by. Once, while walking through the Tropicana, I caught the eye of one of these immortal beings who danced with the *Folies Bergere*. Celestially floating across the casino floor like a seraph, this divine creature slowed just long enough to gaze down at me and smile. Hers was the face of a princess. I wished I could be as beautiful as she was. Perfect, ruby-red lips. Pointy cheekbones. Eyelashes that reached the expanse of her glittery blue eyelids, brushing against those thin, manicured eyebrows. I wanted to be her and wear all those hot pink feathers.

She reached down and casually grazed the bottom of my chin with her long, red, fiberglass fingernail. I swear the blink of her false eyelashes sent a heavenly breath of wind across my cheek—the bright flash of her dazzling, white teeth set my heart aflutter. She lingered only a moment and whispered, "Darling…" before she continued on her way. I was twitterpated as I watched her, admiring the shape and swagger of her flawless tush in the fishing line that Vegas likes to call a costume, with all those feathers trailing along behind her, walking elegantly away in heels so high that she could easily reach up and touch the stars.

She was gorgeous. They all were.

Are.

I believe with all my heart that one hasn't lived until she has performed on a stage under a shining spotlight wearing a rhinestone gown, hair extensions, false eyelashes, and stilettos, wiggling her… yes, her feather boa.

You've all stood in front of your mirrors singing into hairbrushes pretending you were Madonna, or head-banging and strumming out *Highway to*

Hell on your air guitar with AC/DC, or lying across a straight-backed chair wearing an off-the-shoulder sweat shirt while your best friend stands on a ladder above you and pours a pitcher of water over your head. Maybe you only did that last one once.

I, however, strutted for miles back and forth in my room on my tip toes, undies tucked tightly into the crack of my butt, plastic flowers strung onto my tee tees (or not) balancing an old, feather duster on top of my head that I duct taped to one of my mother's old headbands. Those showgirls can-canned their way into my bloodstream. It's never been any different, and it's never going away.

How devastated I was to learn then that all those beautiful women, including my grandmother who chose the music business over Jesus Christ and the church, were sinners and going straight to Hell and were *not* people that I should try to emulate in any way, shape or form according to my parents. That whole scene fell under the category of "debauchery," and included dancing, which was a great, big no-no in their world. In addition, gambling was a sin. Alcohol was a sin (except for when Jesus turned the water into wine—and that was more akin to grape juice than wine, I was duly informed). Skimpy clothes were definitely a sin and, if shoes with heels that high were not a sin, they were at the very least not sensible.

I had to wonder if the lady who taught my Sunday School class owned a pair of fishnet stockings. I doubted it. She was a nice enough lady. She didn't have fake fingernails, although she did smile at me and cup my cheeks in her hands. It didn't have quite the same impact on me as the angelic Amazon with all the glitter. Her hair was gray and short, and she wore Vaseline on her lips. I don't know if she had any eyelashes, but she had VERY sensible shoes. With rubber soles. They were brown. And flat.

But you know what I loved about her? She told us stories, she gave us hugs, and she always gave us cookies. They weren't the cookies out of a package from the store. These were homemade like my Grandma Polly's. We sat in a semi-circle on the floor around her, munching on our cookies, sitting criss-cross applesauce. We were mesmerized at this strapping young Jesus, robed in white with a purple sash and brown sandals. You know how we knew He was strapping and robed in white with a purple sash and brown sandals? Because we could SEE him! On the flannelboard!

For my readers who have no idea what I'm talking about, this "flannelboard" contraption is yesteryear's... shall we say? Power Point presentation? You know, back before the advent of fire and the wheel—when we were still hammering away on stone tablets. Our teacher made Bible scenes come alive on that flannelboard: Jesus feeding the 5000, Zacchaeus getting stuck in a tree, Lazarus being raised from the dead. She had a standing Jesus and a sitting Jesus. He, too, sat criss-cross applesauce.

Jesus was amazing. He was magic. He spit on mud and put it on a blind guy's eyeballs to make him see. He felt a woman touch the bottom of His robe—she was very sick, but she got better. He didn't eat or drink for a long, long time and the Devil came and tempted him in the desert with rocks. He kneeled down next to a big boulder in a beautiful garden and prayed because He was really sad. Then a whole bunch of people came, and somebody got his ear chopped off, but Jesus put it back on. I don't think He was even mad about it because He was very kind.

He died on a cross on a Friday, but He came back to life again after they put him in a cave behind a different boulder, and there was a lot of light and angels and soldiers, and that was on a Sunday. And He loves us because He's still alive after all these years. And He knows everybody's name and how many hairs everybody has on their heads.

Every week, we sat in awe.

I was told we should love Him, so I did. I was a very good girl. I was told we should all ask Him to live in our hearts. And I did that too. I was told we should be baptized. So I got baptized.

It's a little much for a girl to make any sense of. As you can imagine, it became a challenge to sift through all the components of my life and decipher between the sanctified and the insane. I was raised by parents who took us to a church where people ate donuts every Sunday, spoke in tongues, fell backwards onto the floor, ran down the aisles of the church and swung from the chandeliers. Okay, Maybe they didn't eat donuts *every* Sunday.

Assimilating the craziness of the casinos and the craziness of church was relatively easy. The clanking of coins in the slots was not that unlike the clanking of coins in the offering plate. The heavenly streets of gold and gates of pearl? Yeah, I've seen 'em a million times on the Strip. God setting out a banquet table before us in the presence of our enemies probably looked a lot like a buffet. Tammy Faye Baker was just as beautiful to me as any showgirl on the Strip, and the soldiers' costumes for every Easter production I've ever seen most likely came straight from Caesar's Palace. The dissonance in my life was not between the showgirls and the Sunday School teachers. The dissonance in my life was more likely that I was baptized by the guy who had been molesting me since as early as I could remember.

Thank you, Captain Buzzkill.

Chapter 2

I Came By Life Honestly

"SISTER, YOU'RE WHITE. You know that, right?"

This from the young African-American gentleman looking at me like I had clearly stepped outside my mind. We were standing outside under the giant horse waiting for a table at PF Chang's. I saw him, tilted my head in friendly recognition, pointed my finger and informed him, "You look *exactly* like my little brother!" He truly did—tall, dark, and handsome.

"I'm not kidding! My brother is your height, your build, has your jet-black hair, your dark skin, your dark eyes. You could be his twin!"

He looked around to see if anyone else was in on this joke. Only it wasn't a joke. I conceded, "My whole family is dark—I don't look like any of them. *You* do, though!"

If Mr. Hooper from Sesame Street sang, *One of these things is not like the other…* about our family, all the kids in the television audience would be pointing right to me. Even the knuckleheaded kids.

Maybe I was the knuckleheaded kid, because it no more occurred to me that I didn't entirely belong in my family than it occurred to Gilligan how to get the hell off that island. The explanation that I was like my Grandma Jean was what my mother used to appease me, and it worked like a charm.

Until I got in trouble one day.

The man I'd believed was my father flew into one of his angry fits. The incensed look on his face, the fist clenching tightly the collar on my shirt, his enraged breath in my face, and the slap of the belt across my bare butt—all topped off with a snide, "I'm not even your father."

If I could travel back in time, I would go back to that moment and burst into song: "Zippity doo Daahhhhh, Zippity-ay! My, oh my, what a wonderful day...."

But the day he said that to me? It broke my little heart.

I felt rejected—which, if you think about it, is how he was trying to make me feel, so I guess I had the correct response if it's still true that adults can manipulate kids into thinking or feeling or doing pretty much anything they want. I knew in that moment that my mother had not been honest with me about me looking like my grandmother and being like her. I wasn't even sure in that instant whether or not she *was* my grandmother.

"Is Mom still my mom?" I asked.

"Yes. She was married to someone else before she was married to me, and they had you. Your mom's been divorced."

The unpardonable sin. Well, there were so many of those...

"Where is my real father?"

"You're *mine*. You belong to *me*."

The insidious look on his face made it crystal clear that I shouldn't bring it up again. I wouldn't even be allowed to debrief with my mother about what I'd just been told. I felt in the days that followed that I would never be allowed to know who my real father was. I didn't know his name, first or last. I didn't know what he looked like or if he was married to someone else too—maybe he had more kids—half-brothers and sisters. I didn't know if they even knew about me or where he lived or what he did for a living or if he was good to his other children. But here's what I knew for sure:

I knew his eyes were blue. I knew his skin was light. Like mine.

One day when my mother's husband wasn't home, I went into the kitchen where she was just standing, looking out the window above the sink, seemingly lost in her own thoughts. What were her thoughts? Did she think? What could she possibly tell herself in her own quiet, private moments?

Quietly I asked her the question she could have lived her whole life without hearing. It floated softly, slowly through the air and landed across her countenance like a shroud, forcing her to acknowledge all that she'd hoped had been removed as far as the east is from the west.

"Who is my father?"

She didn't look at me or even answer my question. Instead she said, "He never loved us. He never wanted us." It would be her only reply. Denial was easy for my mother. Whenever she wanted something to disappear or pretend an event didn't happen, she had but to shake her head and make it all go away. She was nailing this coffin shut. She, like her husband, may as well have said, *This is a closed door. You will not open it.* Her concern was not for my emotional state but for the climate of our home. Her husband was a jealous man prone to explosive rage.

Don't poke the bear.

Best to slap on a smile and act as if nothing is amiss. Redefine to suit. Throw a little something in there about Jesus to lock it down and make it good.

What could I do, then, but turn to the one person I knew would hook me up because she was nosey and knew everything and she got to do whatever she wanted and say whatever she wanted however she wanted to say it, and no one could stop her and she *never* got in trouble for anything: *my aunt!*

At twelve years old, she was the final authority on pretty much everything. The next time we were at Grandma Jean's house, I found her in her bathroom sitting at the vanity in front of a big oval mirror with the gaudiest gold frame. I'm sure it was a precise replica of the infamous *Mirror, Mirror on the Wall.* Behind that was—please believe me when I tell you—poodled wallpaper. Poodles. About fifty of them across the expanse of the bathroom with black, curly poodle-fur. Diva-poodles in various bathroom poses: taking bubble baths in pink bear-claw tubs, drying their delicate poodle tails with petite pink towels, having their hair styled with elfin pink hairbrushes, spraying it with what looked like Aqua-Net... It horrifies me still to think of it. Maybe it was trendy back then?

As she sat there brushing her hair, I flat out asked her what I wanted to know.

"Did you know my mother was married before?"

The brush froze halfway through a stroke of hair, and she eyed me suspiciously in the mirror.

"Yeah. How did you find out?"

"I got in trouble, and he told me. Did you know my real father?"

"Yep."

Then I said something that surprised even me. "I hate him."

"Why? I liked him. I thought he was cool."

"Because he's never even talked to me. Mom said he never loved us, and he never wanted us."

"Hmm." She contemplated that last little tidbit. Finally, she shrugged her shoulders and said, "I don't think that's true. He was always nice to me. He was funny."

I'd had enough of this conversation and the poodles and the brushing, and I started to go back out the door until one more question occurred to me. "What was his name?"

She put the brush down and turned around in her chair to face me. "Don. Donnie Lofton. That was your last name before you got adopted."

I let it sink in. *Lofton.* It sounded nice. A normal name. Nobody could make fun of it.

"You look like him, you know," she offered.

"I know."

That was the extent of my knowledge about my father for several years. To mention my father or my mother's divorce was forbidden in my house. My mother's husband would not allow it, and to do so would be considered a personal affront that would set him off like a stick of dynamite. The notion of my mother having been married to someone other than him was a source of shame and was not to be broached. The mystery of it all began to make me feel as if I were some sort of "secret disgrace" for our family. It was just one more secret in the house of my childhood. There were plenty of other things we didn't dare talk about. To anyone. Ever. Having a different father, admittedly, paled in comparison to the most shameful secret I had been keeping.

It might occur to someone, say, a college senior majoring in psychology maybe, that living under such a shroud of shame would be emotionally and psychologically harmful for a child. Children exhibit bizarre and unhealthy behavior sometimes when their minds and spirits can't release what is happening in their lives. They pee the bed. They start having trouble in school. Their personalities seem to change. But here's what I figured out. I figured out that if I was different, then someday maybe I could have a different life than the one I was now living. How I ever came up with that in my formative years, I'll never know. But the fact that I wasn't like my family slowly became a relief and a comfort. If home was my Hell, school became my Heaven and, until I hit algebra and geometry in middle school and high school, I did very well in school.

I remember seeing the kids' movie, *Matilda*, (based on the book by Roald Dahl). The tiny girl for whom the story is named was unfortunate enough to be born into a family who was very different than she was. She loved to read and did well in school. Her parents were shady and mean and didn't care about her. She had a wonderful teacher, Miss Honey, who saw something beautiful in Matilda, and lavished her with understanding and affection. In the end, her parents discarded her, more or less, relieving her of her horrible life with them, and she got to live with Miss Honey and be raised by a nurturing, loving person.

Kudos to Matilda. My childhood, like many others, simply had to be endured. I merely had to survive it. When I got out on my own, I knew I would make different choices and that the power and control would eventually shift into my own hands. When it did, I found my real father.

I am so grateful I had the presence of mind to take advantage of the education that was offered to me by this crazy country that believes that everyone is entitled to a free education regardless of race, gender, socio-economic status, religion or even ability. You can say what you want about public education, but many countries in the world don't even attempt such a gargantuan endeavor. A person can take advantage of that phenomenal opportunity, or she can piss it away. Such is our freedom. Somehow, though, by the grace of God or maybe just my father's DNA, I chose to do well regardless of the obstacles in my way. My grades were good enough to go to college where I stuck it out for four whole years, managed to hook up with my first husband and get knocked up in the process.

Upon college graduation, I moved to Missouri with my then-husband and got hold of my Aunt Ora. She wasn't really my aunt, but a very close, life-long friend of my great grandmother's. What was handy about Aunt Ora was that she used to deliver the mail in the same town where I had figured out my father lived. This town was small enough that she knew everybody, which would include my father, his brother, and my grandparents.

I told her, "Aunt Ora, I know you know where my father is."

"Well, of course, I do! He's uptown with your grandma and grandpa," she answered.

"Listen," I told her, "I would like to know who he is. I'd like to get in touch with him, but only if he wants to. He might be remarried—he might have more children. They might not know about me, so if getting back in touch with me is going to make it hard for him, then he doesn't have to call me. I completely understand."

After all, he never wanted me, right?

"Oh, I wouldn't worry about that. I'll let him know."

That Aunt Ora—she was the crust on the biscuit.

She went straight over to my grandparents' house and gave them my phone number. When my father came out of work that day, so the story goes, and saw his parents standing there waiting for him, his heart sank to his knees. He thought someone had died. Why else would his parents be standing outside his work waiting for him to come out?

With his heart pounding in his kneecaps, he made his way toward them. They met him halfway, waving a slip of paper at him like a victory flag. He tried to wrap his head around the fact that they were absolutely jubilant, their smiles wide and their eyes bright and giddy.

"Guess whose phone number this is on this here paper!" Without speaking, he took the slip from his mother's hand and saw my name. His heart dropped from his knees, landed on the gravel beneath his feet, and stopped altogether.

A man goes about his day like any other day. He welds in the hot warehouse all morning and sweats through his shirt all the way down his back. He clocks out and swallows his lunch in three or four bites while his shirt dries stinky and stiff. He clocks back in and welds all afternoon and soaks his shirt through again. At five the whistle blows. Sweaty blue collars all clock out. He walks out to the car, and his whole life changes.

He dialed my number and hung up about a hundred times. When he finally got the courage to let it ring, *my* life changed forever.

My husband and I had just moved into a small brick house we were renting. I was almost eight months pregnant with Geoff and we were going out to dinner for my birthday before we hit our first Lamaze class. I was teaching at a private Christian elementary school, while Geoff's father finished a master's program at the local university where he also taught some freshman level English classes. I had just put on my coat, which barely wrapped around my belly. He was standing with the keys ready to walk out the door.

The phone on the end table rang as we were leaving, and I thought twice about picking it up. We were pressed for time if we wanted a nice dinner that we couldn't in a million years afford before our Lamaze class for this baby that we couldn't in a million years afford. But something I can't explain made me reach for that phone.

"Hello?" I answered.

I thought I heard a short breath on the other end and then, "Hello darlin'. My name is Don Lofton."

I almost dropped the phone. I knew I couldn't just stand there with nothing but dead air between us. Seconds were slowly ticking off the clock. I had to say something, so I said the first word that came to my mind.

"Dad?"

His breath on the other end of the line was audible. It was his turn to fill the space between us with nothing. Finally, he spoke. "Happy birthday, honey," he said.

"You remembered today is my birthday?"

"This is your 24th birthday. I've remembered this day every year since you were born."

This from the man who supposedly never wanted me. But the fact of the matter was, not only did he remember that it was my birthday, he'd never forgotten precisely how old I was on this day for the last 23 years.

Can you say, paradigm shift?

"Wow. Well, speaking of being born, you'll never believe where we're going after dinner tonight. Our first Lamaze class! I'm pregnant! I'm having a baby late November or early December."

I never thought you could hear a person smile over the phone.

"Oh, I *am* married, by the way!"

His easy chuckle was a very nice birthday present. We didn't speak long, but he managed to let me know in those ten minutes that he did love me, and he had loved my mother. Details and questions and confessions would come later, but, for now, I knew that I had mattered to him. Before we hung up, I asked, "Dad?"

He seemed blown away that I would so easily call him this, but I've never been inclined to call him anything different from the moment I heard his voice.

"Yeah, darlin'?"

"You're eyes are blue, aren't they?"

"Yes, they are. Like yours."

"Like mine."

Our phone conversations that followed were mammoth marathons. We had ages of time to recover. He told me he had been stationed in Thailand during the Vietnam War when I was born. Lyndon B. Johnson was the President. The Baltimore Orioles just swept the Los Angeles Dodgers in the World Series. Newton and Seale formed the Black Panthers. Grace Slick joined Jefferson

Airplane. And my dad opened a telegram from the Red Cross, which read, "Baby girl arrived. Mom and baby doing fine." This precipitated some R&R in town to celebrate the glorious occasion. That may have been the first time, in fact, that I'd ever heard the phrase, 'three sheets to the wind,' which was how he'd described his condition the night I was born. He bought me a tiny, infant Thai outfit and gave it to a pilot who was coming home. He asked that soldier to send it to me when he got stateside, but I don't know what ever happened to it. Did the pilot send it like he promised? Did my father write his address down correctly in his drunken stupor? Or did my mother find it in a box one day and decide to dispense with it without ever telling me, knowing her possessive husband wouldn't approve? I would give anything to have that outfit—the first present my father ever got for me. I'll never know what happened to it.

Since then, my father has given me many presents, the best of which are answers. I look like him. I have a string of feistiness that runs through me that, if I'm being honest, doesn't hold a candle to his. After all, although I've definitely stood up on a bar top with my cowboy hat and boots on and shaken my bootie for the patrons in true Coyote Ugly form, I've certainly never stood up straight and tall on a bar top in a rowdy, rival Kansas beer joint and started a brawl by screaming at the top of my lungs, "KANSAS AIN'T NOTHIN' BUT A BUNCH OF SUNFLOWERS AND SONSA-BITCHES!"

God love his heart.

My dad was an impressive kind of guy in many respects, and figuring out who he was, helped me figure out who I am. My dad wasn't rich. He wasn't what society would consider 'educated' necessarily. He wasn't the boss of anyone. But he lived his life on his own terms. He was smart, which was probably why I did well in school. And he was brave.

My dad grew up in the furrow of his older brother, Ronnie. Ronnie and Donnie. Donnie and Ronnie. The kid had to be tough—tough enough to sit by himself in the old cemetery late at night. Uncle Ronnie would drop my dad on some gravestone somewhere so he and his girlfriend could go… do whatever it was that they did for however long it took them to do it. The poor guy was only seven years old. I guess it had to be scary enough for him so he wouldn't run off somewhere. Sucks to have to take your younger brother with you when you're running around town all hours of the night. Not sure why he couldn't have been left at a neighbor's house. So here's this little pistol, trying to be brave, sitting all by his lonesome on some old grave somewhere in the middle of a cemetery where the ghosts could keep an eye on him. I'm sure my dad was out there flippin' off the zombies and spittin' chewing tobacco on the ghouls and pissin' on the demons. By the time his brother got back to him, he was wild with terror and ready for a fight—to the sheer delight and amusement of his brother! It's no wonder then that Donnie grew up fearless. Ronnie made sure he survived all that spewed out from the sulfur-ridden hollows of Hell. Nitroglycerin comes in small packages, I've been told, and Donnie Lofton learned never to shy away from a challenge. He didn't even mind looking around for a good one.

My dad and I would talk on the phone for hours. Story after story after story. I had plenty of my own. He would listen to my own antics and laugh and tell me, "Darlin', you don't even know why you act the way you do. But I do. You're just like me." He grew up late, and I grew up young. We met somewhere in the middle.

Each story he told me seemed like one of my own fingerprints. Every time I talked to my dad, he would give me another little piece of the puzzle of my life. It was comforting to finally have some explanations as to why I was the way I was. Growing up, I didn't look like my family. I didn't want the same things. I always felt different. Meeting my dad reassured me that I wasn't different—I was like him. I was anchored in someone else. It was a series of gifts that he gave me every time we connected.

Someone had come before me—someone who made me and knew me and understood me. The tragedy here is that I could never replace the years that were lost, and I've been the one who has had to pick up the tab for that. I'd like to tell parents to be careful of the choices that you make for your children, for those children tend to grow up and try to fill in all the holes that time has eaten through their lives.

He told me stories of the war. Of having to make a trip into Vietnam once a month to salvage parts for the airplanes he worked on. I thought he'd stayed in Thailand—I hadn't known he had to actually go into Vietnam-country-proper. He explained, "Well, honey, when they shot those planes down, it's not like those Vietcong ever brought 'em back!" He loved the History Channel and even expressed a desire to return to Vietnam and Thailand to experience it in a more positive light. He talked about the times when the rain would suddenly burst out of the clouds and every soldier would stop what he was doing, run back to their barracks to get a bar of soap, run back outside and strip down, buck-ass-naked wherever he stood to shower in the downpour. It didn't matter if they were eating, relaxing, or working. He laughed at the poor schmucks who were still lathered in soap when the rain stopped as suddenly as it had come.

He looked every pilot in the eye and asked him how he felt about his mission before he allowed the plane in the air. "Are you feeling good about this one, sir?" he'd say. The pilots would almost always say, "Absolutely! I'm coming back." Only one time in the year he served did he have a man say, "You know, I don't have a good feeling about this. I don't think I'm gonna make it." My dad grounded his plane that day. He "found" something wrong with it. That soldier didn't fly. Not that day, he didn't. It's how my dad coped. He spoke reverently about the bravery of the men he'd met. He said when his tour of duty was over and he flew home, there was no fanfare. No flags. No banners.

Wrong war for all that.

My rebel-rousing dad didn't fear war, he didn't lament the lack of accolades when he came home, and referred to jail simply as, 'three hots and a cot.' He certainly didn't seem too concerned if he ended up there on occasion. He knew everyone on both sides of the steel bars and got along with most. It makes me wonder if the number of Loftons who have never been incarcerated are fewer than the number of Loftons who have? I may never know, but I have my suspicions.

And maybe I'm walking around with just a little bit of that mettle in me. I'm sure I didn't get it from my mother.

❧   ❧   ❧

Interruptions on the Time-Space Continuum

As aforementioned, Grandma Jean was swinging the world by the tail during this timeframe. Sometimes she was even swinging it by the nuts. One wonders if my jet-setting grandmother sucked all the ambition from the room (or perhaps it just skips a generation) since, surely, the pendulum could not have swung any further between Grandma Jean's approach to life and my mother's.

Not a jetsetter by any stretch, my mother plain and simply loved the hometown of her childhood. The small town feeling of her home in America's heartland was just her speed. Whereas her mother couldn't see enough of the world, my own couldn't see the need to be anywhere else. Being dragged between New York, Los Angeles and Chicago was not my mother's idea of a good time. She was sixteen when her mother suddenly became pregnant, and those jet-setting days were behind them all. My grandmother set her sights on Vegas, a place my mother believed to be a desolate dirt hole in the middle of nowhere.

Diamond in the desert, her *ass*!

My mother begged to go back "home" to live with her grandmother, our Gram, and graduate from high school with her friends. That wish was granted.

A few months into her senior year, it must have occurred to my mother that Grandma Jean expected her to join her in that God-forsaken, treeless, cactus-ridden dust bowl of a town after graduation. She needed a plan. Just three months before she was to graduate from high school, Gram walked in on my mother, then seventeen, sneaking out her bedroom window—a young man was apparently standing in the yard below, waiting for her on the other side. Not my father. She was sneaking out to elope with another gentleman, which would have allowed her to stay in the Midwest where she wanted to be. Gram was quick on her feet in those days and strong as an ox. She ran to the open window and dragged my mother back through it. My mother was on a plane headed straight for Vegas faster than she could lick a sucker down to the stick. She did not graduate from her hometown high school with the friends that she'd loved her whole life. She graduated with total strangers in a class that was bigger than her entire high school back home in a city that she hated. I've always thought that was phenomenally sad for her.

One perk about being in Vegas that my mother couldn't deny is that the nightlife there blew doors off the nightlife in her itty-bitty countrified hamlet. After high school, my mother with her new Vegan girlfriends, came upon some serviceman at a pub. The ladies huddled around a table with their mile-high bouffant updos and their smoldering cigarettes and flirted shamelessly with several soldiers who were stationed at Nellis Air Force Base. *Sans* my mother, that is. She couldn't be less interested. While her friends glanced coyly at the boys over their Jackie K cocktails (apricot brandy, triple sec, bitters and cream with a splash of grenadine, in case anyone forgot) my mother, bored straight out of her go-go boots, stared in the opposite direction completely detached. The year was 1965.

The soldiers bought the girls another round and came on over. A certain redhead, with striking blue eyes, noticed just how beautiful my mother was. Maybe it was that "you-couldn't-get-me-to-acknowledge-you-if-you-lit-yourself-on-fire" demeanor that attracted him to her. In any case, this gentleman started out with literally no chance of ever becoming my father until the group started making small talk, and he happened to mention that he was from the itty-bitty, countrified hamlet right *next* to her own hometown.

Her ticket home!

My father told me once, "When your mother heard me say that, all of a sudden, she got all *kinds* of friendly. She latched onto me like dill on a pickle."

I don't have a whole lot of information about their courtship, but this one noteworthy item I gleaned: One cold, February night in 1966, the stars aligned, the egg dropped, the angels sang, and *bam!* I was a zygote.

Now, you'd think that my mother could drop this on Grandma Jean without too much hassle, right? After all, my grandmother had had her own illegitimate child just three years previously, with a married man no less. When one considers the times vs. Jean's age bracket, she clearly emerges as an extremely ahead-of-the-times, feminist, forward thinking lady. She didn't wait for Helen Reddy to roar in numbers too big to ignore. Who had time to wait for these chicks to get their shit together and start marching? My grandmother didn't wait for the movement or the marching. My grandma was her *own* movement! She certainly had the means to care for my mother and her precious, growing zygote. Surely, my mother could come to her with her "predicament." It was not as if my grandmother would ever turn her out.

No way, Jose Feliciano.

My mother made my father give Grandma Jean the happy news about my impending arrival. Although she thinks I'm the greatest thing since Clairol hair bleach now, she was less than enthused about this news when she first heard about it. But, of course, she rallied. She, being the glorious, self-reliant, corporate canopy-shattering feminist that she is, assured my mother that she did not *have* to get married. A woman didn't need a man to take care of her. For the love of tie-dye, it was the sixties! There was a revolution (that my mother apparently skipped), and times, they were a-changin'! She offered to let my mother stay there in her beautiful home, burn her bra, and raise her baby-zygote in the most exciting city in the world!

My mother would rather have hawked up her spleen.

My grandmother was a realist. Practical. Progressive. To this day, she's all business and has accomplished what she has because she did exactly what she wanted. My mother, perhaps out of sheer rebellion, was a romantic. Serendipitous. Susceptible. Not to mention, homesick. She, too, did exactly what she wanted.

She married that soldier from home, turned her back on Lady Vegas, and eventually made her way home soon after I was born. Far from the glitz. Far from the glamour.

In so doing, my mother would become the single-most motivating person in my entire lifetime—she became everything I didn't want to be. As she did to her mother, I would do to her.

I am persuaded, then, that I came by my life honestly.

Choices. Interruptions along the time-space continuum that alter the trajectory of our lives, altering our propulsions, sending us to God-knows-what.

My dad's parents were thrilled to have us back, and my mother was thrilled to be back. Four seasons. Old friends. Familiar places. Friendly faces.

Not a cactus or a marquee in sight.

While my dad was serving overseas, my mother rented a small apartment for the both of us, and we certainly weren't deprived of company. In fact, an old friend of my mother's from high school heard she was back in town. This dashing young man from high school walked straight up the sidewalk to my Gram's house.

You've heard the saying, "You can't con a con?" Here's the thing about my great grandmother. God rest her soul, she was every bit as wily as her daughter, my Grandma Jean. Those two, even though they didn't share the same Turner blood, were still somehow cut from the same swath of fabric. When her husband was alive, my Great Grandpa Poo-Poo (God strike me dead if I am lying about his name) was adamantly opposed to their Jean Louise being a famous singer or a movie star or moving to New York or Hollywood or any such nonsense. Those two, mother and daughter, conspired together, and Grandpa Poo-Poo got snookered plenty when Gram sneaked Grandma Jean to every single singing contest in their niche of the woods. And it wasn't like Grandpa Poo-Poo was a dimwitted man. He was the town's mayor back in the day.

To say my Gram was a shrewd woman doesn't begin to cover it.

Dashing be damned, this young man was trouble, and she knew it the second she opened the door and saw him flash his million dollar smile.

"Hi, how are you today, Alice?" he said charmingly.

Blank stare.

"Uh... I heard your granddaughter is back in town."

Raised eyebrow.

"You wouldn't happen to know where I could find her, do you?"

"I wouldn't tell you where my granddaughter lived if the world were filled with piss and she lived in a tree."

Door slammed.

Not only did she know this guy was up to no good, she also knew that, such was his cocky arrogance, this guy would march his arse straight over to her in-laws' house and find out where my mother was. Why *shouldn't* they trust him, she could read his mind in that pointy little head of his. He was a student in Bible college, after all, studying to be a preacher, a man of God, a shepherd for Christ's lambs.

Gram always thought he was a jackass who didn't want to go to Vietnam, so he enrolled in Bible school and conscientiously objected or some such bullshit.

She got on the horn and warned my paternal set of grandparents that he was on his way.

"Billie, this is Alice. There's a young man on his way to see you who thinks the sun comes up just to hear him crow. He wants to know where my granddaughter and the baby are. I'll bet you a blue million he's up to no good. Don't tell him a thing!"

Grandma Billie, unlike my Gram however, had no guile in her. As my father recalled, she trusted my mother implicitly and loved her very much. She didn't have the vivid imagination that my Gram had and couldn't conceive that there was any harm. When this young man showed up asking for my mother, it didn't take him any time at all to suavely convince her that his intentions were pure. He had our location in less than five minutes.

If I could travel back in time, I would go back to that moment and do my darndest to thwart that entire chain of events, so help me God. I have to wonder what life would be like if that scenario had not played out like it had. Of course, my Grandma Billie had no idea then that this would be the very man who would ultimately rob them of many, many years with me, years that would never be replaced. And if she ever knew the horror he would impose on an entire generation of a family, she never would have told him where we were.

My mother's letters to my father in Thailand soon began to mention this Cassa-freakin-nova. According to my father, it didn't take long before the letters were more about this new Rico Suave than they were about anything else, so he started to suspect that something might be going on back home, regardless of his Bible school student status. Several of his buddies had already gotten their "Dear John" letters. He figured his young wife was just working up her courage to drop the napalm on him.

My father returned from the Vietnam War in August of 1967. I was nine months old. When he got off the plane at the airport, his parents and my mother and I were the only ones there to greet him. Apparently, Gallant Gus stayed his ass home for this one.

My dad knew his marriage was over within the first week of being home.

The two lovebirds played it cool, thinking my dad wouldn't be the wiser if they took him to a revival meeting, of all things, where Reverend Romeo was doing the special music for the church meeting...with his girlfriend in the audience. And her husband sitting beside her.

After prayer meeting, they decided to do a little late-night swimming. My mother and father were sitting on one end of the pool with their feet dangling in the water as super-swimmer-singer-conscientious-objector-gonna-be-a-preacher boy did his best swan dive off the diving board. Always performing. Always the star of the show. My mother made her three millionth comment about how good-looking he was.

"Are you in love with him?" My dad was never one to beat around the bush.

"I don't know," she admitted with a slight shrug of her shoulder, her feet still swinging back and forth in the water.

That was enough for my dad. Instead of going home with my mother that night, my dad went to his parents' house. In fact, it was super-swimmer-singer-conscientious-objector-gonna-be-a-preacher boy who drove him there. When they pulled up to the curb outside my grandparents' house on that dark street, my dad said to my mother's new boyfriend, "Why don't *you* marry her? She seems to think an awful lot of you."

"Oh, no. I'm not ready for a ready-made family."

In other words, "Oh, whoa! Wait! No! Hey, I'm just fucking her." Of course, he wouldn't say the f-word—he was a good Christian man who had just declared pastoral ministries as his major with an apparent emphasis in the laying on of *hands*! And my mother was too delusional to see it.

He did eventually marry my mother, however, after knocking her up—although he did his hearty best to squirm out of that one too. I wished he *had* squirmed his way out of it. He convinced my mother that he had every intention of marrying her, but all but packed her bags for her and sent her back to Vegas to be with my Grandma Jean. He told me he hitch-hiked clear across the country to break the news to my once-again pregnant mother that he had *no* intentions of marrying her. But yet another unfortunate event altered the momentum of my life once again, forcing our paths to align.

My uncle, a good man whose intentions were pure, convinced his young buck of a brother-in-law to do right by the woman in the sight of God and the church and take responsibility for his actions and his child.

My uncle's intentions were generous. The outcome was disastrous.

To think that he was gone! Out the door! We were *done* with him! He was but one conversation from being out of our lives forever! I wish he'd have been allowed to simply go. But, for the second time, a well-meaning person interrupted that time-space continuum to the detriment of an entire generation. It's like being one number away from winning the stinking lottery. We've got a brand new Ferrari, but no one has the key. The biggest banana split *ever*, and me without a spoon.

But would it have mattered? I have the notion that my mother would have just gone out and found someone else just as destructive, just as twisted, just as vile. This guy wasn't the first "visitor" to our little apartment. He, sadly, was simply the last.

So, I have to ask myself, what does it matter that my Grandma Billie told this asshole where to find my mother? He would have found us eventually. It was a small town. They had mutual friends. Does it matter that my uncle convinced him to marry this woman he had gotten pregnant? Probably not. My mother would have found a way to rope him into our lives—this predator-preacher, who prayed.

Who preyed.

No reason for these wistful thoughts of what could have been. Of what *should* have been.

You Should Really Think About Skipping This Part

You can skip this whole next section if you prefer. It's not like I'm dying to write it anyway. If you're the kind of person who would rather just duly note that I was abused as a child and leave it at that, I invite you to head straight for the next chapter. I am not offended in the least, and here's why.

The cutesy song we all sang in Vacation Bible School, *Be Careful Little Eyes What You See—Be Careful Little Ears What You Hear*, is more than just an admonition for children to refrain from inappropriate conduct. It's damn good advice. I've seen and heard things I wish I hadn't—things that haunt me now and will for as long as memory serves. When I reveal the sordid details of the abuse I suffered, I have the potential to lay the weight of it upon people I care about. And, frankly, it's heavy. There is nothing that obligates you, the reader, to carry the burden of my past pain, and I hope you will not carry an ounce of it.

I don't.

However, this *is* my story. This *is* what happened to me. I am removed from it so that I can tell it objectively, without prejudice or derision. I tell it so that those who have been enslaved by the sick and twisted appetites of others can also be liberated and have a life abundant in peace and in hope and in health. I tell it so that others can be free. There are little girls and boys and young ladies and young men who have endured all I have endured and worse. Some of these young people have been brave enough to tell someone they could trust. In many cases, allegations are brought to the prosecutor's office to decide whether formal charges will be brought against their perpetrators. These kids, then, must tell perfect strangers in very precise terms the graphic details of their most shameful, humiliating, and dehumanizing moments. And those are the hardest words they've ever had to speak.

Some can't do it. Ever. As a result, the people who have hurt them so egregiously get off scot-free. And so, these sadistic pedophiles maintain their proximity to these precious children who could not bring themselves to speak the words to send their abusers away and, in many cases, the horror continues even more violently than before. These abusers are free to retaliate. They are free to prey upon, groom, and molest other little girls and boys who won't tell, other young women and men who are too ashamed. As a result, lives are shattered for generations.

Maybe if they read this, they can find the courage. This is what I would have had to tell a police officer, a prosecutor or a doctor. But I never did. My abuser has never answered for his actions in a court of law, though he has surely escorted those who have been found guilty in court to *their* jail cells. That's because he's a law-enforcement officer. As of this writing, he's a cop. I Googled his name once out of the blue and found a picture of him in his uniform standing next to his patrol car. I read his bio and wanted to puke. It tells how long he's been with the department and his certifications. He gave props to the town's former marshal who had "taken him under his wing and kept him out of trouble," and then went on to say, "Now it's up to me to return the favor." That marshal took him under his wing all right—that marshal took him into somewhere private and molested him. I distinctly remember him telling me this officer's name, which I will never forget, and telling me that he was the town marshal. Imagine my shock when I read online how his own abuser had become his hero—someone he grew up to emulate. Someone for whom he would "return the favor."

Well, he certainly did.

And this is the man around whom certain family members have rallied for years. After all, it's so much easier to believe that I am lying or crazy or have "fallen into Satan's hands" with these ridiculous stories. Troubled. Deceitful. Lost. That's an easier pill to swallow. So, another reason I tell this story is to stand up to those who stubbornly cling to the notion that I am unfairly maligning my mother and her husband, fabricating and exaggerating these events. It is to stand up and tell the truth, whether it is acknowledged or not.

This is what I know and so does he: it happened. And it happened exactly like this.

*** WARNING ***
This is your last chance to skip this section. Once you know it, you can't un-know it.

I don't remember a time when my mother's husband didn't sneak into my room at night. It never *not* happened. He put his hands where he wanted and always slithered out having satiated himself at my expense. By the time I was in kindergarten I had an astute understanding of the adult male anatomy and how it functions. He was always naked around the house. It was nothing for us to sit as a family and watch television with him completely nude. No one said anything, even when he wanted us to sit on his lap or sit behind him to massage his legs and back.

My mother knew about the sexual abuse of all her children as well as her younger sister and did nothing—said nothing. Not a word. Her husband developed an incredibly inflated sense of entitlement since he was never questioned or held to any accountability for his actions. This enabled him to quite easily start bringing me into their bedroom while he had sex with my mother. I have seen them have intercourse countless times. He would touch me while he was having sex with her. Eventually, he began to make me touch my mother while they were having sex.

She didn't protest. Not even once. She participated and said nothing. Ever.

He came to wake me up every morning and made me touch him while he masturbated. For a long stretch when he was unemployed, he came to pick me up from school, took me for ice cream almost every day, and molested me as soon as we got home. It was during this time that he penetrated me with his fingers. It hurt so badly I burst into tears, but he didn't stop. He just stared at me with eyes so blank, so void of empathy—void of any and all compassion—that I knew he felt nothing of my pain. He cared nothing. He was completely anesthetized by his own compulsion, and didn't hesitate to jam his fingers in even further. My tears weren't ever acknowledged.

I was nothing.

He made me put lotion on his feet every night and made me touch him while he masturbated in the bed with my mother and me both there. When I was still very young, he made me perform oral sex on him, and when I got to be about 10 or 11, he did the same to me. He told me he was educating me and that it was very important that we did this. He said it would help me in my future relationships. He also said that he felt that this brought us closer together and formed a bond between us that was very strong—a bond that he valued.

I didn't know for a long time that he was also molesting my sister and brother and aunt. I thought he was just abusing me, and I thought it was because I wasn't really his biological daughter. Come to find out, he preyed on four of us.

That we know of.

My brother and I had a conversation once where he told me how I needed to forgive the man I have come to refer to as my stepmonster for everything he did to us and move on. I said, "Yeah? Well, he's never fucked *you* up the ass!"

My brother's response: "Yes. He has."

He ruled that house with an iron fist, and no one questioned or crossed him. It was nothing for him to flail his arms and send everything on a shelf or a counter top crashing to the floor—even if it was our dinner. My mother and I would quickly scurry to clean everything up.

If he were in a rage, he wouldn't hesitate to hit us. I got punched in the stomach once in Sears because I was complaining. I saw him hit my mother one time in the arm where he left a fist-sized bruise. When we got spanked, he pulled his belt out of his belt loops in one sickening yank, and we had to pull our pants down and lay across his bed to wait for the blow. If our fingers got in the way, they were left with welts just like the ones left on our butts.

He was to be feared above all, and we were all afraid of him. No one could stand up to him. No one could question him. And no one could stop him.

❧   ❧   ❧

And...We're Back

Concurrent with the abuse, we were in church every time the doors opened, where he sang in the choir and sang solos once a month and we had to hear everyone tell us what a great guy he was. Our job was to agree wholeheartedly.

The chasm between what people thought he was and what he really was, was deeper than the Atlantic, longer than the Nile. One could walk to the moon before they would ever reach the extent, the length, the breadth or the width of his deception.

Whenever I would resist or tell him that I didn't want to do any of these nasty things, he would become incensed and scream at me, "WHAT? Do you think I'm CRAZY? Is THAT what you think? DO YOU? Is THAT what you THINK?"

"No," I would tell him and start to cry.

He put his face in mine and pulled me closer as I flinched away. "DO YOU THINK I'M CRAZY?"

"No!" I would be forced to insist.

He lowered his voice to barely a whisper and, through grit teeth, would warn me, "If you ever thought I was crazy, I would take that gun out of the closet, and I would BLOW MY BRAINS OUT!"

"I'm sorry, Daddy," I would cry.

I'm sorry.

And I would let him do what he wanted.

I don't wish him any harm now—I think forgiveness takes care of angst and vengeful thoughts and has brought me into an amazing place of peace and wholeness—but I can objectively say that if he *had* blown his brains out, it would have solved a lot of problems in that house and in the future. The bottom line is, this world would have been and someday will be a better place without him in it.

From somewhere I found the courage to ask my mother once how she could allow her husband to do such wretched things to me.

Sweetly and sincerely, sickeningly so, she told me, "I can't make him do what is right in the eyes of the Lord. I can simply keep praying for him. The only thing I can control is my own obedience to Jesus. My job is to submit to the authority that God has placed above me. No matter what, he is still the spiritual leader of this home according to the Word, and I must respect that."

Good to know that God Himself signed off on the whole fucked-up situation. She was being obedient to her husband *and* God when she laid silently, pretending to be asleep, while her husband sneaked out of their bed and crawled into mine.

Duly noted.

My mother could pray for her degenerate husband all she wanted, but I prayed to be rescued. Incessantly, I never stopped praying to be spared from the torture for the duration of my childhood. Never did God answer—unless that answer was no. He did not rescue me from my abuser or his subservient wife. My perpetrator's "free will" and my mother's compliance to her "spiritual head" apparently trumped my own safety and well-being, in my young mind. That flannelboard Jesus was somewhere else sitting criss-cross applesauce or maybe even answering Stepmonster's prayers that he would never, ever get caught and end up in jail.

But I will say this. One prayer that God must have heard and answered was, "Please don't let me grow up and be insane and live in a mental hospital." It was my greatest fear. I just knew I'd be Jack Nicholson's roommate in *One Flew Over the Cuckoo's Nest*. For some reason, I was convinced that that was what happened to little girls like me who were having affairs with their mother's husbands whether they wanted to or not. So I always prayed, "Dear Jesus, please let me stay sane." It is a bona fide miracle that not only did I stay sane and avoid Nurse Ratched, I found my voice and became a writer. Abusive parents are dipshits if they think for one second that their children won't grow up and bust them out someday just like I'm doing right now. And I say to all young people who are enduring childhoods like the one I had—the sooner you *do* bust these people out, the better you will be. I can pretty well promise that you will go through absolute hell and your family will most likely be broken, but you are *not* the one who broke it up. Your abuser is. Telling someone who can help you is your best chance to avoid being a broken adult and possibly passing the abuse on to your own children. Break the cycle. You *can* do it, but you have to find your voice.

The closest I ever felt to "healthy" was when we *pretended* we were healthy in front of other people—at church. Church became a phony sanctuary for all of us. It was the only semblance of normalcy that we knew—such as it was—so I gladly engaged in it. It was Disneyland, the Happiest Place on Earth, complete with my flannelboard Prince Charming who loved me and chose me. I was

Cinderella at the ball. Disneyland closes at midnight, so as long as I left right after the fireworks with both my tiny shoes, I was never in any danger of being discovered as the cinder-faced girl, imposter that I was. But something happened in that pseudo-sanctuary. The Prince really did touch me in that beautiful ballroom with the music and the dancing and the bounty.

Like the hymn says, I was convinced that I should, "…trust and obey, for there's no other way to be happy in Jesus but to trust and obey." And if I did trust and obey, then I could "stand" on the promises of my Prince—that He could take a cinder-girl and make her a princess.

I knew that I should always be "…leaning, leaning, safe and secure from all alarm. Leaning, leaning, leaning on the everlasting arms."

Oh, I sang. Just like my grandmother, I sang.

Here's the downside, though, about being at the ball with the coachman rat that brought me every week: I had to join his "singing ministry." I know people may be curious as to why he shared the stage with me when he had the ego of a "solo" guy, but I was his ingénue, his creation. I was a trophy to him. I was his little girl with the big hair and the big voice. In his warped mind, he created me, and he owned me, his puppet. He taught me when to raise my hand in worship and when to close my eyes. I learned precisely when to smile and when to tear up. But, damn it all—I *wanted* it to be real!

He booked us anywhere he could find a venue, but our regular gig, ironically, was at the state prison in Jean, Nevada, to "minister" to the inmates, all those forgotten souls behind bars. What sane man would take his 14, 15, 16, 17, 18-year-old daughter out to a maximum security *prison*? Sane, I believe, would be the operative word there. I always thought how twisted it was that he got to leave after our concerts when he should have stayed inside those concrete walls with the barbed wire tops.

The two people at the center of my suffering will certainly be horrified that I have shed light on their darkness. They will lie and deny it the way they have been lying about it for years, yet privately implore me to forget about all of it and let it go—to forgive them like Jesus has. All I can say to them is this: I have forgiven you. That has nothing to do with what I'm doing now. All three of us know that every incident of abuse as I have described here is the solemn, tragic truth, no matter how many times you've lied to our family. No matter how many times you've tried to convince them that I am the liar, I am not the liar, and you know this. After all, we were all there, weren't we? The bottom line is this: this is my story. I have every right to tell it. It is as I have said. Simply put, if you wanted me to tell a different story, you should have given me a different story to tell.

❧   ❧   ❧

God Doesn't Even Know Where I Am

Having rounded the corner of my eighteenth year, I realized that time was a precious gift and that all the time I'd been given thus far in my life had been stolen from me. I had been expected to mother my sister and brother. My own mother willingly offered me up to the selfish and twisted desires of her husband. The money I made at my part-time job was often spent on food for the family and even some of the household bills, not only putting me in the role of caretaker and sexual chattel, but often provider as well. I had to share in the responsibility of everything under our roof, and no one stopped to ask me whether or not it was all right with me. It just was. I hit a wall the day I looked in the mirror and lamented to myself for all that I'd missed out on. I hadn't even been allowed to go to my own senior prom because dancing was sinful and why would anyone even want to go to her prom, knowing that Jesus would not be welcome inside for all the debauchery that occurred there with the boys who were only out for one thing. No dress. No corsage. No pictures. No memories with friends.

My reflection in the mirror was beyond devastated and well-past despairing. It was blank. A quiet resolution rested upon the demeanor of the young woman looking back at me from some dark and distant place. My eyes bored into her to see if I knew who she was. I did.

She was my mother.

Like her, I, too, was a woman who accepted whatever came. Nothing to do about it. Nothing to do except to convince the world outside that I had not a care in this world—that Jesus would reign supreme, whatever in the hell that meant. I had no voice, no opinion, no power. My soul was a chew toy clenched between the powerful jaws of a Rottweiler. But as long as no one suspected, I could almost make it through every day convincing even myself that I was just fine. My mother had taught me well. And I was a very good student.

So, when my good friend Robbie skied himself into a tree, head-first and helmetless—and landed in a coma for three days—I presented myself at church on Sunday as the ever faithful, hope-filled, standing-on-the-promises-of-God believer, proclaiming the victory of healing in Jesus' name. Proclaiming was very important—the louder the better. All I managed to do was stand on the promises of my own screwed up theology. Our ubiquitous church attendance played into my own self-delusion. You see, I knew that our family pretended to be a lot of things, but I wasn't just pretending to believe. I was convinced that my belief was Robbie's only chance. If he didn't make it, it was because I didn't have enough faith. I didn't dare not believe for his full recovery—his life depended on it. The fate of his whole world hung precariously on my gossamer resolve, on how much faith I could gather from every nook and cranny of my mind and heart. After all, couldn't I at least come up with the minimum mustard-seed amount necessary to move mountains? Heal the sick and the afflicted?

Raise the dead?

The phone call came.

When the world took a nosedive, there was nothing left for me, the misguided believer, but shame—standing in the gap of disappointment. That gap can be an abyss. That abyss is where I crumbled knowing that Robbie had been taken off of life support, an eighteen-year-old young man who wouldn't be going on to college and medical school after all. I was an eighteen-year-old girl who carried the guilt of his death and the shame of my own fabricated façade of a faith and a life. My theology was shattered. I learned the hard way that Almighty God is not our errand boy. This is earth. People die. Little girls get molested by Bible-thumping assholes who are beloved by all the people at church where you show up like the sunrise—twice on Sundays and Wednesday nights—and fill your head with all kinds of pretty little lies. The reality is, shit happens. And where is God in all of it?

Hell if I knew.

I was lost. That was the only thing I knew for sure. I thought of the passage in the Bible that describes how the Shepherd will leave the flock to go find that one sheep that is lost. I was that sheep. However, my faith could not sustain any sort of notion that God would come find me. Instead, I was convinced that God didn't even know where I was. He couldn't find me. I'd fallen off a cliff somewhere.

And why should I believe I was even worth God's effort? After all, it's not like the Divine ever listened to a word I said, right? My prayers bounced right off the ceiling and came crashing back down on my life with all the momentum of my own bitterness. The phrase, *God doesn't even know where I am…* began running through my head. My internal tape recorder was on auto-rewind, and the thought repeated itself over and over and over again in my mind… *God doesn't even know where I am…*

Very shortly after Robbie died, after my "faithquake," the step-predator and I were asked to provide the music ministry for a Full Gospel Businessmen's meeting that was being held at the Hacienda Hotel in one of their small convention rooms. I never had a choice of where we "ministered." Refusing was what I wanted to do, but that obviously was not an option. Being fake seemed the simplest and the most familiar. Just perform like I always had. In bed. On stage. Sitting in the pew. Lying on my back. I was so good at it by now. So, I put on a dress and drove down with him on a Saturday morning and sang my harmonies right on queue. I closed my eyes and lifted a hand with the crescendo of the music. I laughed, spoke my Christianese with just the right accent, and sat down next to my abuser, smile intact, and leaned into him as his arm went around my shoulder as was expected of me. His Karate cologne burned my nose, and my stomach churned when he rubbed his hand up and down my arm.

Still, I smiled.

The CEO of Ocean Spray juice drinks was the guest speaker. I don't remember his name, but he was a slight man in an expensive suit and pure white hair. His voice, ironically I thought, was soft. The microphone squealed as he leaned into it. The look of surprise on his face, like he was suddenly awake on this early Saturday morning, evoked buoyant laughter from the crowd of men. Stepmonster gave me a little pat, reveling in the success of our performance. Everyone had given this man their rapt attention. I'd turned my tape recorder back on. The robotic mantra that I had rehearsed for two weeks was automatic, almost drug-induced, to me now: *God doesn't even know where I am.*

After the meeting, we all had that standard Kumbaya moment where we stood around in a circle, held hands, and prayed. Of course, my hand was firmly in the grip of my molester and singing partner.

Somebody's muffled voice floated somewhere over my head. "Heavenly Father, we just wanna thank You for this day…" He doesn't even know where I am. "We thank You for the many blessings in our lives…" He doesn't even know where I am. "We ask that You forgive our iniquities and cleanse us from our sins…" He doesn't even know where I am…

Suddenly, this Ocean Spray guy who was standing across from me next to the guy who was praying, broke the circle and walked right through the center of it, looked at me with his eyes very intense, and stood right in front of me.

"I feel very compelled to pray for you right now," he told me. This is from a high-powered businessman, not a preacher.

This did not impress me. Not because I was in a bad spiritual place, but because every boneheaded Vegas whacko that has ever been attracted to the Pentecostal movement has approached me with "words of wisdom" and messages from God, usually after I walked off some stage after a rousing musical performance. Here was one more. And besides, *God doesn't even know where I am. I'll just play the game a little longer. I wonder what we're having for lunch. I wonder if I'll be the one buying it. After all, God doesn't even know where I am.*

"Absolutely," I replied convincingly. "I'd love to have you pray for me." *God doesn't even know where I am.*

He took hold of both my hands and started to pray. *God doesn't even know where I am.* He just prayed some generic prayer—nothing at all relevant or life-altering. He just prayed. *God doesn't even know where I am.*

Mid-sentence and without warning, he stopped praying and let go of my hands and looked at me ardently. My eyes popped open and locked with his.

"You know what?" he said pointedly. He looked so deeply into my eyes with such a steeled confidence, I had a feeling that, somehow, he had just read my mail.

He lifted his finger toward the ceiling and said almost chastisingly, "God knows EXACTLY where you are!"

My heart stopped pumping blood through my body and, instead, started to pump something akin to an iced, cherry slushy, chunking its way through my constricting veins. My lungs became bricks in my chest preventing inhalation—exhalation. And my ears suddenly stopped hearing any other sound except for some cool wind, blowing gently, bringing me something... true, and laying it at my feet. A gift. My spirit entwined itself with his in that moment. I was convinced that this total stranger knew everything about me. He knew. I was the Great Poser. No secret was it to him that I didn't mean a word of what I had sung that morning. The pain of my tortured existence was no mystery to him. My disguise hadn't fooled him. We stood there with only the other, and everyone else fell away into some dark backdrop. He knew who I was, and I was completely exposed.

He had my strict attention.

He told me: "God knows EXACTLY where you are. You are right in the palm of His hand. Right now you are going through a desert experience in your Christian walk. But there will come a day when springs of Living Water will flow up from your soul!" He said it with strength and authority, chasing any shred of doubt from the dark corners of my mind.

I am well aware that this is classic Christianese, and I bag on that groupspeak all the time. But even so, these words were unquestioningly spoken with the command of a Higher Jurisdiction.

I was like buttuh.

And he was done. He never spoke another word to me again. What else was there to say? Almighty God stopped the world from spinning, got off His throne, came down to me in some back room of the Hacienda Hotel in Las Vegas, Nevada, and told me, "ENOUGH!" And He gave me a promise to hold onto as I walked out of the doors of that hotel, got back into the car with my abuser and drove home to continue living under the same roof as he did.

The promise that one day, "springs of Living Water would flow up from my soul" was something I have kept in my heart every single day since the moment I heard it. Those words have been branded into my heart. They have sustained me through the ever-continuing, black, insidious excruciation of my abuser's free will. I still got molested—even at 18 and 19 years old. But those words gave me hope when I considered the possibilities that I might someday escape this torture and make something of my life. They afforded me the confidence I needed to stop pretending to be something that I was not, letting the chips fall where they may, and they comforted me when, through the years, the real me began to emerge and was no longer embraced by the religified status quo.

In the meantime, I had figured out that God was not going to interrupt the choices that my stepmonster was making, for whatever reason I couldn't understand. He had not intervened on behalf of my physical safety my entire childhood. That could only mean that I would have to escape from that situation myself. I had to leave somehow. I started looking for ways to break away and get out from underneath my stepmonster's possessive, iron grip and my mother's codependent, debilitated indifference. Even though I didn't know where or how or what they would be, I did hold one certainty in my heart and in my mind: God would always know exactly where I was. And somehow, He would keep me right in the palm of His hand. He would eventually lead me out of this dry, barren desert, and someday, springs of Living Water would flow up.

From my soul.

Chapter 3

Through the Desert to the Promised Land by the Beach

THE DAY I packed up my white Datsun B-210 with what precious little I had and moved the hell out, I honestly had no earthly idea how my parents and my sister and brother would make it without me. It couldn't matter. I had to go.

From the moment my friend from Ocean Spray uttered that amazing promise, it didn't take long to understand that God was not going to drive up in a taxi and cart my ass out of that house. I had to break and stretch and struggle out of that cocoon that had trapped me for too long. Even though I was only moving fifteen minutes away into my Grandma Jean's house—scary juju and all—I managed to free myself from the bondage of my parents. I paid Grandma a little bit of rent and, by "little," I mean a *little*!

What a difference.

Gone were the oppressive days where every minute of my time was meticulously accounted for. I went from having every iota of my life controlled by a sick and overbearing man who had to know whether or not any boys were ever within ten feet of me to complete freedom with my grandmother, who didn't seem to be affected in the least whether I was home or not, what I was out doing, or with whom. She had always given my mother and aunt whatever freedom they wanted because, let's face it, she was busy. By the time I took one of the little bedrooms in the back corner of her house, she wasn't any less busy. She still had a business to run. Her life was as consumed as it ever was booking gigs for The Platters, sending out promotional material, doing interviews and radio spots, canvassing new acts, talking to agents and industry people, writing checks to lawyers who haggled in court with other groups over the right to use The Platters' name. We were in the decade of plenty—the 80s. Ronald Reagan was the President and, although my grandma is a staunch democrat, she liked the guy. He was a show biz fellow from her own era, after all. Money was plentiful and Lady Vegas was rolling in it. The Platters had regular gigs at the Four Queens, and we were down there watching them perform more often than not.

I found myself instantaneously in a rut. I was working part time as a telemarketer, selling air/hotel packages for several properties on the Strip and downtown, going to UNLV part time with no declared major, and keeping myself busy with my newfound freedom. But it started to feel like I was jumping my pogo stick right in the mud. My life was quickly becoming monotonous and inane, and it was getting pretty hard to ignore. It seemed that I had spent so much time and energy on escaping my childhood home that I had no idea what to do once I did and got a flat tire straight out of the gate. College had always been a dream and a priority. I love those UNLV Runnin' Rebels, but I was drowning in that place. I needed a smaller school.

Preferably by the beach.

Although my church encouraged most of its young people to attend a private, Christian college in northern California, a couple people from my youth group opted for a tiny college in Southern California, still affiliated with our denomination. Definitely warmer than northern Cal. This is where I wanted to go. I wanted to put some distance between me and the dread of my childhood as far away from my past as I could get.

People have asked whether or not I was concerned at all about leaving my sister and brother in the home of a pedophile. I must confess, in my naivety, I believed they would be safe for two reasons. First of all, they were biologically his, and I stupidly believed at that point that he was only molesting me because he was not actually related to me by blood. I never thought he would do something like that to his "own" children. And second of all, my uncle—who was a preacher—was taking a new church and asked him to be his minister of music. Where?

Southern California.

WTF?

My uncle, along with the rest of the world, had no idea that this man had wreaked havoc on my body and my mind and my faith and my childhood. And I didn't realize then that he had already done the same to his own biological children. Nor did he even keep his insidiousness within the four walls of our home. Years later, I would learn of yet *another* family member, a total of five that I *know* of, who was slightly more fortunate and escaped his advances. What is so troubling now is not knowing how many others there are out there who have been preyed upon by this man. I didn't know the half of it. My uncle certainly didn't suspect anything. He had no idea that his brother-in-law had such a twisted appetite for children. Why wouldn't he offer him a position working for the Lord?

And I remember distinctly thinking, *Well? Has God finally answered my prayers and sent this opportunity to consume this man's mind and time and energy to prevent him from acting out in such ungodly ways?*

And then almost immediately thinking, "Pssh. Impeccable timing, Lord. The horse has already bolted out of the corral, and You're just now closing the gate? It's a little late, don't You think?"

But it was enough for me to believe that if he did start "missing" me, my sister and brother would be safe underneath the umbrella of church work.

When I got that acceptance letter from that Bible college in Southern California, I packed up once again—it took all of about 26 minutes—and bid Grandma Jean and Lady Vegas goodbye and drove west, knowing that my parents were about to do the same. My dorm room was reserved and, sight-unseen, I got up early on a Saturday morning, took the 95, and wove my way through the Spaghetti Bowl to the 15 South with a cassette tape of Petra blasting *More Power To Ya* through my lousy stereo system.

The freeway stretched out ahead of me like a black snake lain out in the barren sand. The words, "Right now you are going through a desert experience in your Christian walk. But there will come a day when springs of Living Water will flow up from your soul," came to my mind as I set out upon that barren wilderness of the Mojave Desert. With hope in my heart for a new beginning, I said goodbye to each major exit: *Goodbye Charleston and the donut shop we used to stop at after church. Goodbye Sahara.* I couldn't count how many times I'd gotten off at that exit to get to Trinity Life Center. Every Sunday and Wednesday night of my life it seemed. *Goodbye Flamingo.* No more driving down to UNLV for classes. *Goodbye Tropicana.* Back in the day it was the exit we took to get to the airport. That was almost the edge of town then. There wasn't much between that and the Blue Diamond exit, which literally spit me out to nothing but gazillion-year-old dirt, sagebrush, and Joshua trees scattered about intermittently.

And you know what's strange? I no more missed my hometown than a big, fat dog misses a tick. I wouldn't doubt that I have attachment issues. Maybe it's because I'd been raised in that town where we blow up our historical landmarks when they get old and we're all hankering for something new? I had vague memories of the Dunes Genie that used to stand alongside the very freeway I was on now, beckoning drivers to come play 18 holes of golf. Whatever happened to *that* guy? Did *he* get all sentimental and sappy when he left? I daresay not. The golf course he watched over is long gone, and the hotel has been replaced. The Desert Inn, the Sands, the Stardust, the Landmark—all gone. Can't say as I missed them. Now I was going away. Would Lady Vegas miss me?

Would I miss her?

I was Petra'd out by the time I'd gotten to Baker's Tallest Thermometer in the World. No time to stop. Besides, I knew how hot it was. Three digits, and after 110 degrees, it really doesn't matter. I switched over to Undercover: *Holy, Holy, Holy,* tapped the dash of my car, and encouraged her to keep puttering along. Like a faithful friend, those tires kept rolling along that asphalt, hotter than hell. We didn't stop until we got to the McDonald's in Barstow, where I pulled up and parked between the train and a busload of 80-somethings. It took all of 10 minutes to pee and grab a Big Mac. I was on a mission.

My life was about to start.

Got back out on that black snake with Barstow behind me and the sun directly overhead, burning down on the scenery that hadn't changed in miles and miles and miles. Second Chapter of Acts—*Mansion Builder, of course*— carried me through Victorville. I turned my A/C off to make it over Cajon Pass. With sweat quickly forming under my bare thighs against the seat, I cranked my window down—dry, blistering air blowing through the car was better than baking in it—and navigated carefully up and then down those long, winding curves.

Not too long after, my surroundings finally started to change. I flew under the sign that said, *91 West—Beach Cities.*

The beach…

The searing heat seemed to diminish, and it didn't seem so Tarzan hot anymore. It smelled different here. It felt different. A contemplative mood had found its way to my heart and, by the time I hit the 55 South, Keith Green was banging on that piano and singing about that prodigal son. I got to the end of the 55—it was the end of the freeway in those days—and hung a right onto Fair Drive. I couldn't have agreed more with Keith: *Oh Lord, You're Beautiful…*

And so was this campus.

I've heard it said that the place of one's birth isn't necessarily the place where she's born but, rather, where she first learned to live. The place of my birth is Southern California College, Costa Mesa, California, 1986, now Vanguard University.

In the end, I landed about four and a half hours away from Vegas—but a blessed ten minutes from the Pacific Ocean—and an hour and a half down the freeway from where my parents lived in a small, inland town.

What could I do but assume by "faith" that everything was as it should be?

Being by the beach quite possibly made up for every rotten thing that had ever happened to me. Southern California is gorgeous, and I loved it. I loved the air. I loved the people. I loved the pace. I loved the water. I loved the freeways. I loved Disneyland, the weather, and the fish tacos. I loved the beach. I loved my classes. I loved my *life*! I loved it! A reprieve had been granted to me.

One of the resident directors stepped up to the microphone every day in chapel for the first month and said the same thing every day: "Everything. Is. Going. To. Be. All. Right."

That woman scared me.

She felt the need to reassure the incoming freshmen that they would survive the transition in their lives. Kids showed up and cried, and I looked at them like they were escaped mental patients. Maybe everybody else sitting around me had parents who made it hard to walk away from their childhoods, but not me! I was fine as frog hair split five ways! And, frankly, the more she tried to reassure us, the more she freaked me out. I wasn't waiting for everything to be okay. This was as okay as I'd ever been in my life.

I got up and could literally *taste* the salty water rolling into my dorm room on the ocean breeze. The perks of being on the 7th floor… The education was great and all that, but let's face it. It's where a kid can wear shorts, tank tops, and flip-flops all year long and sit on the beach for four whole years. When I went there, Vanguard had just under a thousand students, and the feeling of family and community enveloped me and provided something I'd never known before—my first tantalizing tastes of sanctuary. Freedom. Hope.

I declared a music major and auditioned for the Vanguard Singers, the traveling group for the college who performed and promoted the school in churches all around California, Arizona and Nevada. This group of about 40 singers and instrumentalists traveled every other Sunday. We were our own roadies, which sucked, but what can you do? Our director, Noel Wilson, bought us all breakfast croissants from Jack in the Box, loaded us up in vans, and took us all over the place for a full day of performances—usually two services on Sunday morning where the host church would feed us lunch. Then we'd pack up all the equipment and head out for another church—who would feed us dinner—and we would once again set everything up, perform, tear it all down again, pack it all back up in the truck, and return to the dorms late in the evening.

It was, unequivocally, the time of my life.

Performing on stage without my stepmonster was surreal and thrilling and fantastic, and now, when I stepped in front of the microphone and sang about Jesus, I meant every word that came out of my mouth. To say that the music was outstanding is an understatement. Noel is a brilliant composer and one of the first examples I knew of what a true Christian man is. He fathered this lost little girl in ways that her real father couldn't and her step... I can't even say it... wouldn't. Many of the men on that campus fathered me: Virgil Ziegler, Phil Robinette, Vince Gil. God put these remarkable men in my path simply to let me see that there *were* good men in this world who were committed to Christ and lived a life that exuded true kindness and compassion. They were smart, every one. And they were authentic. They are pillars in my life that remind me that the greatest impact we can have on others is to simply *be*. So many mistakenly believe that we have to engage in some exalted task in order to please God or be in His will or simply to "make a difference" in the lives of others. I'm not sure that's true. Often we make the most impact just by being *who we are*. These men showed me the face of God. They were a safe place to land. If there was goodness in the world, it was here. My concept of being "close to God" was believing that I had to do what my parents did and chase after those "signs and wonders." If there weren't a good miracle around that was obvious to everybody, they'd just conjure one up to show anyone who might be impressed with their proximity to God. These men were different. They were just... walking. Causing no harm. Their laughter was not sinister; they had no ulterior motives. They simply loved God and loved us. Loved me. They were sanctuary. And that was the miracle—simple pilgrimage.

I was happier than a pig in... well? The sunshine. Little did I know that this newfound bliss was really just ambrosial anesthesia. Laughing gas. Jesus juice. I was too inebriated to catch what was really happening to me. I didn't even feel it when I was pulled off of that bloody gurney I'd shown up on and placed ever so gently on the operating table that I had no idea was waiting for me. The Great Physician was standing over me wearing a white gown and rubber gloves, a scalpel in His steady, healing hand. I looked right past his surgical mask. All I could see were His eyes looking lovingly into mine as He plunged into my heart with that first cut.

❧   ❧   ❧

Right to the Edge of Nowhere and Back

The academics of college really started to rock my world—not because the work was too rigorous for me. I did well. But the sheer volume of knowledge that existed was overwhelming to me. We had professors at our school who had helped translate the Bible into the New International Version and could fluently read, write, and speak in no fewer than 15 dead languages, thousands of years old. I remember one gal who taught my Old Testament Survey class who floored me every time I walked in. She lectured about *I AM* one day and I thought, *If this chick gives an alter call right now, I swear I'm going forward.* I doubted my psychology professor was even saved, but she was brilliant all the same. She didn't fit into my "mold" of Christianity, but by the time I was done with one semester, she had pretty well ended up demolishing a few of my paradigms— thank God.

My favorite part of the day was my music classes. Not theory, mind you, but my choir classes. Nothing like kicking out some great harmonies with talented singers and, afterwards, grabbing one of those chocolate ice creams in the short, white Styrofoam cups with those little wooden spoon paddles on your way to the quad to see if you had any mail.

You usually didn't.

We were done for the day a little before 3:00 in the afternoon, and I had agreed to hit the beach with some of my new friends. The mailbox had just a half-sheet of paper with a message scribbled on it, and I had to run up to my room real quick to grab some 55 sunscreen and a towel.

The message said for me to stop by the financial aid office at my earliest convenience and talk to someone about my account. It was on the way.

"Why don't you have a seat?" I was told.

"Is there something wrong?" I asked. I knew I had filled out my financial aid paperwork meticulously. Thankfully, the fact that my parents were poor as dirt came in handy. I got a hefty package from Uncle Sam.

"You're about $1000.00 short of being able to stay here at Vanguard. Is there any way you can get us that money and remain enrolled in your classes?"

She might as well have asked for a million.

"I... uh..." Thoughts of running home, putting a couple bucks down on the table and rolling the dice flashed through my mind. Of course, the city wasn't built on winners. "I don't have that kind of money right now."

"Hmm. This is very unfortunate."

"I am getting a job. I can make payments," I offered.

"Unfortunately, you need to have $1000 by the end of this week or you'll be withdrawn from your classes here."

And go where?

Back to Las Vegas? To what? My grandmother's house? To do what? Work in a casino? I wasn't even 21. To be swallowed up again by UNLV? I couldn't even park at a school that big. Should I move to that armpit of a town where my parents lived? Back to the hell of my childhood? To another church where I would have to pretend again for everybody that my family was happy and healthy and that we all loved Jesus?

There was no fucking way.

I had burned the ships behind me when I came ashore to this new land. I told my financial aid counselor, "You don't understand. I have nowhere to go. I have *nowhere* to go!"

"There's really nothing I can do," she said flatly, looking back at me over the thick black rim of her glasses.

I walked like a zombie back to my dorm room and fell face down on the bed. I lay there for about thirty seconds in stunned silence before I began to wail from a place of hopelessness that I'd thought was all behind me. My roommate was in class, so I was alone. Boy, was I ever alone. The thought of leaving this place shattered any hope I had for my future. My whole mind was destroyed just thinking about having to pack up my clothes, my toothpaste and shampoo, and my comforter, which were all the possessions I had in this world, and drive back down the road to nowhere. To the barren wilderness. To nothing.

I sobbed hour after dismal hour. And how could I pray? Prayer didn't work for me. How many times had I prayed that I would be safe in my own home? If

God didn't intervene for an innocent child who was being ravaged by a sick and selfish monster, what the hell could I expect God to do for that child now? Write a $1000 check?

Right.

Hours went by and the sun set over the ocean just five miles away. I just lay there on my bunk, not moving, barely breathing. I'd cried all the tears I could squeeze out of my eyes. My crying had stopped. My caring had stopped. I had no plan. No hope. Still lying in the dark, I heard a light knock on the door and decided to ignore it. The knock came again and whoever it was finally opened the door and told me that I had a phone call on the payphone at the end of the hall.

Who gives a shit? What? Is it my *mother*?

Slowly, I pulled myself up, set my feet to the floor and sat there for a second. My swollen eyes squinted from the bright lights of the hallway. I walked down to the phone, lifted the dangling receiver, and held it to my ear.

"Hello?" I managed.

The voice on the other end happened to be the choir director at Trinity Life Center. He said, "Someone told us that you needed some money to stay in school there at Vanguard, so the music department here wants to send you a music scholarship in the amount of $1000 toward your tuition to make that happen. Would that be okay?"

Would that be okay?

I took the phone away from my ear and held it out in front of me, staring at it as if giving it a good once-over would make the mystery of what I was hearing any more clear.

Just when I thought I'd cried all the tears I could muster, here they came again. I couldn't answer him. I couldn't even speak. The soft, grateful sounds of my weeping told him I would surely take him up on his generous offer.

When the president of Ocean Spray juice drinks told me, "God knows EXACTLY where you are," it was the first time in my life that I knew God had spoken directly to me. When I heard these words come across the phone line on the 7th floor of the girls' dormitory, I knew that God had, for the first time in my life, taken notice of me and moved on my behalf.

I was staying.

❧   ❧   ❧

Prince Charming, Paper Tigers, and the Fairytale Vacuum

I was Cinderella who thought she had gotten kicked out of the ball at midnight, but somehow managed to get behind the velvet ropes once again and back into the party! After that $1000 check cleared and the rest of my financial aid rolled into my account, this cinder-girl's glass flip-flops never touched the pavement. Seventy-five degrees all year long. Singing and traveling all around Southern California. Bible stories suddenly coming alive and relevant because I was relearning them in a real, historical context, and having the time of my life with new friends who knew like I did that we were all saved from the eternal fires of Hell and ready to spread that message to everybody else.

Except few of us ever saw or talked to anybody else for the four years we were there. We were sans heathens for the most part except for maybe a few *Lutherans* that had been accepted to our school and were still trying to figure out the Holy Ghost!

To say Vanguard was a vacuum of sorts is not meant to be derogatory in any way. For me, it was a long-awaited safe haven. I would not have changed my experience there for all the sushi in the world.

Although…I did meet a boy. He arrived mid-semester of my freshman year on a white stallion. Okay, it was a yellow Datsun 280z, but he was just looking for somebody to rescue, and I'd always wanted to be somebody's princess. His major was Pastoral Ministries, but I was pretty sure I couldn't end up with a preacher. When he changed his major to English, I got way more interested in being swept off my feet. Very cerebral, this man. Had been a marine. Devoted completely and wholeheartedly to his Maker. Hilariously funny. Truly, those were great qualities, but, really, I was only looking for someone who wouldn't hit me or molest our children. In my world, that was the highest I could ever set the bar. What else did I know? Truth be told, we attempted to rescue each other. I needed to be rescued from my entire worldview, and he needed to be rescued from a relentless self-loathing that made him question me all the time as to how I could love someone like him. I mistook that for humbleness and just knew I could love him right out of that! Unfortunately, neither of us had the good sense to know that a person has to make that journey into health all by himself. Herself. And healthy people don't hook up with unhealthy people. That's why they're healthy. They don't take on other people's issues, they don't believe they can rescue anyone, and they don't look for anything outside themselves for the solutions to life's big problems.

I was about as healthy as a pus bubble.

This pus bubble, though, was happier than she'd ever been in her life! In my psychology class, I learned about this really *boss* coping strategy called repression. People who had experienced hellacious abuse and trauma actually had the ability to "forget" about their horrible pasts. They could block out entire episodes in their lives.

This was the coolest, damn thing I had ever heard.

In that fairytale vacuum, people could be healed and delivered of all of life's ills. Of course, since I was starting to toy around with this whole *prayer* thing again, I laid down that night in my bunk and asked for God to erase any and all memories of my abusive childhood. I'd heard all my life that God could simply wipe a person's slate clean! Fantastic! Wipe it clean, Lord! Wipe it clean! Because, honestly? I, to that point, unluckily remembered every gruesome moment of those years and thought this repression would be my healing—my restoration. My repair. I prayed that when I woke up the next morning, all recollection of the pain would be gone.

It wasn't.

I wasn't shocked or surprised. To me, it was just one more prayer that God refused to answer. My distrust of God was always close to the surface, even though I acknowledged the fact that He'd clearly intervened on my behalf in helping me remain there at Vanguard. I had no clue what moved His mighty hand and what prayers bounced right off the ceiling back in my face. Truth be told, I'm still not absolutely certain.

People have to understand... In that subculture and with the whacked out way I was raised, the solutions to all our questions and struggles back then could be resolved according to the formulaic, pat answers that we all memorized by heart. We went to chapel, we prayed a lot, we were obedient to God by following all the rules and submitting to the authority that God had established above us. In the meantime, we didn't work on our shit—we just threw ourselves face first into this big cosmic plan with the notion that we'd tapped into the source of all truth. Whatever happened, we certainly couldn't lose with God at the helm, right?

Trouble was, I'd never even seen a helm, and I certainly didn't know where mine was or who was standing at it. If I was going to stick with how I was raised, I had to appoint either God or Satan to stand at the helm of my life. Those were pretty well the only options.

Not sure how relevant that whole "repression" class was for me, but a few classes later, a much more specific subject came up: child abuse. Specifically, the sexual abuse of children. What the hell was all this talk about child abuse? I was trying to put all that mess behind me and walk in God's light! On the beach in God's light! The anesthesia from my soul surgery was wearing off, and I wanted to go back to dreamland! Swim in the beautiful blue water, sit on the sand at Huntington Beach, and watch the sun set majestically over the Pacific Ocean!

I began to suspect that instead of circumventing this big pile of shit that was my past, it might be that God wanted me to sift through it.

Frankly, this did not raise my opinion of Him in any way.

Like so many other victims, I had been prepared to take the secret of my sexual abuse to my grave. I was ashamed and humiliated by what I'd been forced to do and all that had been forced upon me. I didn't blame myself, per se, but I would die a thousand deaths before I'd rehash all of it for someone else. I didn't want anyone else to ever know.

I have no idea, then, what crazy notion possessed me to talk to my boyfriend about the information that was now swimming around in my brain and intruding on my spirit. I tried to sound as clinical and detached as I could, but the instant I started throwing out statistics and facts about this subject, something clicked and he knew. He just knew.

He didn't acknowledge any of the percentages I was quoting but, instead, interrupted me and asked me flat out, "Has anything like that ever happened to you?"

The "no" lodged in my throat. I had been fully prepared to lie and deny everything, but something in his eyes told me that he wouldn't believe me if I did.

"Yes."

I could almost audibly hear the bricks crumbling to the ground as that wall around me collapsed into rubble. And my hero responded by putting his arms around me and telling me I was beautiful and cherished and blameless, even though I knew he didn't really believe any of those things about himself. That should have been my first clue that my Cinderella-marries-the-handsome-prince story might not end in a happily ever after. I was just thankful that he created a sanctuary for me out of sheer compassion so, obviously, I had to marry him. He made me feel safe. Those were the qualifications for my Prince Charming in my own fairytale vacuum, and like we all did, I hinged the whole thing on God and praised Him for bringing us together.

One problem. He was hell bent on confronting this monster, and the very next available Saturday, he lifted me up behind him on his valiant steed—okay, he put me in the passenger's seat of his two-seater—and drove out to my parents' house for the showdown.

The further east we drove, the dryer the air was. The dryer my throat was. The dryer our conversation was. I was ill over it. I did not want to do this. *No one* challenged this man who could rage like a hurricane and lay out anyone stupid enough to cross him. I fully expected the two of them to come to blows over this. I contemplated who would bleed out first as he drove relentlessly, mile after wretched mile.

We pulled up to the parsonage where my parents lived rent-free as part of their compensation for their ministry work at my uncle's church. He wanted to go straight to my sister to ask her if the abuse was still happening. He wasn't going for that whole "God-would-surely-prevent-a-minister-from-hurting-his-children" theory. In fact, he thought that was the stupidest notion he'd ever heard in his natural-born life. I didn't see how such vile duplicity was possible. Surely, he couldn't lead such a double life. Surely he'd relinquished those sick tendencies.

My boyfriend was nowhere near me on that issue.

We found my sister in her room. No posters on the walls. A cassette tape of Amy Grant played softly in the background. My sister was sprawled out on an unmade bed drawing in a notebook. She really was the "pretty one" with her long, chocolate brown hair and thick eyelashes, strong and sweet over her mischievous eyes. He didn't beat around the bush.

"We're here to talk to your dad about molesting your sister, and we want to know if you've ever been sexually abused by him."

A stiff wind could've knocked her over into a whole new family.

"Have you?" he repeated gently.

"Yes."

"And has he molested you since you moved here? Since he's been in the ministry?" I watched her struggle with telling him the truth—much like I did when the questions were pointed at me.

"Yes," she admitted.

You know? I think a faith that *can* be shattered? Probably ought to be. And this is "Exhibit One" for why that is. Who did this girl have to turn to? Where could she have gone? She walked around in a "Christian" environment six out of seven days of the week between her Christian high school and church. Everyone knew her dad and her uncle were in the ministry at one of the local churches, and literally no one had a clue that she was in Hell.

We went back into the living room where the predator was watching TV. We stood together in front of this man who had seemed so formidable for my entire childhood. I had every reason to figure that he'd put us both out on our asses. Suddenly, I was six standing there in that living room. I was about to witness Armageddon.

"This isn't really a social visit," my boyfriend began. "I need to talk to you. I think we should go into another room."

I choked down the bile rising up in my throat and followed my fiancé and the monster into the next room—his bedroom, of all places. My boyfriend and I sat on the edge of his bed, and he sat in a chair across from us not even two feet away.

"I know what you did to your daughters," he said calmly. Too calmly. "You have been molesting them for years. Not just touching them inappropriately but serious, invasive, unconscionable abuse. You have done horrible, horrible things to your own children."

In a moment that exploded in my head, I flashed back and heard that maniacal voice: "DO YOU THINK I'M SICK? DO YOU? If I knew you ever thought I was sick, I'd take that gun in the closet, and…" My eyes darted to the closet where his clothes were strewn about and found the top shelf. He could use that gun any way he wanted. My heart was a jackhammer trying to pound its way out of my chest. I could hardly breathe.

With eyes that filled with tears and an expression of complete and utter remorse, this man who I thought would come apart at the seams with rage said earnestly, "I'm going to tell you the truth—I'm not going to even try to lie…" The sincerity with which he spoke could have convinced the most jaded cynic: "…since I've been in the ministry working for the Lord, I have not touched my children. The Lord has taken the desire away and I've lived above reproach since living here and working with the church." A tear rolled down his cheek.

I was baffled at this claim that I knew was a bold-faced lie. My boyfriend's face showed no expression, no emotion. This is obviously what he had expected all along.

He matter-of-factly stated, "Your daughter has already told us that you have."

The monster was stunned. He looked bewildered for a split second, as if he never anticipated that we wouldn't fall hook, line and sinker for his deception. He could have won an Academy Award for Best Actor, and he knew it. Then, as if it was the only thing left to do, he hung his head in shame and wouldn't look us in the eyes anymore. I was floored. Here was the man I'd lived in fear of my entire existence, and he was rendered completely impotent in nine short words: "Your daughter has already told us that you have." He was nothing but a paper tiger. The first time someone dared to shed light on his perversion, he shriveled into nothing. He might as well have been a napkin that we'd wadded up and thrown into a fire. Bringing him down was just that simple.

All at once, I was incensed. What in God's name had I been afraid of all those years? *THIS?* It was outrageous to me! And how did he sit there looking straight into our eyes and *lie* like he did? I'd never seen such genuine, heartfelt sincerity in all my life! And it was all *BULLSHIT!* He could have convinced any jury, any judge that he had overcome his atrocious compulsion. I was so relieved that we'd already talked to my sister because, if we hadn't, she would have been the one we would not have believed. In that moment, I counted everything he'd ever told me before as a lie, and I would never believe a word he spoke from that day forward. Anyone who could lie so convincingly had to be dismissed forever. Absolutely, positively sociopathic. He had deceived me into thinking he was all-powerful. He'd deceived me into believing that the devil had made him do all these awful things. He was nothing but a sick pervert, incapable of telling the truth about anything, and I promised myself that I would never be fooled by him again.

I wish I could say that this story ended with a phone call to the police. I wish I could say that we'd pressed charges and had him hauled off to jail with my mother. I wish the night had not ended the way it had with him being the focus of the "forgiving circle." He called a family meeting to ask our forgiveness. Oh, the drama. He put his head down on the kitchen table and wept and begged our forgiveness. My mother cried and begged our forgiveness. We all had to go around in a circle and tell him that we forgave them both, including my brother, who I had not known until I sat down next to him that he *too* had fallen prey to his own father.

A revealing day.

"The Lord has shed a light on my sins, and I beg your forgiveness." His body shook with convulsive tears. "Please, I'm *begging* you! The Bible says that all have sinned and fall short of the glory of God! And that one sin is no greater than another. If we don't forgive one another, then our Heavenly Father will not forgive us of our own sin!"

Well, that certainly is how *some* people read it.

My mother reached her hand out to gently stroke his temple as he sobbed. He couldn't seem to speak anymore, so she said her piece.

"I have to ask for forgiveness too because I knew what was going on, and I didn't say anything." Repentant tears streamed down her cheeks as well.

"I forgive you," my brother said.

His father looked up gratefully, then turned expectant eyes toward me, imploring me silently to say the words.

"I forgive you," I said.

This broke him again. Another twenty-second bout of crying ensued. He lifted his tear-stained face and looked toward my sister.

Silence.

"Please," he urged. "I *need* you to forgive me!"

Her face didn't even move. Not an eyelash. She just stared blankly at him.

"I am sorry for what I did! Don't withhold your…"

"SHE DOESN'T HAVE TO FORGIVE YOU! NONE OF THEM DO!" my boyfriend screamed, cutting him off. "THIS ISN'T ABOUT YOU! IT'S ABOUT THEM!"

My hero.

I'm not sure what we thought we accomplished there that day. In hindsight, we should have pressed charges. He should have gone to jail. He should have been made to pay for his crimes against children. He should have stood before a judge and been made to answer for his actions. But because we didn't press charges that night, I have family members who refuse to believe me now and they are convinced that I have lied about what happened to us. Because we didn't press charges that night, he went on to work in law enforcement and found another church to "minister" in music. Because we didn't press charges that night, he has been able to convince a good many people that he is a good and harmless Christian man who loves God and loves his children, and I am a liar. Because we didn't press charges that night, I am left to ponder all that our family...

...has lost.

æ   æ   æ

When Do We Learn Not To Want?

I hear all the time, "Every path leads to Heaven," and it's a beautiful notion. It truly is. It beats the hell out of, "Turn or burn!" for sure! I gotta say, though, I believe that just the opposite is true. I don't believe *any* path leads to Heaven. Rather, I believe God literally comes and gets us from whatever path we're on—and that includes Christianity. I was *on* the path of Christianity, and had to have God come and "save" me right out of it, and that was a pretty big job.

Have you ever seen *The Pursuit of Happyness* with Will and Jayden Smith? This father-son team portrayed the life of Chris Gardner, who successfully completed an internship for a brokerage firm while concurrently homeless and caring for his young son. His life by day was spent among the wealthy; his nights were spent among the impoverished in shelters and on the streets. At one point in the movie, Mr. Gardner was able to get $250 for selling medical equipment. While cashing his check, he saw that his little boy was eyeing a candy bar on the counter by the cash register. Yet, when he asked his son, "Do you want that?" his son's facial expression immediately changed from wishful yearning to casual indifference.

"No, thank you," he quickly replied.

The exchange only took a split second, but it was long enough to stop my heart.

That, perhaps, was the moment that that sweet boy learned something very debilitatingly tragic: He learned not to want. That child wasn't born with that tendency. Babies come into this world wanting. The second they pop out, they want back in. They want to be fed. They want to be changed. They want a toy. They want to be held. They want their baba. They are virtual wanting machines. So when does that change? For this man's son, that may have been the very instant he realized that he was not eligible for candy. Candy was for *other* children. Maybe he didn't deserve it. Maybe he wasn't that important. Regardless of the reason, he knew then that he was not entitled to good things. And, invariably, it happened—he learned not to want them. He learned that good things were for other people, never for him.

I cried when I saw that scene, and I cried hard. You know why? *Because I am that child.* Somewhere along the line, I learned that I was not eligible for good things. Good things were for other people. Maybe I didn't deserve good things. Maybe I wasn't that important. Like this child, regardless of the reason, I learned that I was not entitled to receive good things. Somewhere, at some time—and I don't remember the precise moment it happened—I learned not to want.

Many have taken this tragedy in human development and created a whole prosperity theology from it: God wants to give you the fancy car you've been drooling over. You'll get that job, that girl, those backstage passes. God will give you whatever you ask Him for—in whatever color you want it. "Name it and claim it!" was the catch phrase back in the day. As if God is our almighty errand boy.

That's so *not* what I'm talking about.

I'm talking about walking around with no idea that I was God's beloved. I'd grown up my whole life being told He loved me and He came to give me abundant life. And you know how you have a concept locked in your brain, and it's solid in there, but you don't really feel it and you couldn't really explain it if someone asked you to? That's why I have such a hard time now listening to Christianese—the jargon of our own exclusive subculture. Our groupspeak takes deep and meaningful truths and trivializes them, and the problem is exacerbated when we can't seem to authentically live out those truths.

I remember a lady who used to come into the restaurant where I worked in college. She was platinum blonde, loud and brassy. Her perfume choked anything unlucky enough to be caught in her wake, and her thick, nasally, New York accent could scrape the chicken grease right out of the frying pan. She'd yell across the counter to our cooks, "YAY-SU-TAY-A-MO!" (That's *'Jesu, te amo'* or *'*Jesus loves you' for those who don't speak Spang-nasal-ish). She'd walk in like she owned the place, throw her Gucci clutch on the table of her choice, plop herself down in the booth, and while not sparing us even a glance as she used her pocket mirror to make sure the glittery blue eye shadow was smeared on evenly, she'd greet us all the same way: "Jesus, LUWUUVZ you—Gimme some CUWAAAFEE!"

Hallelujah, give God the glory, she was done being a witness for the day!

I can't fault her one bit. I essentially did the same thing. I could talk about the love of God with the best of them. And I wasn't even aware that I wasn't even aware of how God really feels about me. I would proclaim while being completely clueless:

"Jesus died for my sins! Oh, how He must love me!"

I never delved into the depths of myself where my thoughts melded together with my feelings—where my mind met my soul—to admit what was *really* true for me: Jesus stood by and did nothing while I was being ravaged by a monster.

Oh, how inconsequential I must be. How unlovable. Of no value.

How many years did I walk around pretending not to be dead inside? That's why the "Name it, claim it" bullshit is so infuriating to me. I tried it. It doesn't work. I thought that if I just kept naming and claiming God's love for me, then maybe someday it would actually *be* true and *feel* true. And those were the rare moments when I was at least *approaching* honesty and self-examination. Most of the time, I consciously or subconsciously deluded myself and never broached that kind of authenticity. I would vacillate on a continuum between knowing I was empty and believing that the shallows in which I waded were truly the extent of the depths of God's love and relevance to me and, even more twisted, that I had tapped that depth. Put simply, either I was nothing to God or I had traveled as far as I could into His love.

Whenever I heard someone talk in church about experiencing what was "undoubtedly" the touch of God in his life, I thought somewhere in the very back of my mind that he was pretending, just like I was. Or worse, I considered the possibility that God simply loved him more—that that guy was *truly* God's beloved.

So, what did that make me?

What else could I conclude, then, but that good things were for other people—never, never for me. Rescue came for those whom Christ loved... more.

Blessings? Abundance? I couldn't even find safety. How could someone like me ever hope to enjoy the lofty promises of God or be "filled" with anything other than what I already had? The pain of that was too great to bear, and that was why I pushed it down as far as I could and pretended that He loved me too—that I was important to Him. That He could see me. That He could hear me. That He would be interested enough to pay attention to me and deliver me.

There was no such thing as want because, as everybody knows, it sucks to want. My mother was adamant about never wanting anything for her birthday or Christmas or their anniversary. That's because her husband rarely gave her gifts. Those special occasions would come and go without fanfare or celebration. He got everything he ever wanted: musical equipment, ham radios, steel-tipped cowboy boots, guitars, man-toys... She didn't even get tampons. She taught us to fold toilet paper several times over and stick it in our underwear once a month. She got nothing even though she was the one who worked the majority of the time to support us. She never got new makeup. She said she didn't want it. She never got new clothes. She said she didn't need them. She didn't have anything that was just hers to pursue. She didn't have time for a hobby or any kind of interest that she could call her own. And if she couldn't even give herself permission to need, then how in the hell could she ever begin to want?

She taught me well.

I cannot tell you why I had to endure a living hell that stole my entire childhood. Or why Jesus did not strike my stepmonster dead or at least send a lightning bolt straight up through his small intestine. If I were God, it truly would have been so. All I can offer in the way of an explanation for my own suffering or the suffering of anyone is that shit happens on this earth. I do not believe for a minute that "everything happens for a reason." Oh sure, I believe there is a reason, or maybe a better way to say it is that there is an *explanation* for everything, but I don't mean that in the way that most people do when they say that. A reason for child abuse? Here's your answer: People choose to fuck with their children every day for any number of "reasons." Those are tough words to read. Tough to write. Some might be offended. But I have to ask—is the reader mortified because of the reality that it happens or because I wrote it the way I did? It's happening. In churches, in schools, in organizations. Every minute. Right this second, even as you read this. And there's your reason, folks. There is *not* a silver lining behind every cloud. That is a pretty little lie. We're constantly looking for some cosmic "lesson" that we can learn from our experiences to ransom some semblance of meaning and purpose for our pain and suffering or in trying to understand the suffering of others. But I'm here to tell you that I believe this universe is random. Like the Indigo Girls claim, "Anything that has happened to anyone else can happen to you or to me..." That's the truth. And, "The way that it is, is meant to be—the Philosophy of Loss—" is complete and utter bullshit. I've been told time and again that God wanted me to *learn* something from my abuse. Hmm. Maybe that's why I always felt like the dimwitted pupil that He was always browbeating instead of feeling like I was, in fact, His beloved?

Volumes have been written in every language about why bad things happen to good people, benefits and detriments of our free will, and the goodness or evil of mankind. I don't get wrapped up in it. Won't touch it. I'm not even going to attempt to suggest that because free will, which was given in perfect love, reigns supreme, or so it seems, and that's the "reason" behind all the heartache in this world. That would sound like I'm trying to offer up a defense for God for what He does or doesn't do, and if I'm God's defense lawyer, then we are all in a butt-load of trouble. Whatever the reason, my abuse altered the very design of this innocent child and, therefore, I am left to question whether or not I can or will be everything I was meant to be and whether or not Christ can or will ever bridge the gap between what I could have been and what I am. It's a question that everyone who has been marginalized in any way must ask if he or she is being truly honest.

I saw a woman on the news once who was being interviewed for a story on child sexual abuse. She told the journalist that years after her abuse ended, she went back to the man who had molested her and thanked him for it because she would not have become the person she was today without having gone through that. I just about puked and sincerely hoped that she went back to counseling.

We hear people all the time say they wouldn't go back and change a thing about their pasts, that they have no regrets, and they wouldn't be the people they are today if they hadn't had those life experiences. I'm fine with that to a point, but I have to draw the line at abuse. Believe me, if you come from that background and you are healed and successful and whole, it's not *because* of your abuse. You are healed and successful and whole in *spite* of your abuse! Someone or something intervened on your behalf and made a way where there was no way. You figured *something* out. There is a quantifiable difference between the clouds that open up and rain hardship upon the rich and the poor, the young and the old, and a force of evil that stops at nothing to destroy the inner sanctum of our hearts and sabotage all that which we could have been. In all my years in education, I have taught literally thousands of children, and let me *assure* you with absolute certainty that no good thing comes of it. No good thing. Insurmountable hurdles are thrown up onto the paths of these precious souls who are just trying to find their way back to love and safety.

So where did this leave me? Was my abuse so debilitating that it destroyed all my chances of ever becoming Madonna? Or Oprah? Or Mark Zuckerberg?

Or maybe even just being in a position to leave the world better than I found it?

Do I pull myself up from my bootstraps? Send good thoughts out into the Universe, knowing they'll all come rushing back to me and bring me joy? Should I live only for others, forget about myself? Be Gandhi? Vote libertarian? Become a nun? Wear crystals? Put fairy dust under my pillow? Chase every wind that blows?

Or *what*?

Trust God?

Yeah. Be my guest. Let me know how that works out for ya.

Even with the voice of God telling me that He knew *exactly* where I was—even providing the miracle that allowed me to stay in college, I still could no more trust God than I could swim the English Channel or get back to a size two. It's not even that I didn't want to trust God. I most certainly did. I just didn't know how. I didn't know where to start. People say all the time that they found all their answers within themselves, but I'm pretty convinced that I knew nothing. I was completely and utterly helpless, and all that effort that I was making to pretend that everything was glorious and that I was "walking in victory" like I'd been taught to do all those years was starting to wear me down. That exterior of 'faith' began to crumble. And you know what? I think, to the relief of Almighty God Himself, I just didn't give a shit anymore.

∾   ∾   ∾

Thelma: You awake?

Louise: You could call it that. My eyes are open.

Thelma: Me too. I feel awake.

Louise: Good.

Thelma: Wide awake. I don't remember ever feelin' this awake.

~Thelma and Louise

∾   ∾   ∾

The Preacher-Boy, the F-Word and the Almighty Come-Apart

My new husband and I settled into our single-wide castle at our school's "married housing," a metal box, 12 x 28 feet, where he had to endure each new recipe, and I had to change how I'd always folded the towels. The space was small, the sex was dull, and the baggage of my past took up most of the room.

My husband was the only person I'd ever told about my abuse and the only person I had ever wanted to know. But he couldn't carry all that weight by himself, and he confided in his best friend Rob. Rob was a Pastoral Ministries major and had been my husband's roommate in the dorms as well as the best man at our wedding. He was gravely concerned as to how I was coping with my past, and he came over one night to talk to me.

Holy awkward, Batman.

What neither of us initially realized that night, though, was that awkward was just the opening act for the anger that lay just underneath my cracking exterior. Being angry with God was another one of those unpardonable sins, as far as I'd been told. Inexcusable. God had given us everything. He paid the ultimate sacrifice. He offers the world eternal peace and joy even though we're just a lowly and sinful lot. We don't deserve His kindness and mercy and, therefore, would be out of our minds if ever we held angst in our hearts toward Him. If ever we felt anger bubbling up in our hearts, we repented immediately (before we *really* pissed Him off) and did our hardy best to squelch that anger down and get our attitudes back in check. STAT! He expected us to walk in His victory—not blame Him for all the ills in the world that we just bring upon ourselves because of our dimwitted and ubiquitous iniquities.

But, if you really want to know the truth, I was just jonesin' for a chance to double up my fist and belt God right in the face.

When Rob got to the "advice" part of our conversation, he suggested, "We just need to pray through this…"

Now, you'd think that would be sound advice coming from a guy who was a Pastoral Ministries major, right? Makes sense, after all. But I'm really leery of sentences that include the word, "just."

I looked at my friend sitting on my couch, kindness and love and empathy emanating from that dark and handsome face. This man is Jesus in blue jeans. All that kindness and love and empathy were too little too late for me.

I flat flipped my lid.

"We need to pray?" I asked, oddly quietly, before I went into a tirade that went on for several minutes that included the f-word at least fifty times, my volume increasing. "JUST *PRAY*? We need to JUST PRAY? WHAT THE

HELL DO YOU THINK I'VE BEEN DOING ALL MY LIFE, ROB? FUCKING PAINTING MY NAILS? YOU WANT ME TO PRAY? WHY? TELL ME WHAT GOOD IS PRAYER! PRAYER DOESN'T DO SHIT!"

Poor guy. He sat there with his hair blown back from the g-force of my sudden fury. Before it was all said and done, he probably at least considered the possibility that I was demon possessed. His mouth popped open, but before he could respond, my pain exploded and splattered anguished sarcasm all over the furniture, the curtains, down the walls and dripping in sick, slimy clumps all over him.

"YOU GOT ANSWERS FOR ME, ROB? *DO YOU*? TELL ME SOMETHING ABOUT PRAYER THAT I DON'T KNOW! OPEN UP THAT BIBLE AND READ TO ME A VERSE THAT I HAVEN'T READ!"

He looked down at his Bible and turned it over and over in his hands. Letting out a trepidacious breath, Rob shook his head trying to think of a response.

"TELL ME, *PASTOR*! WHAT THE FUCK DOES A GIRL HAVE TO DO TO MOVE THE ALMIGHTY HAND OF GOD! HOW BAD DOES SHE HAVE TO GET FUCKED OVER BEFORE GOD GETS OFF HIS ASS AND DOES SOMETHING ABOUT IT? YOU THINK I SHOULD PRAY? FINE! LET'S PRAY!"

I slapped my hands together, lifted my tear-stained face toward my speckled ceiling, and I screamed as loud as I could: "DEAR HEAVENLY FATHER! WE THANK YOU FOR THIS DAY! 'CUZ MAYBE THIS WILL BE THE MAGIC, FUCKING DAY THAT YOU FINALLY SEE ME! MAYBE THIS WILL BE THE MAGIC, FUCKING DAY THAT YOU FINALLY GIVE A FLYING FUCK ABOUT ME! MAYBE THIS IS THE FOUR MILLIONTH, NINE-HUNDRED THOUSANDTH, GAZILLIONTH FUCKING PRAYER—SINCE ALL THE OTHER ONES HAVE OBVIOUSLY BEEN SOME FUCKING CARROT ON A STICK—MAYBE THIS IS THE ONE YOU WILL FINALLY FUCKING HEAR! THE ONE THAT WILL FINALLY MAKE YOU MOVE ON MY BEHALF? DO YOU THINK, *GOD*? DO YOU THINK THIS COULD BE THE ONE?"

I ripped my hands apart and shot both my arms, fists clenched, toward Heaven, pumping the air as I screamed hysterically, "IS THIS PRAYER DESPERATE ENOUGH FOR YOU? IS IT LOUD ENOUGH? CAN YOU HEAR THIS ONE? AM I FINALLY BROKEN ENOUGH FOR YOU? AM I FINALLY PATHETIC ENOUGH FOR YOU? AM I FINALLY *NOTHING*

ENOUGH FOR YOU SO THAT YOU CAN BE MY *EVERYTHING?* HAVE YOU FINALLY GOTTEN ME WHERE YOU WANT ME? WILL YOU FINALLY FUCKING MOVE NOW?"

It was very much like the scene in *Forrest Gump* when Gary Sinese's character, Lt. Dan, rages against God during the hurricane on the mast of the boat and dared God to "…do His worst!" I know people who were so offended by that scene that they actually got up and walked out of the theater, refusing to watch any more of that movie because they weren't going to sit and watch God be mocked or hear His name blasphemed.

I fell in a puddle on the carpet and hemorrhaged tears and snot and sweat with an acute awareness that I hadn't gotten what I wanted from God, I probably never would, and I was pretty sure I had now secured for myself a spot in Hell for all eternity. Mine was just one meaningless and miserable existence from womb to tomb with no purpose, no sense, no reason. A waste of a life. A waste of a soul.

Suddenly, I heard Rob stammer, "Uhh…"

I had forgotten he was even there.

I knew what came next. "Uh, I gotta go. You're obviously not in a place right now where you can receive anything from the Lord. But I'll be praying for you."

Only, that's not what came.

He stood over me as I sobbed and touched my shoulder so gently.

"Um…" he started again. "Uhh… Baby steps. W-w-we're going to take baby steps here."

Now, I don't know if Rob received that from the Holy Spirit in that moment or if he got it straight out of *What About Bob?*, but that part of it doesn't really matter. In the fear-based, legalistic world I was raised in, I half expected him to get up and walk right out the door, washing his hands of me— just like those people who walked out on Lt. Dan in the midst of his storm. Just like all those people who are no longer reading this and have slammed this book shut in complete disgust. After all, anyone who would curse God the way I just did should *expect* to be in the dire straits I was in. Confessions are important, as long as they're edited for content and tone, right? Just one more reason I didn't deserve good things.

But Rob didn't go anywhere. He stayed right there. He put his hand on my shoulder and said softly, "This is okay. You're okay. You're gonna be all right."

See, here's what Rob knew then and what he surely knows now: God is a pretty Big Boy. He can handle our meltdowns. In fact, looking back, I think God looked down on me in that moment and said, "It's about dang time…" We always think about how long we wait on Him. Maybe He laments how long He waits for us. I don't know. But I know He was there sitting on that cheap linoleum that night. He saw me. He heard me. And I don't think it was because I threw a fit or was finally desperate enough for His liking. I think it's because I was finally just being *honest*. I think it was less important to God that I was throwing the f-word in His face and accusing Him of sheer cruelty and neglect than it was that I was finally, truly reaching out to Him—even though it was in complete rage. I beat my fists into His chest until I wore myself out and cursed Him with the ugliest memories I could fling into His heart and tried to hurt Him as badly as I hurt—and He had His arms around me the whole time. Why would He do that?

Maybe because… I was His?

I was His.

I hated Him. I blamed Him. But there was no way He was ever going to let go of me over such trivialities like blame and rage that He'd already conquered. Starting on that night, I began to understand incrementally that my hatred and blame and rage had already wounded and left bruises on Him long before that night. See, this whole conversation had already happened—I had heard it all my life, but I still didn't *know* it. He'd borne my grief and carried my sorrow for centuries, before I was ever born, even though I despised Him and turned my face from Him. And what was even more powerful is when I eventually came to understand the *rest* of the gospel: that not only did He wave away my transgressions, but that transgressions that were committed against *me* also ripped across His back. He bled and suffered and He anguished in every way that God and man together could anguish over what happened to me. You see, He doesn't just take away the sins that we commit—*He HEALS us from all the sins that we have ever suffered at the hands of someone else!* That is good news, folks. That is *great* news.

Years later I would learn about the concept of *worship through lament*. Crying out like I did that night turned out to be an act of worship far more effective than singing my solo, *He is Able*, in the Vanguard Singers every other week in churches all over Southern California. And that's a great song. But it was still just me pretending. Naming. Claiming. When I really just needed to lay it out and tell God the damn truth: I really hate You right now.

A few weeks ago, on one of those rare occasions that I was in church, I heard a man give his testimony. He said that he went to bed one night and the last words he said to God before he went to sleep was, "I hate you, I hate you, I hate you, I hate you, I HATE YOU!" He had a dream that same night that he opened up a letter that God had written to him with a rainbow-colored pen. It said, "I love you, I love you, I love you, I love you, I love you, I love you, I love you, I love you, I love you, I LOVE YOU!"

It is important, so important, to understand and accept the fact that I did not get up from that tear-snot-sweat-stained carpet completely healed and whole. I didn't. I got up, still shattered. Still fragmented. *Know* that! I was still in need of a whole lot of wisdom from a good many people like Pastor Rob who, with his beautiful wife, literally walks around in the Light of God's love, providing just that kind of sanctuary for everyone who wanders into their path, their church, their lives—no matter how they're screaming or raging or falling apart. And I *did* need baby steps, as much as I laugh about that now, because I did kinda freak the boy out.

That night with Rob changed my life forever because I had awakened that morning not really believing that I could have something good from God, and when I went to bed that night, I contemplated the possibility that I could. When I had awakened that morning I hadn't really known—where my mind meets my soul—that God truly loved me. But when I went to bed that night, I knew I'd felt a spark of hope that maybe He knew me—that He had always known me. And He had loved me all that lonely time. Thinking back on my childhood, I pondered the religion of my parents, their God, their Jesus. Their Devil, the belief system that allowed them to live their lives the way they did with all they justified to themselves.

And then I pondered the Guy who showed up that night on my kitchen floor.

⮧   ⮧   ⮧

Satan, My Sibling

Well, of course, Satan would obviously decide to take up residence in Las Vegas. It's Sin City, and there's no state income tax. Where else do you think he would live? What's more, I'm pretty sure he lived at our house. He went to school with us. He played with us. He ate with us. He was there when we woke up in the morning and when we went to bed at night. He slept in my closet or under my bed.

I made sure my closet door was always closed after dark, and when I went to bed I stood at the light switch by my door, turned it off and was immediately airborne, making a Superman leap from that spot onto my bed just in case he was underneath it waiting to grab my ankles as I soared over his horned head on the way to my pillow.

He was the one who made my mother's husband come into my room at night.

He was very powerful. He could make anybody do anything. No one was able to resist him except for that flannelboard Jesus in the desert, sitting criss-cross-applesauce. Satan, my sibling, was the big brother who goaded us to do something wrong, but he never got in trouble for it. We did. Mother warned us about speaking our doubts out loud because, even though Satan couldn't read our thoughts, anything we *said* was fair game. Satan never had to pull his pants down and get the belt on his bare butt, even though he was the one who put it in our minds to do whatever we had done.

Nobody ever put a belt to my mother's husband either, come to think of it, and what he did was worse than what any of us ever did. Satan talked him into doing some pretty hellacious shit.

You would have thought we'd have been safe from Satan at church. We were certainly there several times a week—twice on Sundays and Wednesday nights. But you know, it's the strangest thing. Satan was there *too*! Oh, they talked about him a lot. About how he was destroying the world and destroying families and how we had to get the victory over him or else. We never did, though, which is probably why they had to keep talking about him. We just couldn't git'-er-dun for some reason. Not sure why. We pretty much lived out the "or else."

Jesus lived at our house too, though, and in all fairness, we spent just as much time and energy on Jesus as we did on Satan. Except Jesus, who supposedly was the more powerful of the two, evidently didn't pay as much attention to us as we did to him, whereas we had Satan's strict and undivided attention at all times. The two were supposed to be in this big battle over us. And, either Satan stomped Jesus' ass for the better part of twenty years, or Jesus was too busy saving other people's families. He didn't seem like much of a force to be reckoned with or a real spiritual presence of power and authority. I mean, I'm sure he was great at a picnic and all—all somebody has to do is show up with just five loaves of bread and some fish… But He watched over us mostly like a bobble head on the dash of our car as we traveled down the highway of life.

Let me describe our family portrait.

Stepmonster is sitting regally in the center on a great, big, royal throne. He was always the center of our family. You can't see my mother because she is hiding behind her husband where a good, godly wife should always be, mouth shut. My brother is hoisted high up on Stepmonster's shoulder in a place of honor. You know, because of him having a penis and all. My sister and I are on our knees on the floor each holding tightly to one of his legs, looking up adoringly at our devoted father, with the biggest smiles on our faces that anyone's ever seen, ready to do whatever we are told. The smiling was *very* important! We needed to make sure everyone knew what a great dad he was and how happy he made us. That was our number one job. Then there was our sibling, Satan, who stood smugly over his shoulder, talons deeply embedded in Stepmonster's anesthetized chest. And Jesus? Well, Jesus was kind of off to the side, really. He was supposed to be the center, but there he stood out of the way. I think maybe he was just shy, and truth be told, just a bit insecure.

We spent our time and energy on Jesus because, of course, we were Christians, although that little guy was always a mystery to me. But I did my best to be faithful to him. Better that than inadvertently ending up in Hell for any doubts I might've had. I certainly made it a point not to detach from him when I detached from my parents during my teenage years, which was the most bizarre thing. I just woke up one day, looking over at the two of them and realized, "Ya'll are fucked up!"

I wasn't sure in that moment why it no longer mattered to me what they thought of me. It just didn't. I looked at my stepmonster and thought, *You're not worth the powder to blow you up.*

I looked at my mother and thought, *I have bigger problems with you than I do him. He's just twisted beyond recognition. He just does according to his nature. But you? You are a mother. You held us inside your own body and then offered us up to his sick appetites. And for what? Because you can't take your next codependent breath without him? Because you don't know who you are without a man to tell you? You're sicker than he is, so you can kiss my ass too. Your services, such as they are, are no longer required.*

I looked at Satan and thought, *You know what? People in this house give you entirely too much credit. You can just stay the hell away from me because I'm done with you too.*

And I was.

Finally, I looked at this Jesus and said, "And *you*? I just can't figure you out."

This silent, solitary revolution was fought and won sitting across the table from them without a single word spoken over a bowl of generic corn flakes on a Tuesday morning at some point during my sixteenth year. I walked out of the house to go to school that day with just a small taste of freedom. I felt lighter. I felt a smidgen of hope. I knew that there was something after this that would not include them. None of them knew it, but I knew it. There certainly was no need to explain it to them. It just was.

Makes you wonder what's going on in your children's minds, doesn't it? My parents certainly had no idea of what I was not telling them. For all they knew, I was still that doormat they laid out daily.

I thought, *I merely need to survive this part of my life. Just survive.* Sometimes that's the best a kid can do. My thoughts naturally turned to my eventual escape—college, my plan of action. Home was Hell—I made school my Heaven.

However, upon graduating from high school, even though I had survived, my heart shattered against the wall of regret over the child who had never really lived; who had been ridiculously sheltered, but never safe; who wasn't allowed to dance, who had to buy groceries for the family from her own money; and whose responsibility it was to satisfy the sadistic compulsions of a monster who should have been the last person in the world that I needed to be protected from.

When I finally did escape to college, Stepmonster and the rest of the family, of course, took that position as the music minister for my uncle's church, packed up all of Satan's shit and took him with them when they left. I'm sure Jesus probably tagged along too. One had to wonder what else he had to do. He didn't seem all that motivated to me.

Currently, they all live in the Midwest in case anybody's worried about where Satan resides at this very moment, and I believe they are pretty well settled there. This is where Stepmonster took a job in *law-enforcement*, if you recall, right after his "music pastor" stint.

You remember.

My parents are, at present, going to a wonderful church where Stepmonster sings regularly and leads worship and are very relieved to have escaped the insidious wickedness of Las Vegas, a city associated with such sin and debauchery. The Easter Bunny leaves colored eggs in the bushes, and Elvis is alive and well.

I haven't spoken to my mother or her husband, really, since 1996. I haven't had anything to do with Satan, my sibling, since... Geez! 1983?

It's been nice. I can't say as I've missed him. Our paths just never cross these days. We don't go to the same church anymore, which is refreshing. He doesn't get credit for anything I do or don't do. I get the credit for all of it. See, I do this really whacked out kinda thing now called *taking responsibility*! I do that for pretty much everything, except for when I'm being whiny and weak. But even then, I do the decent thing and blame other people or world events or the weather or some other crazy situation. I've put Satan in the same category as PMS—I don't blame my woes on either one of those entities. I kicked Satan to the curb, and I keep the Midol handy. I'm sure, though, that even while living with my parents in the Midwest, Satan still finds reasons to spend many long weekends in Vegas. But he certainly doesn't come around me anymore. I leave him alone, and he leaves me alone.

As for that sad little Jesus who lived with us, I don't know whatever happened to him. He seemed to wither away into oblivion after I went to college. Maybe he moved along with my parents and he's sitting silently in some corner he's found where he won't be in the way. Mouth shut. With my mother.

It was when I got to Vanguard that I was introduced to this other Guy and, ironically, His name was Jesus too. He was way more of a badass than the guy I grew up with. Way tougher, way cooler, way more vocal, way more mojo, way more everything. There were rumors that He got really pissed off one time because these people were using His Dad's house to sell a bunch of whatever they were peddling, and He went postal. I mean, it was *game ON!* Only it didn't seem like a game the way he handled it. He raged. There's no other way to describe it. He went crazy as a sprayed roach, flipping over their tables and sending their money flying. He got a hold of somebody's bullwhip and thought He was Indiana Jones snapping the bejeezus out of people, no pun intended. Those people went tearing out of there like their lives depended on it. Maybe their lives did? Who knows? He wasn't dinkin' around, that's for sure.

When I started talked to Him about what went down in my house growing up, He got that same frenzied look in His eye. The whole episode at His house was nothing compared to how He tore through *my* house. He flat got rid of the *shit that didn't belong!* People talk about when "all Hell breaks loose," as if nothing could ever be worse than that. Maybe those people have never seen all *Heaven* break loose. But I have. Trust me—it trumps. He was definitely a disaster of "Biblical proportions!"

When I told Him about Satan and the Jesus I grew up with, it seemed like He knew who Satan was, but He didn't seem to know the other guy. I asked Him if He knew my parents.

He didn't answer.

He doesn't tell me everything.

He did say He knew me, that He's always known me. But you know? I wasn't dinkin' around either.

"Why then," I asked, "did You take twenty years to introduce Yourself? Why didn't You come to me sooner? Why didn't You take that bullwhip and run my stepmonster out of that house? You're so powerful! How could You just sit there and watch?"

"Hmph," He smirked slightly and looked into the distance as my accusation pinged off of Him. He put that scarred hand up to His chest and rubbed under His ribcage in a circular motion. It seemed like He was transported temporarily back in time to another place, remembering something... painful. Finally, His eyes still on the horizon, He said, "I asked my Father basically the same thing once..."

After a moment He returned from his private recollections. "I was not spared. You were not spared. Many, many others have not been spared and are *not* being spared even as we speak. Mankind is not spared because mankind does not spare himself. You're right, Daisy, in not blaming Satan for what happened to you. Satan cannot force a human being to do one thing or another. He's a poser. He doesn't have that kind of power. I do, though. I'm sure by now you've figured that out. I could make people do the right thing. But I won't."

He stuck His thumbs in the loops of His jeans and tilted His head as He looked at me. Finally He added, "So, if you need to blame someone other than your perpetrator, I suppose then that the blame should come to Me."

"I do blame You."

"I know you do."

"If someone breaks into my house, even now, and wants to hurt me, will You intervene on my behalf?" I demanded.

"I'd strongly suggest that you always be aware of your surroundings. Lock your doors. Get a dog. Don't ever allow yourself to be taken to a second location."

"You watch Oprah?" I asked, remembering her giving that same advice to women around the globe.

"I watch everybody."

"How safe am I with You?"

"Impenetrably."

"Will You protect me?"

"Ultimately."

He waited resignedly while I crossed my arms against my chest and turned my face away from Him, contemplating His words.

"Do you trust Me?" The silence between us was its own voice.

"Sometimes," was finally the best I could do.

He nodded thoughtfully and looked back at the setting sun. "Shall we walk?"

Special Delivery

Wouldn't you know I got knocked up half way through my senior year of college? One balmy, March night in 1990, the stars aligned, the egg dropped, the angels sang, and *bam!* I was the proud owner of a brand new zygote. Ah, the cycle of life…

My husband got the news while still in bed on a Tuesday. Significant events occur in my life on Tuesdays. He was reading. He was always reading. An English major, I'm sure he was reading some 14,000-page classic novel that only he and Shakespeare and Einstein and Professor Ewing were capable of understanding. He read every page of every assignment in every book for every class he's ever taken in every year of college he's ever attended. And he's got more degrees than quills on a porcupine, so he's read a ton.

I would love to say that my husband found out there was a baby on the way on a Friday night over a candle-lit dinner with someone in a tuxedo serenading us with beautiful violin music. Instead, he found out from my screams, which were literally peeling the paneling back, "HOLY SHIT! SWEET MOTHER OF GOD! THE STICK IS TURNING BLUE! THE STICK IS TURNING BLUE!" Incidentally, I had been stuck in "cuss-mode" since the breakdown with Rob on the kitchen floor of that single-wide trailer. As you can see, I've never fully recovered. I've had potty-mouth ever since, but I always thought it was better than succumbing to insanity. Or serial killing.

The night before I'd told my best friend David, a man after God's own heart, that I was going to be peeing on that stick. I stood outside of chapel that morning and, with the slightest hint of a smile, nodded to him to affirm that, indeed, I was preggo. His knees hit the ground, completely elated.

My best friend—more of a brother to me, really—and I were so connected in college that to separate us would be lethal. I don't believe in reincarnation, but if I did, I would know that David and I have made this trip several times and have found each other on every single journey. We were amoebas together. We were insects hatched together. We were plankton and jellyfish and hippopotami. We were ducks and cows and big redwood trees. We were Tom Sawyer and Huck Finn, Bonnie and Clyde, Sampson and Delilah. I'm sure that this time, we've got it right.

The day we met, he assumed I was a conceited little snot. We definitely have different spins on the story. However, since I *write*, history will always be remembered the way I tell it, although the claim is always there, "Well, Daisy, there's always the Oprah interview where I will set it straight or the National Enquirer… I will be the 'source close' to Daisy Rain Martin!"

I'll burn that bridge when I come to it.

I assure you. The other version counts for nothing. It's like this:

Three years earlier, David joined the Vanguard Singers a few weeks after the rest of us. I had shown up right at the beginning with the other singers, sick as a dog and unable to sing a note, sounding like a bullfrog. It took those two weeks just for me to feel better and get my voice back. David walked in and sat down as inconspicuously as possible and found me sitting up on a table in the front of the room surrounded by a few of the other singers. Someone wondered out loud what my voice really sounded like since no one had really been able to hear it due to my laryngitis. In complete and total jest, I said flippantly, "When I'm sick I sound like Leslie Philips. When I'm well, I sound like Amy Grant." Everyone laughed like they were supposed to except for this new guy whose eyes rolled like cherries on a slot machine and thought, *Who does this girl think she is?*

And, anyway, the last laugh is on David, because now I sing like Celine Dion.

I don't know at what point he began to believe that I was okay, but I'm eternally grateful that decision was made, because we've been best friends ever since.

Sunflower seeds, literally in the millions, were consumed while watching this new talk show we were hooked on hosted by some chick named Oprah Winfrey—and you gotta love a dude who has an appreciation for our girl,

Oprah. The only time we ever skipped her show was that day we went down to Hoag Hospital in Newport Beach and get me a blood test to confirm what the pee-pee stick had already told us. The two little old ladies at the information station would barely look at us. We stood there waiting patiently to be acknowledged. We weren't.

"Why can't we get any help here?" I asked. "You'd think Nancy Reagan was here or something."

We looked over to some brouhaha on our left. Lights. Cameras. Nancy Reagan. I'm not even kidding you. That's exactly how it went down. Google it and see if Nancy Reagan wasn't at Hoag Hospital in the spring of 1990.

My husband and I didn't have anything better to do after graduation so, instead of hanging out in Southern California and becoming yuppies, we took David home to a town not too far from where Rush Limbaugh is from, I believe. This, as you recall, is where my husband applied for and was accepted into a master's program at the local university where they also offered him a job as a teaching assistant, and, really, who wouldn't offer him some such thing because he's the smartest guy ever. We transplanted ourselves from one fairytale vacuum to another—we'd been Hoovers in California, but now, equipped with Jesus and our college degrees, we were Kirbys! Of course, in that part of the country where they believe anything out of California is either a fruit or a nut, some dubbed us Dirt Devils. It's where sushi is still called bait, after all. My husband worked and went to school at the university there, and it took all of about ten minutes for me to get a job as a teacher at the private, Christian school that was affiliated with the church we attended. David's whole fam-damily went there and, since we were living in the Lancaster family basement, so did we. Those poor Lancasters. They sent one kid away to college and after four years, they ended up with that one back, plus two more with a baby on the way! And that, dear friends, is how the Lancaster family rolls. They loved us.

Actually, they loved me and couldn't wait to spoil this new baby.

By the time Thanksgiving rolled around, I was rolling around too. I looked like a toothpick with an olive stuck on it. And wouldn't you know my contractions were about five minutes apart as we sat down to a big turkey dinner!

My doctor had told me not to eat anything if I thought I was in labor, so I told myself that the tightening in my belly every four to five minutes was Braxton Hicks. That turkey was delicious! The mashed potatoes? Divine! The yams? The green bean casserole? The biscuits? You gotta love Midwestern cooking. By the time the pumpkin pie was served, my contractions were three minutes apart.

So, of course, I had a piece. With Cool Whip.

I think what really threw me off was the fact that these "pains" weren't really painful. Sure, my entire torso was constricted so hard every few minutes you could bounce a quarter off me, but it didn't really hurt. I've seen women on TV screaming and threatening to rip their husbands' arms off and beat them to death with the bloody stubs. I just wasn't there. And I was hungry. So I ate.

After dinner, when I finally mentioned that I'd been having contractions, be they true or false, for the last three hours, the family surrounded me on all sides, and pelted me with questions:

"What were you thinking?"

"Why did you eat?"

"How long did you say you were having contractions?"

"Why didn't you tell somebody?"

"How far apart are these contractions?"

"Did your water break?"

"Did you lose your mucus plug?"

"Have you lost your mind?"

I answered truthfully, "I was thinking I was hungry. Because I was hungry. Three hours. Because I was hungry. About three minutes apart. No, no, and no."

They all froze momentarily, eyes all as big and round as I was, and you could hear the ticking of the cuckoo clock on the wall in what had been a very noisy room just a second ago.

Mama Joan broke the stunned silence, threw her forefinger in the air, and yelled, "GITTER UP! WE'RE GOIN' IN!" The family erupted in chaos with people running back and forth, looking for their keys, and barking orders as to who was going in what vehicle.

"WAIT!" I screamed. "I have to shave my legs!" I ran into the bathroom and locked the door before anyone could stop me. I had kind of been holding off on doing this because, for one, it was winter; and two, I didn't want to have any stubble growth between my last shave and whenever this baby decided to come. I didn't listen to the screams and the pounding on the door for me to get my arse out of the bathroom and into whatever car had been deemed to take me to the hospital.

Finally, fourteen people piled into a van and three cars, and away we went speeding down the quiet streets of Smallville—the crazy caravan from hell—taking corners at 45 miles an hour. It was no small matter whenever the Lancaster family converged upon the emergency room and took it over.

Now, you can sit in an emergency room with an arm lopped off for hours upon hours. But if you say, "My chest hurts," or "I'm having a baby," those are the magic words, folks! People on the other side of that counter move! One of those two statements is your golden ticket straight upstairs! Luckily, I said the latter, and some dude in scrubs threw me into a wheelchair and broke the sound barrier getting me into the elevator.

My contractions still didn't really hurt, so I enjoyed the ride.

I was actually pretty cavalier about the whole thing. Happy as a clam. A great big, round clam. Panic was everywhere around me, and I was calm as a cucumber. Clams. Cucumbers. Salad. I must have been hungry again. I was calm enough to realize that it was my little brother's birthday. I thought, *How cool! I'm about to give my brother a nephew for his birthday! That's a pretty good present!*

I got upstairs, got undressed, and twenty people all got up to their elbows in my vagina. Sadly, it was after midnight and no longer my little brother's birthday. But, it was...David's birthday! I could give the Lancaster family a little baby boy on my best friend's birthday!

Perfect! Still happy.

Alas, due to a colossal lack of progression, my husband ended up taking me home, and we went to bed. Where he slept. Him. Sleeping. I tightened up every two minutes. I peed. I lay down. I peed some more. I went back to bed. He still slept. Some moron at our childbirth classes advised the pregnant women to allow their husbands to sleep as long as possible because we would be needing them to be as alert as possible through the delivery.

Oh, the knee-jerk obedience of a born-again, 20-something, subservient, voiceless, "just-tell-me-what-to-do-and-I'll-do-whatever-you-say-because-I-have-been-taught-by-this-patriarchal-subculture-to-put-my-own-needs-on-the-backburner-and-be-a-pleaser" bullshit. Let me have a baby now and see if my husband gets to check out the back of his eyelids while I roam around the house in the middle of the night!

I peed and walked. Walked and peed. Peed and walked. Eventually, I found my mucus plug in the toilet. You know, nobody really warns you as to how incredibly disgusting that really is. And that's all I have to say about that.

The early morning hours found me bored out of my mind, still not in pain, and marginally sassy about the whole labor process, wondering what the big deal was.

Then my water broke.

The next contraction came instantly. My knees hit the floor as I held onto the kitchen table for dear life, and I must have said the f-word about sixteen times.

Who is surprised?

I thought somebody took a sledgehammer to my abdomen. There was no more sass as my husband dragged himself out of bed and drove me back to the hospital. And might I mention here that that breathing shit they taught us in those childbirth classes was about as helpful as tits on a boar.

I said those magic words one more time at the front desk and a different dude in scrubs threw me into a wheelchair, breaking the sound barrier once again to get me in the elevator so that twenty more people could be up to their elbows in my vagina, for a grand total of forty vagina people. This time, I was staying.

They sent in a sweet little girl to shave my hippity-hoo-ha. I assure you, you do not know the height and depth and width and breadth of your faith in God until some teenager comes in with a razor and a soap bucket to play barbershop while humming Tiffany's *I Think We're Alone Now*. God be praised, the procedure was a success.

Shortly thereafter, another teenie-bopper bounced in to give me an enema. Again, my faith in God was tested, but I must have gotten an A on this test because, I have to admit, I really kinda liked it. The turkey dinner was no longer an issue, and I felt tons better. Giddy, even.

After that it was pretty uneventful. In the next few hours my contractions actually started coming about four minutes apart. Then ten minutes apart. Then I was lucky (if you could call it that) if I could get one or two contractions in an hour. They ended up putting me on Pitocin.

Let me tell you something about Pitocin.

Satan drinks it for breakfast in the mornings. Its toxins are extracted from volcanoes. It sank the Titanic. It caused the stock market to crash in 1929. It's some evil shit. Some nurse put it in my IV, my contractions came back—and they were *pissed!*

At one point, I looked up at my husband and said, "I'm sorry. I'm really sorry." You know why I was sorry? Because I knew that I was going to die. I had come to grips with it. I was going to die and leave him to raise this baby by himself. I was really sorry about all that, so I thought I'd let him know before I left.

Some saint of a nurse finally called the anesthesiologist to come in and give me an epidural.

Let me tell you something about epidurals.

God drinks them for breakfast. Its sweet nectar is found in beautiful flower-filled meadows. It saved Dorothy from the wicked witch of the West and got her back to Kansas.

And her little *dog* too!

It made the Clampetts rich and got Fleetwood Mac back together.

As fate would have it, I slept peacefully and my husband wandered. Peed. Wandered some more, bored out of his mind. He'd called back the Lancaster family, and they were all holding vigil out in the waiting room. All 57 of them. David spent his entire birthday in the hospital waiting for a birthday nephew. The morning hours became afternoon hours. Those became evening hours. Evening hours became night.

David's sister Deanna, who has become my own and is not someone to be provoked, accosted one of the nurses and demanded, "I want to know just how long you're going to let her lay in there until somebody DOES something!" It had been almost thirty hours, and exhaustion was taking its toll on all of us. She'd had enough and so had the family. She demanded that the doctor be called, and he showed up PDQ. He looked just like Richard Dreyfuss.

They let me start pushing at about eleven o'clock, and I pushed for an hour and a half before collapsing back on my pillow. Silly me. I thought the doctor was supposed to deliver my baby. It suddenly occurred to me that the person who was going to deliver this baby was me! My husband couldn't do it. The doctor couldn't do it. The nurses couldn't do it. The only thing was—I couldn't do it either. The next contraction came, and I just let it take me over. Suddenly, three nurses and a husband were screaming in my face, counting to ten and coaxing me to try harder. Loudly. And somebody had breath that smelled like coochie, and it was making me sick to my stomach. The doctor was somewhere with what—I don't know—probably a catcher's mitt or some damn thing. And I came uncorked.

"Get away from me! What the hell do you think I'm doing up here? Painting my nails? I'm doing the best I can! BY MYSELF! Nobody's even helping me! Everybody's yelling at me!" They backed off, and I looked at my doctor down between my knees, my feet clear above his head in the stirrups. I managed to lift my head just enough to scream at him, "AND I'M NOT PAYING YOU, YOU KNOW!"

I didn't give a royal rat's ass if he *did* look like Richard Dreyfuss.

He smiled and nodded, patted my knee and said, "I know, honey. I know." He came up to my head and pushed the hair back from my face. He looked at the tears in my eyes, wiped the sweat from my forehead with a cloth, and saw that I was done. He patted me on the cheek and went to call the surgeon.

You'll never guess what happened in the next thirty seconds. Some lady came in with a razor and a soap bucket to landscape my lady parts once more! But this one was no young whippersnapper. She was 147-years-old. I politely explained to her that I'd already had my faith in God increased yesterday. She said that had been underneath and all around my moneymaker. Since I was now having a C-section, I needed to have a clean strip across the top. So, I endured one more white-knuckled, faith-building, standing-on-the-promises-of-the-Lord-Jesus-Christ moment. When she was done, I was left with a Foo Manchu.

After that, the scurrying ensued. People in. People out. I had to change gurneys so I could be wheeled down to the operating room where my arms and legs were strapped down to the table with thick, black bands. Monitors were attached to my chest and clippy things were attached to my fingers. An oxygen mask was strapped over my face to help me breathe. Everywhere I looked someone was busy, but no one was panicking. Except for me.

"Doctor, how was your vacation?"

"Great!"

"Where did you go?"

"The Bahamas."

"That's why you look so tan."

"Hello?" I piped in. I don't think they heard me because no one answered. Another contraction was coming.

"Look how little her tummy is! She didn't get very big at all."

"She's tiny."

"Hello?" I couldn't get the breathing cup thing off my face because my hands were strapped down. Meanwhile, everyone bustled around with all their different jobs, talking and laughing and complimenting the girl in the bed on all the weight she didn't gain. The contraction took hold fast and I screamed, "I GOTTA PUSH!"

They heard me. All twenty of them shut up, quit doing whatever they were doing, turned toward me, and yelled in unison, "Noooooooooo!"

"Get that anesthesiologist in here!" the doctor ordered. And just like in the movies, he said it:

"STAT!"

Somebody screamed STAT for *me*! Looking back, it was the very coolest part. Some guy came running in and pumped more juice into my epidural and life was instantly better. I suddenly knew I wasn't going to die. My husband came in and took his seat up by my face. The curtain went up, the doctor went in, and my son came out. It didn't hurt a bit. It just felt like I'd had a giant tooth extracted from my abdomen. The instant I heard my son scream, I thought, *I could do this again...*

Someone said, "One-fourteen A.M." It wasn't David's birthday anymore. It was officially Aunt Jennifer's on Geoff's paternal side of the family. At least I was able to give somebody a nephew for her birthday.

The nurses cleaned him off and wrapped him in a blue blanket. My Geoffrey. Someone put him down by my face so I could see him. God blew me a kiss when I saw that baby for the first time, and I'll never forget what it felt like. I laughed because Geoffrey's tiny eyebrows were scrunched together and his mouth was puckered in a pouty little scowl. His dark eyes were roaming the room, checking the place out. He wasn't impressed—I could tell by the look on his face. He was seriously looking for a way to go right back where he came from. The nurse put his cheek against mine, and I made myself memorize what it felt like. So soft. So perfect. The tears came.

My sweet baby boy. Every maternal instinct I would ever have for the rest of my life came to me in that moment. I didn't really have any when I was wheeled into that room, but I had everything I needed when I was wheeled out.

Everything I would ever need.

ॐ   ॐ   ॐ

"But I Thought..." The Decimation of All Previous Presumptions

"Calvin?"

"Yeah?"

"Can I hold my baby?"

"Sure! Just hold on a minute..."

"Calvin?"

"Yeah?"

"That's my baby."

"I know, I know! But he's just reeeeally happy with Paw Paw right now."

"Yeah, but... I wanna hold him. Am I gonna get a turn soon?"

My brand new baby boy snuggled contentedly in Paw Paw's arms, and Paw Paw Calvin never took his eyes off of him.

"You can't give Dad a baby," David offered too little too late. "You might not get him back."

Grandma Joan was next. In true Lancaster tradition, she scooped the new baby up and gave him his very first bath. They were the best grandparents any baby ever had, and my little boy was lucky to have their home as his first home. They just added Geoff to their list of grandchildren: Bubby, Sissy, Little Bubby, and now? Micro-Bubby.

When Micro-Bubby wouldn't stop crying, Aunt Deanna pressed him up against her "pillows" and rocked him right to sleep. He loved those pillows. My pillows got sucked right back up into oblivion. Well, I'd at least filled up my 32 B cups for a few months anyway. It was nice while it lasted.

When it was time for Geoff's baby dedication at church, David sang an original song—I have it on my iTunes, and I treasure it. All the kids' baby dedications were graced with his poetic words:

Watching you grow there's so much I see inside of you
That I wish I could be
To laugh and to play, To love with a tender heart that's oh, so true
With your tiny, gentle hands, you've touched my life
And I wanted you to know
You're a gift from God, it's plain to see
You're the heartbeat that He's given me
And I only want the very best for you
And someday when I'm old and gray
We'll laugh at all our yesterdays
And I'll thank Him for the precious gift of you.

It's nice to be able to quote an entire song and publish it in a book and not have to worry about getting sued for using intellectual property. And why don't

I have to worry? Because we are family. True siblings. Calvin and Joan are our parents. Our children are their grandchildren. Grandma Bailiff loves us all. And so do Uncle Rick and Aunt Barb. One big happy family. The Lancasters took me in with open arms and gave me the best gift I could have ever been given.

Being part of the Lancaster family was healing to me. Their love and acceptance was a balm that covered my childhood wounds and created new and fresh places in my soul. We were literally grafted into their lives. We went to church together, shared meals and holidays, went to the kids' sporting events. I was in Heaven once again. This "home town" feeling was so foreign to me, having grown up in Las Vegas, and I slathered it on like tanning oil and baked in it the way I would in the searing desert sun. God knew I needed a family so He, in His infinite generosity, gave me one. Now the Lancasters claim all three of us: Deanna, Daisy, and David.

Even though my husband and I immersed ourselves in the ministry of the church, we never quite fit in with the subculture there. We certainly had not a shred of what the church calls, "legalism," a Christianese term that refers to the strict adherence to the "rules and regs" of Christianity in an effort to display for others a certain "proximity" to God. You know, drinking, dancing, chewing—or going with those who are so doing? Yeah, *that*. We weren't big "rule-followers" and didn't gauge our faithfulness to God by any of the suggested or accepted criteria. That was already a block I'd been around. Didn't feel the need to traipse around again.

Lord knows my potty mouth certainly hadn't improved.

My husband and I managed to find the one other freethinking couple at our church. I'll just call them the Joneses. Anyway, we found people whose thinking was more like our own—FREE in JESUS! Mr. Jones was the campus pastor for the university, and they led a Christian Greek organization there called Chi Alpha. Pretty soon, they asked us to partner with them in their ministry and, of course, we accepted the call. We preached. We prayed. We sang.

We were pretty busy, shepherding all these sheep. As a result, we started to detach from the church we'd been going to and even from the Lancasters. This was a double-whammy for Deanna because David had suddenly taken a job back in Southern California. We Lancasters are a tight-knit group, so when the freeways and the weather and the ocean beckoned and David left, Deanna was very, very hurt. Our brother was gone, and she was losing me too.

I was torn. My heart was solidly with my newfound family. But let's tell the truth here: they were way fonder of Geoffrey and me than they were of this man I'd married. It wasn't hard for him to pull away from them and take me right with him. After all, a good Godly wife does everything her husband wants her to do. It says so in *I Misogynist, Chapter 6, Verse 66*. (Now, before he reads this and his eyeballs pop out of his head, let me be crystal clear: The use of the word "misogynist" does *not* refer to him, but to the patriarchal rhetoric to which I'd been subjected my whole life. He certainly is not sexist in any way. The biggest misogynist in this scenario was me! I was acting according to my own paradigm of how I believed a Godly woman should conduct herself.

So, we pulled away, told everybody God was leading us in a new direction and believed it with all our might, broke Deanna's heart, and became best friends with the Joneses.

And one beautiful summer day, I had just returned to our apartment after turning in my application for the nursing program where my husband had just earned his master's degree. He sat me down as soon as I walked through the door and told me, "Mrs. Jones and I are in love. We want to be together. She is having this exact conversation with Mr. Jones right now."

My world bottomed out. Just that quick. I knew he meant it by the look in his eyes.

He added, "I don't love you. I see now that I've never loved you."

"But you married me…"

"I think if you look back, you'll see that you pretty much pressured me into that."

I'll say it for you: *Wow*.

"I'm leaving you! And I'm taking my son!" I screamed at him. I only said that to snap him out of whatever insanity he'd stepped in. I didn't even mean it.

He simply replied, "I'll get the suitcase out of the closet for you."

Geoffrey and I were on a plane that night. Back to Vegas. I felt like God had lifted me up and put my feet on higher ground in that town. And now He was slamming me back down into the muck and the mire of my childhood hell.

The shit hit the fan. The rumors. The conjecture. The judgment.

I got one phone call upon my return to Vegas: from Deanna's husband Chad—my brother-in-law, for all intents and purposes. He may tease me like his own little sister, but that man loves me. A *lot*!

"Why didn't you just come *home*?" he implored me. "Back to us? You know you always have us."

I broke a lot of hearts.

Hurt people hurt people.

However, David was only four and a half hours away—three hours flat the way he drives. He called as soon as he heard the news.

I had gotten home to my Grandma Jean's house on a Monday night. On a Tuesday, my mother's husband made sure to tell me, "I guess you don't feel all high and mighty now, *do ya?*" On a Wednesday, my aunt had me out to the Cheyenne Saloon to drown my tears in country music line dancing. On a Thursday, I informed my soon-to-be-ex-husband, "I want everything. You get nothing." And by Friday night, I was sobbing in my best friend's loving arms. David had driven in to be there with me right after the workweek ended. Just to be there.

The world had stopped spinning. David got off, and came to my aid like we had promised each other we would way back in college over peanut butter ice cream one rainy night while studying Lord-knows-what in the student union. He definitely made good on that promise.

We and the Joneses were four well-intentioned people who had run a Christian ministry outreach on a secular college campus. Had we preached? Had we "brought the word of God" to those who were in need of something that we had to give? Had we given praise to the One who was the Healer and Holder and Keeper of individuals and families and anyone who trusted in Him? Did we lead the singing and lay on our hands and prayed for those who sought out help for their troubles?

What the hell just happened?

I never thought I'd be in the center of some church scandal—that's for danged sure. It's amazing how quickly circumstances can change and how instantly a person can completely disappear—simply vanish—from a group he or she was wholeheartedly vested in. That's what I did. I ceased to exist.

Chapter 4

God Sits in Non-Smoking

TIME MOVES ON—whether you want it to or not. It's relentless. It has no mercy. It doesn't care that you just want to crawl into bed and wake up in twenty years when everything has blown over. That blasted desert sun keeps coming up over Sunrise Mountain every twenty-four hours. Like clockwork. Can't go back. Can't fast-forward. Each excruciating moment must simply be endured.

On Day Nine after my marriage fell apart, I decided to go get a job. I believe it was a Tuesday. I waited tables in college, so I left Geoff with a friend and spent the entire day filling out applications and talking to managers from nine different restaurants. I came home with my choice of five jobs that day. I didn't really have a preference, so I just picked one. If Father Time was merciless, at least Lady Vegas took pity on me and tipped the scales in my favor.

I stayed with my grandmother for a few months until I got on my feet and eventually found a cheap one-bedroom apartment, 320 square feet, where I slept on the couch and Geoff wanted for nothing. The only thing I wanted was to be a good mom for him so I used that bachelor's degree in sociology to wait tables five days a week, making as much money as I could every day in five hours or less. You can't believe how much money you can make in Vegas in five hours or less.

Legally, even.

I worked the hours I wanted in shorts and tennis shoes in four-hour shifts. Learned to tend bar. Walked out with a butt-load of cash in my pocket every day. Did what I wanted. Went where I wanted. I didn't date a whole lot; I didn't need a man to take care of me—to take over—to help me raise my child. I was hell-bent to make my son the priority in my life that my own mother had never made me. He was number one. Period. Not negotiable. Geoff was my whole life. And for the next several months, we insulated ourselves with our routine: Wake up about 8:00; have some breakfast. Play. Get our baths. Play some more. Drive to daycare by 10:45. Work until 4:30. Pick up Geoff by 4:45 and head to the grocery store for some dinner. Play until midnight—literally—then get up the next morning, and do it all over again.

Since Disneyland was only four hours away, and San Diego just a hop, skip, and a jump from there, we'd take off on a Tuesday, stay with David, and spend a few weekdays at the attractions and the beach while the rest of Southern California was busy at work.

And you know? Time moved on—whether I was thinking about it or not. It wasn't relentless *or* merciful. It just was. That scorching desert sun kept coming up over Sunrise Mountain every twenty-four hours. Like clockwork. I wouldn't go back for the world. And I wouldn't fast forward through even a minute of my life. Each moment was exhilarating, and these moments could finally be enjoyed.

I was totally in charge *of* my life for the first time *in* my life. No father, no mother, no husband. I heard Cher say once, "I answer to two people: God and myself. Anybody else, I don't give a shit…"

I bought a house and invited my brother and sister-in-law to move in with me with their little girl. My brother is the most tenderhearted guy you've ever met. But he does have a tough side.

The day he turned 18, my brother moved out of that parsonage that his parents occupied for free. It's not hard to understand why. At 18, you can legally decide whether or not playing video games at the local Circle K at two o'clock in the morning is a good idea or not. Of course, the lady behind the counter didn't mind. My brother and his buddy were friends with her son, so she didn't mind them hanging around and keeping her company during that long graveyard shift.

A scruffy-looking gentleman stumbled in, so sloshed he couldn't find his arse with both hands, and went straight to the beer cooler. Beer in hand, he then proceeded to make his way to the counter, slamming the 12-pack of Bud Lite in front of the woman. Unfortunately for the man, but fortunately for the rest of us, it's illegal in just about every state to sell alcohol to a person who is already inebriated.

"I'm sorry, sir. I can't sell you this beer. I'd be happy to put it back for you. Have a nice night."

As ignorant-ass, drunk people often do, he made sure that no one was going to have a good night. The guy reached across the counter and planted his fist across her temple, opening up the side of her face and causing a gusher of a head wound.

My brother's friend was the first to reach the guy. In a move he'd most likely learned on the football field, he swooped in and shoved the guy into the double doors. They swung wide open and the guy stumbled out onto the sidewalk in the front of the store. My brother followed right behind and grabbed the guy as he was crashing into one of the front pillars just outside. He threw him onto the asphalt and lit in, pummeling him his three favorite ways: fast, hard, and continuously. The guy barely managed to get up and took a couple of half-hearted swings at my brother, who was so agile and quick, the guy never connected once. With one swift kick to the thighbone, my brother broke his femur and dropped him like he was hot off the stove. A hot mess is what he was. The cops came, took the report, watched the video, called an ambulance, and shook my brother's hand.

One thing my brother can't *stand* is when a man hits a woman. He doesn't *want* to kick your ass because he is sweet and kind and cries at Lassie movies, but he most assuredly is *capable* of kicking your ass should the need arise.

My sweet brother learned from the church what I did: Blind forgiveness and unwavering acceptance—even for those who have egregiously transgressed against you—is the *only* acceptable form of forgiveness according to God. And a true Christian must *keep* forgiving and turning cheek after cheek after cheek, receiving back the person no matter what he did to you or how many times he did it or else you won't be forgiven and will invariably end up in Hell. It's what the Bible says. All sin is the same. To rape a child is the same as having a bad thought or taking a cookie out of the jar without asking. There is no difference between the two in the eyes of God, according to the gospel of our childhood. My brother had forgiven our parents and never spoke about it because we were taught to put those things away forever. That was part of the forgiveness—never to be brought up again. There was no longer anything to talk about, after all. God had cast our parents' sin away from Him as far as the East is from the West. It would have been nice had He done the same thing with my pain, but that's just me. In any case, the subject of our abuse was always taboo, and I couldn't broach it without upsetting him or having him accuse me of harboring unforgiveness in my heart. It wasn't even that I hadn't forgiven our parents—I was still just trying to process all of it and live healthy. He wanted none of it.

He was fine.

My brother and I had always been much closer than my sister and I. She, like I had done, had escaped to my grandmother's house for a while but ended up eloping with a guy from high school back when I was still at Vanguard. Our relationship had always been strained, and talking anything out with her was impossible. We had fought the entire length of our childhood. Affection between us was non-existent. We never even touched each other unless we were in a fistfight, and we fought like alley cats. Sometimes I won. Sometimes she won. We were pretty evenly matched. We didn't share sisterly secrets. We didn't do each other's hair. We didn't talk about boys or school or make-up or fashion.

Obviously.

I did well in school and was constantly performing. My sister struggled academically and was petrified to ever be on a stage. Whenever she had to be the center of attention, tears would flow down her cheeks from nervousness. She would sooner have her pancreas removed by circus clowns with garden tools on an open plain infested with fire ants during a tornado than to have to perform or be in front of people. Friends have suggested that perhaps she felt like she was in my shadow.

I don't know. I wouldn't take that to the bank.

She kept her feelings to herself and never tipped her hand. Who knows what she thought about anything? No one knew her.

She had been largely estranged from our family for the eight years she was married to her husband. I can see now how she worked to keep her worlds from colliding—her past and her present. Her husband's reaction to her childhood abuse was to shield her. He was a young buck who felt he needed to protect her from us—all of us. She pretty well cut ties with the entire family, creating no small amount of suspicion and animosity between us. Looking back, I think she fueled those suspicions. I can see how his anger and distrust of us probably brought her comfort and validation for all the hell she went through. For the first time in her life, someone was incensed by the atrocities she'd suffered and promised her that nothing like that would ever happen to her again. I can certainly see why she would feed that. I'd probably feed that too.

But they, like many young couples, had their own trials and tribulations. Sometimes she would go back to our parents' house and stay with them for short periods of time away from her husband. And, honestly, she told our parents some jaw-dropping stories about her troubles with him, further widening the shaky space between the families. Whether they were true or not, who knows? I don't know if it was a deliberate pitting of one against the other as it was her just trying to cope with all that had happened—trying to be a young wife and a mother and do something with all the pain she'd been handed during her childhood. I'm sure she did the best she could with what she'd been given.

As a result, however, her two families stood diametrically opposed and believing horrible things about one another—just how my sister orchestrated it to be. My sister, for reasons known only to her, failed to make the distinction to her husband between her parents and the rest of us. She did not represent us well to him, and she did not represent him well to us. There was no love lost between us.

When we wanted to see her, we'd go into whatever fast-food restaurant she was working in. Sometimes she'd come out and be friendly, and sometimes she'd hide in the back and wouldn't come out until we left. You just never knew.

I remember going into the Kenny Roger's Roasters where she worked to pick up some dinner for everybody back at the house after a Saturday bar shift at the restaurant. She was standing at the register and smiled at me when I came in.

"Hey," she greeted me.

"Hey." When I got closer, I could see bruising underneath her right eye. "Nice eye, Tab."

Her eyes shifted down like she was ashamed, and she shrugged her shoulder.

"What happened?"

"I was being stupid."

"Hmph."

"I'm not using my discount tonight. You want it for your order?"

"Sure," I said. "Appreciate it."

"No problem. What'll you have?"

I gave her my order and didn't know what to think about the eye. I didn't want to imagine what kind of ruckus she'd gotten herself into. She'd beat the shit out of me and vice versa more than once, so I knew she could hold her own for all the times we went fisticuffs.

The place wasn't that busy, so after she put my order together, she told her manager that she was taking her break and walked out to my car with me. The cold January night brought with it a slicing wind. She didn't have a jacket. Her small frame shivered as she reached into her back pocket for a pack of cigarettes. She tapped one out and put it to her mouth while I put the bags of food into the passenger's seat. I turned back around in time to see her light it up and suck in that first drag. Smoke blew out from her mouth and nostrils as she announced out of the blue, "The doctor says I'm pregnant again."

"Really?"

"I guess."

She had two adorable girls that I rarely got to see. I shook my head in disgust. "Well, that's fantastic. Congratulations." The sarcasm wasn't lost on her. I looked at her—looked right through her. Twenty-seven-years-old, and pregnant with her third baby. Her shoulders hunched in as she tried uselessly to brace herself from the freezing wind, her fingers trembled as she lifted the cigarette to her lips. That portrait of her burned itself into my brain, and I just lost it. Here she was working fast food (which wasn't nearly as respectable as my job in *casual dining*—what the hell my mentality was there, I still have no idea) out here in the frigid cold and didn't even have a damn jacket! She was having another baby? With this guy who couldn't even stand us? What the hell was she doing with her life? She was throwing it away.

I had tried to let Tab do her own thing for the most part. I mean, what choice did any of us have? She was going to do whatever she wanted. Sure, there were times I tried to give advice—if what she said was true about her troubles with her husband, I had certainly suggested that she give independence a try. We had all suggested it at one time or another. After all, I was finding my center, becoming incredibly self-reliant and *loving* it. Maybe she could find the same path, right? I was developing a particular distaste for women who have to *be* with someone or have a man take care of them, and I saw many of the females in my family as quintessential examples of *those* women. The more I took care of myself, the more I wanted to be by myself. And here she was becoming even more dependent on somebody else than she already was, further and further away from self-reliance.

I could say that it pissed me off, but that wouldn't be true. It was fear. Pure terror. I can't explain it except to say that I was suddenly and inexplicably afraid for her, for what would become of her. That fear became an angry fire that ignited deep, deep within my belly. It flamed up and came boiling out of my mouth, "You know what? You need to figure some shit out, Tabitha. You need to figure some shit out!" I stuck my finger in her face. "You're throwing your life away! If you don't get your shit together, you're not going to *have* a life! Do you hear me? You won't have a life!"

I threw my purse across the seat and was barely aware that its contents exploded against the passenger side window. I didn't look back at her. I got into the car and slammed the door shut. I backed out, threw it in drive and punched it, peeling out of there like Dale Earnhardt and leaving her shivering with nothing but that damn cigarette for warmth.

No way in hell I'd ever live my life like that.

This was new territory for me—all this independence, but I was handling it just fine. I was high on *control*. I didn't need a man. Hell, I had a man—he was five. No one else needed to be introduced to the equation. I didn't need approval. I didn't need anything from anybody. I felt as good and happy and secure as I ever had. Why? Because I was the driver toward my own destiny and no longer just a passenger on the journey of my life—not like my sister. Not like my mother. Not like any of the rest of my family.

My life was *fine*.

Never mind I couldn't darken the doors of a church for the first six months I was home. I tried different churches a time or two, but every Sunday that I tried to go, I'd have toxic flashbacks. I'd sit there in the pew, look around, and wonder how many of these people would drink the poison Kool-Aid if they started passing it out. Every song brought me back to a hypocritic-religified childhood that I had yet to sift through—not to mention having to tend to the fresh wounds of being stuck in the middle of a church scandal—and it all left me sickened, every bit of it. Every sermon. Every announcement. Every smile. Every voice inflection. Every handshake. The carpet irritated me. And the taupe walls. And the 3-inch golf pencils in the pews that no one ever sharpened. They were so dull no one could write with them. Useless. What purpose did they serve? Tell me what good they were to anybody? Yet they sat there, week after week, just tempting parishioners to try to fill out a prayer request card or write a dollar amount on the tithing envelopes. The suits, the ties, the combed-over hair. The mascara and the eye shadow and the matching purses and shoes. The little, old ladies with their ruby red lips and panty hose one size too big, gathered around their ankles like elephant skin. The musty smell in the hymnals was an annoyance and the fact that no one ever sang the third verse from any hymn. Ever. Why? Why did the worship leader only have the congregation sing verses one, two, and four? Did somebody have some issue against every third verse of every hymn ever written? Were they not correctly exegeted? Was there some theological conundrum in every third verse that no one was telling us about? What else were they not telling us? Because I was pretty damn sure that

I'd heard and seen and experienced all this before a million, gazillion times. The repetition was exasperating to me, and my spirit started to expect perhaps just a tad more from a God Who was rumored to be eternal.

I had to go find God *outside* of that building.

For the next several months, I spent every Sunday morning at Bedside Baptist with Pastor Pillow and Sister Sheets spending quiet time with the Lord.

Yeah, I like it quiet when I sleep.

Church folk can criticize all they want, but I needed that time away. I needed to sleep. I needed to detox. I needed a break. Rest. Reprieve. Respite. Relief. I needed to find sanctuary with God in my own heart, and I had to get to a stronger mental, emotional, and spiritual place before I could go back to church and be my authentic self—not pretending to be something or someone that I wasn't regardless of what anybody else thought. I had to be sure I could stand up under the pressure of being myself—someone who questioned authority, someone who might have different opinions, someone who might not vote Republican (perish the thought), and someone who would be brazenly honest about the pain and suffering in this world and how sometimes people don't always walk in victory and the church can't make them no matter how hard they preach or how loud they sing or how fast they run down the aisles of the church with their hands in the air or how high they swing from the chandeliers. I was eventually going to go back *just as I am without one plea*, so the hymn goes and if they didn't like it, they should stop singing the damn song! But I couldn't go to church just as I was right then. I wasn't strong enough to go to church. These are my confessions. I spent those six months *bracing* myself for the day I did go back. I wasn't going to play the game anymore. I knew I had to be solid enough not to succumb to the peer pressure because, by God, I was going back a different person—*Just As I Am*. And is anybody interested to know what the infamous third verse of that hymn is? The verse we never sang?

> "Just as I am, though tossed about
> With many a conflict, many a doubt,
> Fightings and fears within, without,
> O Lamb of God, I come, I come."

I come. And finally one day—I did it. I went home—to the church of my childhood. It happened because Randy and Pam Greer, the couple who pastored that church who have always loved me more than chocolate covered strawberries, came into the restaurant where I worked, and I served up their lunch.

If memory serves, they were slightly distraught by some disgruntled members in their congregation that complained about having to pay three dollars a car for parking because the venue for their Easter cantata had been moved to Cashman Field. The community of Vegans that were expected to attend would never be able to fit in their tiny, 800-seat sanctuary. The three-dollar parking charge was imposed by the facility—not by the church, but people still had their panties in a wad over it.

"I don't know, Daisy," Pam said sweetly as I filled up their water glasses. "What do you think?"

"Pssh!" I shrugged. Without even giving it a thought, I put it out there, "Honey, I've got bigger beefs against the church than three bucks a pop for parking!"

The both of them threw their heads back and laughed! Randy reached out and grabbed my elbow and, with the most sincere grin on his face said, "Daisy, you are so…" He shook his head as he tried to find the right description. Finally, he looked at me, gave me a huge smile, and said, "…*refreshing!*"

I stood there stunned, with the water pitcher in one hand and their empty plates in the other—and my eyes filled with tears right there. A Divine moment.

I don't ever really have those moments. Those moments find other people with other lives that are nothing like my own. The tears are always mine, but the moments are not. For the first time in my life, I held both in my hands—along with that water pitcher and those empty plates.

I looked down, and my eyes filled up. I couldn't even look him in the eye and admitted truthfully, softly, "No one has ever described me quite that way…" It was the first time I'd ever felt like someone *delighted* in me—just as I was. And that's the memory I hold dear when I read in the Bible that, *"The LORD your God is with you, He is mighty to save. He will take great delight in you, He will quiet you with his love, He will rejoice over you with singing" (Zephaniah 3:17).*

And suddenly, standing there in that Applebee's, I knew it didn't matter anymore what anyone else thought of me. My path. My struggle. My failing, faltering faith. In spite of it all, I knew. God was with me. He was mighty to save. I didn't have to worry about anything. *He* delighted in me whether or not anybody else did. He quieted me with His love—right there in non-smoking, station seven, because God will flat meet and deliver a single, struggling waitress living paycheck to paycheck with scrawny legs and a sketchy faith in the middle of a busy lunch rush. He *quieted* me with His love. He rejoiced in me. With *singing*...

Randy and Pam hugged me goodbye, and I thankfully put their fat tip in my apron 'cuz they're just cool like that.

And guess where I was the very next Sunday?

❧ ❧ ❧

Where Did I Park My Broomstick?

The Sunday Randy spoke about loving the unlovable, the good Lord saw fit to test my ability to do just that within the first four minutes after the service. I went to pick up my toddler from the nursery where they, "...shall not all sleep, but they shall all be changed," and he was one very cranky little boy. The number of people trying to get in or get out of the sanctuary between services was ridiculous, and in hindsight, even though Geoffrey clearly didn't want to be held, I should have picked him up and carried him out and would have probably completely prevented all that was about to occur. Alas, he wanted to walk like a big boy. We were halfway out the glass double doors when he decided he wanted to go back into the lobby to get a drink of water from the drinking fountain. He turned and pushed up against me, and he was strong for a three-year-old! People were in front of us pressing to come in and behind us pressing to get out. My baby was plugging up the flow.

"Mommy, I want a drink!"

"Geoffrey, there's a drinking fountain outside. Keep moving!"

"No! I want THAT one!"

"No!"

"Yes!"

I reached down and tucked my hands up under his arms just as he went limp and dropped himself in the middle of rush hour like a puddle. I had to straddle the boy and drag his dead weight by his armpits through the throng of good, Christian souls. I finally got us out of the building and away from the congestion. Before I could even blink, two gentlemen approached me looking like they had to poop in the worst possible way.

We've all been there.

They looked to be about twenty years old, dressed casually in Bermuda shorts and t-shirts and sandals. They both held thin, black Bibles and needed haircuts.

"Excuse me," one of them said. "May we speak to you, please?"

"What can I do for you, gentlemen?" I asked struggling, as I wrangled my baby boy into a somewhat subdued body-lock.

"Well, I think it's what we can do for you that is important."

"Oh? And what would that be?"

"Perhaps you're unaware of this, but those earrings you're wearing? They're an abomination to God."

Now, today's modern woman would ask, "Am I getting punked right now?" Thank you, Ashton Kutcher. But since Ashton was only in about the second grade around that time, the question in my mind, of course, had to be, "Am I on Candid Camera right now?" I started looking around for Allen Funt, not nearly as attractive as Ashton but every bit as crafty.

The earrings to which my new friends were referring were peace symbols about an inch and a half in diameter. Fake gold danglies. I wish I knew where they were as I recall all of this because I really liked them a lot. Anyway, my response was one slightly raised eyebrow as Geoffrey strained against me toward the drinking fountain.

"Do you know what that symbol really means?"

I thought I'd take a shot in the dark and guess, "Uhhh, peace?"

"Well," they smiled patronizingly at me. "That's what most people think. That is really the sign of the devil."

Friggin' shoot me now.

How do these people find me? Am I a whacko-magnet? My kid just wanted a drink of water. Is that too much to ask? You want to know what I think? I think God really does send me these people. You know why? Because He's up in Heaven elbowing Jesus in the ribs and saying, "Hey, you gotta see this. It's gonna be good…" And they're both up there, flat on their backs doing the dead cockroach, feet in the air, holding their stomachs, and laughing their butts off. And watch if I don't get Them to admit it on the day of reckoning.

"No," I smiled politely. "I really think they just mean peace. Thank you boys…"

Undaunted, they stepped forward and prevented me from walking away and looked even more like they really, *really* had to poop! "Ma'am, this symbol is used in Satanic rituals! When a woman becomes a member of the church of

Satan, they lay her naked upon an altar. She holds an upside down cross between her breasts and breaks the sides off, creating THIS very symbol! The world has been deceived by the enemy—the Angel of Light, the *deceiver*—into thinking this symbol stands for peace when it clearly does not!"

Clearly.

Did anyone doubt that some chick would be naked? You had to know there would be breasts.

Here's the great thing about being raised up in this subculture. I knew in a split second the source of this information: Mike Warnke is a Christian comedian who I had heard speak at least twice on that very property back in the day. I think he's quite possibly the funniest guy I've ever heard in my life. Truly. He came and spoke to our congregation when I was a teenager about his life as a high priest in the Satanic church where these rituals with naked women and breasts and upside down crosses were part of his testimony. These two over-eager boys, apparently, did not get the memo that Crossroads magazine put the kibosh on ol' Mike's claims just a few years before. Their investigation found Mike's stories to be fraudulent and deceitful and printed their findings for all to see. He's still the funniest guy I've ever heard in my life—that's the darn truth, so I gotta give him that—but I was keeping my peace symbol earrings.

So, do you think for one minute that I would share this insight with my new friends and show them the error of their ways? Oh, hell to the no! See, there's something inside me that wants to make a parking lot out of a situation when I have to deal with really religified, ignorant, knuckleheads who earnestly believe that they are meting out God's will in bringing me closer to the Light, when the fact is, they don't know their asses from holes in the ground. It is most ungracious and un-Christ-like of me, but it does make for some really good writing later! And so, I continue to strive toward the complete demise of a situation as opposed to working toward resolution and harmony and enlightenment, and Randy's "loving the unlovable" goes right out the window. I can honestly confess that I have not experienced one iota of personal growth in this area, and as of this writing, I will choose to antagonize the circumstances as best I can and send the whole messy business crashing and burning into the ground whenever possible. Yes, so that I can write about it. And make fun of people who irritate me.

Where to drop the bomb? Hmmm? Where, oh where?

With a slightly sarcastic smile I asked, "So, do you think I'm deceived?"

These poor boys.

"Not deceived, really. Just uninformed. That's why we came over here—to let you know so that you would never wear those earrings again."

Ah, this looks like an excellent place to drop a bomb.

"Actually, fellas, I will be wearing these earrings again because, you see, I am a witch. And if you don't get the hell away from me right now, I'm going to cast a spell on you tonight when I'm NAKED! If you'll excuse me, my broomstick is double-parked. You all have a blessed day."

I scooped up my squirming baby and immediately smelled poop. Looking down the back of my toddler's diaper, I saw that his little bum-bum was clean as a whistle.

Makes you wonder which one of those boys finally pooped his pants?

Lines in the Sand

Strength is a funny thing. An ant can lift twenty times its own weight, which really doesn't mean a whole heck of a lot if some kid is laying face down on a lawn chair by the pool in the summer with a magnifying glass just waiting for one to walk by so he can zap it into a crispy cootie.

I would have loved to think I was strong enough to take Geoff on a vacation to visit my parents. In fact, I did think that. My feet had gained some purchase on my journey of forgiveness. I was ready to leave the past in the past. So, with all my naivety, hidden in the obscurity of my new-but-still-blind faith, we boarded a plane, rented a car, and made our way to my parents' home for the longest, most God-forsaken seventy-two hours of my life. The plan was to visit them along with my father and the rest of my Lofton family, and then drive down to Nashville to see David, who had just moved there from Southern California, which made the Lancaster family a whole lot happier.

I showed up to Smallsville, and the old ghosts from the past showed up right along with me. Or maybe they'd never left. As soon as we walked through the door, the familial heaviness in the air hit me like a wrecking ball to the gut. It was like walking back into a time warp. Same cluttered house. Same dishes lying in the sink. The dogs were different, but they had the same names as the dogs we had growing up. In the same disheveled living room sat the same dingy furniture. My mother's face wore the same tired, befuddled expression; on her husband's face, the same sinister mien he'd always had. He just knew he owned the world and everything in it, and that included me. It didn't matter one iota that I'd grown up and had a child of my own.

I hated the way he acted with my son. He postured himself as Geoffrey's "big buddy." Pals. He tried to say they had a "special bond." The hell they did.

It made me sick.

He took great pride in telling me that one of the officers down at the station had an interesting conversation with my mother.

"I got a great compliment from your mom the other day."

I always make sure everybody in the world knows whenever I get a great compliment.

"She was down at the courthouse and one of my fellow officers said to her, 'You sure are sweet. Your husband is lucky to have you.' You know what your mom said? She said, 'Oh no, you've got that backwards. He's not lucky to have me—I'm the one who's lucky to have him!' Wasn't that sweet?"

Like hell. Somebody pass the Pepto-Bismol. "Well, thank you Billy Sunday," I should have said. "You're as high as a Georgia pine, and you're an egg-suckin' dawg! If any of us were *lucky*, your goat-smellin' ass would be stranded all by yourself on some uncharted island somewhere in the South China Sea."

But I didn't. I couldn't remember where I'd left my voice. The inertia of family dynamics is hard to interrupt. See, everyone knows what everyone else's role in the family is—right down to the very youngest ones. And even when those little ones grow up, they have a hard time functioning any differently than what has already been established. What had been established in our family dynamic is that we didn't dispute anything that man ever said. You didn't cross him. You didn't call him to the carpet. You didn't defy him. You agreed wholeheartedly with any and every harebrained thing he put out there. If you needed an opinion about something, he'd gladly give it to you. He's generous like that.

I scooped Geoffrey up and made sure he was never alone with my mother's husband or even the two of them. My mother had been there for my abuse and did nothing. Participated even. Blind faith be damned—I wasn't going to gamble my son's safety. The vigilance wore me plumb out. How absurd, I thought, to have to protect my child from my own parents! Lunacy! Life shouldn't be this way.

I was there about five minutes before Asshole told the story about how my mother was so lucky to have him and then announced, "I'm leading music for church this Wednesday night. I told the pastor you'd be doing special music. Do you have a song you can sing, or should I pick something?"

"I have a sore throat." I had no interest in participating in their little game—portraying our family like we were the Cleavers. I'd been fake and false for the first nineteen years of my life. Living more authentically these days, thank you very much (except for the lie I just told about my throat being sore), so I don't think I'll jump through your little hoops this Wednesday night. I told my mother at one point that I really didn't even want to go.

But I didn't tell him that I didn't even want to go. I didn't tell him that I wouldn't sing—I simply made up an excuse and skirted around defying him. Again, I couldn't remember where I'd left my voice.

My mother told me that they'd already told their congregation at church that I was coming and that everyone was so looking forward to meeting me.

"They feel like they know you. They know you graduated from college and that you're a singer. We told them how you and your dad had a music ministry together. We've been bragging on you. We talk about you all the time. It would be rude if you didn't at least come and meet them."

"Well, Mom, why don't you file that straight under 'tough shit?'" I should have said. But I didn't. I couldn't remember where I'd left my voice.

I went. He led worship. He skipped verse three in both hymns. Everybody followed along and praised Jesus, and I was slightly nauseous. We all closed our hymnals, and he stepped down. The pastor of the church came to the podium and announced, "Thank you. You may be seated. At this time, I'd like to introduce to you [name withheld's] oldest daughter who will be singing special music for us." He turned to me and smiled, not knowing that he'd just blindsided me in front of the entire church, and stretched out his hand for me to come.

I stood up and said to my stepmonster loud enough for everyone to hear, "I think you're confused. I believe the last conversation we had about this, I told you I had a sore throat. You're so smug up there on that stage thinking you can manipulate me to do whatever you want me to do for you, but this little shenanigan you pulled just backfired. I do what I *want* to do, and you can't make me do anything I *don't* want to do. In fact, let me tell you what *you* can do! You can fuck straight off!" Then I proceeded to walk right down the center aisle and out the double doors toward the parking lot.

No, I didn't.

You know why? Because I couldn't remember where I'd left my voice. Instead, I slipped right into my old patterns and plastered that fake smile right where it had been for the first nineteen hellish years of my miserable life. I got up from my chair, walked up to that stage, and offered up the first hymn that popped into my head, *Precious Lord, a cappella.* It wasn't like I was prepared with any sort of accompaniment, so I sang it *American-Idol*-audition-style.

I've not sung it since. Not once. Ever. Ever. It's been years. From that time on, anytime a congregation sang it on any given Sunday, I suddenly felt the urge to pee (or puke) and slipped right out of the sanctuary and headed for the bathroom until it was over. I can't stand the sound of it.

Stepmonster had stepped off to the side and smiled adoringly while I performed for him like I always had—exactly the way we all knew I would.

Fucker.

The whole time I was on that stage, I could feel his hands on me going wherever they wanted—doing whatever they wanted. He made me stand up there naked while he drooled and had his way with me, only this time he had an audience. I had to stand there like his whore and pretend that I liked it, while he molested me all over again. It is precisely what he was doing to me. He knew it, my mother knew it, and I knew it. With everyone watching, I had to take my clothes off, spread my legs, and perform for him—to satiate his sick perversions right there in the "house of God." Sanctuary? Not for me. I wasn't even safe from him in church. And it *never* mattered to him that he hurt me. He enjoyed the hell out of it. When he was finished with me, everybody clapped and smiled and nodded their approval for a job well done.

I thought I was going to throw up. I was literally shaking as I left the stage to take the seat next to my mother, who patted my leg as I sat down. Stepmonster walked back to the microphone and said smugly, "Thank you, honey. That was great."

Was it good for you?

Then he proceeded to give his testimony, praise God.

The next morning I got Geoffrey up and wanted to get him dressed right away. I'd kept my hand on him the whole night as he laid beside me on the pullout couch in the living room. I barely slept the entire time we were there. No way would I allow him to be touched. I told him we were going to go to the bathroom to change into our clothes. While I had my back turned to him getting our clothes out of the suitcase, he did what any and all five-year-olds love to do: stripped down, buck-naked, right there in the living room. I turned back around to him doing the nudey-bootie dance, spinning in a circle giggling, "I'm naked, Mommy!"

I grabbed him angrily by the arm and pulled him to me. "I TOLD you! We're going to dress in the bathroom!"

He eyes abruptly brimmed with tears and his bottom lip went south, breaking my heart. Here was my little boy who had done nothing wrong. He was just being an innocent child. Why should he have to pick up the tab for my own fears? And why should we have to live our lives being afraid that this precious baby could possibly be hurt by his own grandparents? It shouldn't be.

It wouldn't be.

We got in that rental car and left them standing on the porch on our way to Nashville where I knew David—truer than the truest truth—would be waiting with his wisdom and his open arms. As I put that gas pedal to the floor to put as much distance between us as quickly as possible, a thought jetted its way across my mind.

I will never go back there again.

A sense of relief flooded through me at the very notion. The idea washed over me like a summer shower, cleansing me from the muck and the mire of the last few days. I basked in it. It was glorious. Then the next thought occurred to me: *What if I never spoke to them again? What if I never had another thing to do with them? Ever?* A sense of giddiness filled my heart at the mere prospect. Glancing in my rearview mirror at my toddler, my gift from God who made right everything that had ever been wrong in my whole life, I could see that he was dozing off in his car seat. He held his stuffed panda bear in one hand and let a cookie drop from the other. I promised him on my life that I would keep him safe always. Not like my mother. I was not like her. Immense joy came over me. The further I drove, the more free I felt. So I did what felt good—I drove. I felt more liberated with every mile. When I got to Nashville, David had the words I needed when I second-guessed myself.

"Aren't we commanded by God to honor our mother and father?" I asked. "I mean, he isn't even my father. Donnie is my father. I don't think I owe him shit."

"You don't. Trust me, you don't," he assured me.

"But what about my mother? What do I owe her? She served us up to that sick bastard our whole lives and now she tells other people how lucky she is to have him. How do I sever the relationship with her and still 'honor' her? Does all this just mean I haven't fully forgiven them?"

"Maybe it's time for you to honor the fact that she never chose you and let her live with that choice, Daisy? Does forgiveness always mean that everybody cuddles in the end? Or does it mean we are supposed to simply release the people from our past who have hurt us? I think you've done that. You couldn't have gone to visit them if you hadn't done that."

"What about reconciliation?"

"What about it?"

"Shouldn't there be reconciliation?"

"Are you reconciled to the fact that your number one responsibility in this world is to keep your son safe?"

"Absolutely!"

"Well, there ya go. You're reconciled. Congratulations. Those people are God's responsibility. You need to relinquish them to Him. God help them."

I looked across the table at him, thinking intently.

"Seriously, Daisy. You need to let them go—in every way that a person can let go. You're holding onto sickness by holding onto them. You're holding onto death. You can't hold onto your child with one hand and all that mess with the other. This isn't even an option. Do it for yourself and do it for your son."

Sweet release.

I chose health.

Long into the night I processed every emotion that came to the surface. Geoffrey slept. I talked. David listened.

"I don't like who I am when I'm with them. I allowed myself to fall right back into the same pattern of unquestioning submission. I'm not strong enough…"

"What would you say to him if he were standing here right now?"

"That he'll never touch me like that again. That he doesn't have any power over me. That if I had that whole scene to do over again I WOULD have told him to fuck straight off—right there in front of God and everybody—because I don't care anymore. I'm done. I'd tell him to fuck off and go make myself a sandwich."

"Maybe you are strong enough?"

"In one day?"

"Sure. Why not? An epiphany is an epiphany, sis."

"I don't know. In my heart, in my mind, it's already done. I've already detached. I'm just trying to play the devil's advocate with myself and ask myself the hard questions like, How are you going to feel when they die? Because they will, you know. They'll die, and I will not have spoken to them for however long it is that they remain on this earth. I am about to cause them the greatest heartache of their lives."

He lifted an eyebrow at this, waiting for the explanation.

"Regardless of what they've done to me, I live my life by the admonition, 'Do no harm.' Period. This will harm them."

"And?"

"I take no joy in that. There is no satisfaction. This is not retaliatory in any way. It's just something I know I have to do, and I have to let the chips fall where they fall. And when they die? How will I feel?"

I contemplated this as the sky darkened to black outside with my brother sitting across from me giving me all the time I needed to work it out. I thought about this long and hard.

"When he dies, I will be completely unaffected. I won't feel sad. I won't feel happy. I won't feel anything. Whenever I think about him now, I'm not even angry. I'm not bitter. But I don't feel any sort of hope for him either. I feel… nothing. I feel nothing for him or against him. It's like he's seared any emotion in me that I could possibly have. When he dies, the world will be just a tad bit better. Safer. Without him in it."

He nodded in agreement, but still said nothing. We sat silently for a long time; the only sounds were the gentle wheezes of baby-sleep from Geoffrey on the couch. Eventually, David got up from the table and covered Geoff with a blanket from the hall closet. I watched my best friend tuck my son's tiny hand underneath the blanket and tenderly pat his head. So much love for this boy. So much safety here—safety I'd never known at that age. He filled his coffee and came back to the table.

"When my mother dies, will I have regrets?" I rubbed my eyes. I was exhausted.

"Will you?"

I shrugged my shoulders. "I have regrets now. I regret the path she's chosen. I regret that she knowingly offered us up to her husband's demands every day of our lives. I regret that she didn't keep us safe. I regret all that's been lost because of her choices. But I won't regret separating ourselves from her and, I assure you, all this regret won't increase *or* decrease when she dies. It won't get better. It won't get worse."

"And what do you hope happens to them?"

I folded my hands on the table top and looked him straight in the eye, "I wish them both every happiness, every success. What is it to me, after all? How does it take away or add to my life whether they do well or not? So, I hope they live long, prosperous lives. I hope they live without pain or loneliness. I wish them peace and hope for the rest of their days."

"So help you, God?"

"So help me, God," I answered without hesitation. "Just so long as they don't call me on Christmas."

≈ ≈ ≈

Though I Walk Through the Valley of the Shadow of Death

I returned to Vegas after that hellacious trip with my parents in a hopeful whirlwind of a place. The prospect of cutting off all ties to them was always on my mind. I wanted to run it by one last person before I did—one of the other pastors at Trinity, Dean Sanner. Randy and Pam brought me back into the fold, but Dean and his wife Jenell were the ones who ran a singles' Bible study on Monday nights. That was easier for me to do on a regular basis. No hymnals, no hype, no 3-inch golf pencils. Just good teaching with good friends. I met with Dean a time or two to talk through what I was about to do. He didn't tell me what to do or how to do it, but his counsel was good and sound, and he provided true sanctuary for me.

He was not the only one looking out for me.

I quickly settled back into the routine of work. Applebee's, even with all its crazy antics, had been a sanctuary for me too. It was easy to drop my problems off at the door—they'd always be waiting faithfully for me at the end of my shift, after all. My favorite customers had been waiting for my return—one was John Bear. He came in and sat at my bar nearly every day, telling stories and entertaining everyone—such a kind and gentle spirit. He was a medicine man for his tribe, the Paiutes. Their reservation was not far from my home in the northwest. I'd only been back a few days when John came in the Saturday after I got home with a gift for me.

"Daisy, I made this for you this morning. It looks like a dream-catcher, but it's not. I had to hang duck feathers on it because white people aren't allowed to own eagle feathers. I want you to hang this up in your house in a window that faces east. When the sun rises and shines on your house, this will bring protection to your home."

Our eyes locked when he said that. He looked deep into my spirit, and something in his eyes told me he was dead serious. This was not a joke. He knew something.

"What's going on, medicine man?"

He didn't try to hide his concern. He said frankly, "I'm having dreams about you and your family. Just do this for me. Do it for a superstitious old man."

His demeanor was too serious to ignore. In the way of his tradition, from a place of love, he was doing what he knew how to do to protect me from something.

"I'll hang it in my kitchen window. The sun comes up on that side."

He nodded and said nothing more about it. I put the gift in my bag underneath the bar and ordered his lunch.

"So, what have you got going on for this Memorial Day weekend, John Bear?"

"We're having a powwow on the rez—not just for the Paiutes but for the other tribes in the valley. You should come tomorrow. Bring the kids."

"Maybe we'll do that. My ex-husband is in town visiting Geoffrey. I'll bring the whole fam-damily."

I went on with my shift, but John Bear had definitely gotten into my head with this gift of protection. That evening I put a nail above my kitchen window and hung John's "protection wheel with duck feathers" as I'd called it.

Geoff's father was staying there at the house with us. After we'd had dinner and played with the kids and finally put them to bed, he and my brother's wife and I stayed up talking. My brother had to work the next day and needed to get some sleep. He wouldn't be able to join us for the powwow.

Without my brother, we could talk about just how I was going to sever ties with my parents. They were super supportive and didn't know why I hadn't done this years earlier. Geoff's father was especially pleased that Geoff would not know them—one less worry for us as parents.

"It's not like I can just call them on the phone and say, 'Hey, I'm not going to talk to you guys ever again.' That would require talking to them!" The nonsense of it made us laugh. "And I'm certainly not spending any more time or energy or money to go do it in person." Lord knows that would be a soup sandwich. "I think the best way to do it is just to write them a letter. That way I can just say what I want to say without being interrupted. I can drop it into the mailbox and be done with them forever."

And so it was decided. It was too late to draft anything that night, but I knew I could pour out all I needed to say after the powwow the next day or even Monday. Since Monday was Memorial Day, I knew the mail wouldn't run until Tuesday, but it didn't matter. I knew that by the end of the week, I would be free of them forever and everything that needed to be said would be said.

That night I slept like a dead log.

The three of us took the kids out to the rez the next day for John Bear's powwow. If you've never been to one, let me put a plug in here. You need to! Find one! They're wonderful! There's dancing and headdresses and drumming, food and festivities, jewelry and laughter and, in southern Nevada, lots and lots of dust. We bought the kids moccasins, and I bought a beautiful jade necklace. The Paiutes were consummate hosts and got our children to dance while we ate and watched them laugh and jump about without inhibition like children should and so easily do. I was very grateful to John Bear for how he loved our pale faces and our children and wanted to share his beautiful culture. Our children couldn't keep their eyes open by about three o'clock, so we said our goodbyes and took them home.

We hadn't been back very long when the phone rang. I picked it up to hear my aunt screaming hysterically on the other end. I couldn't even understand her.

"What happened? I can't understand you!"

"She's DEAD! She's DEAD!"

"What? Who? Who is dead?"

More undecipherable rantings burned up the line. Or, more likely, my mind was not able to absorb the meaning of the words and I subconsciously refused to understand.

"Wait! Slow down!" She just needed to take a deep breath. This was all a misunderstanding. No one was dead. If she'd just stop screaming and calm down, she would see that she's making a big deal out of something that was probably nothing. Nothing at all. Nothing to worry about.

My heartbeat started to speed up, and there didn't seem to be anything I could do about it.

"Just tell me slowly what's going on. Slow down. Just talk."

"She's. Been. SHOT!"

"WHAT? WHO?"

"TABITHA! She's been shot! And she's DEAD!"

I stood absolutely frozen from my own blood that had turned to ice. If someone had touched me at that moment, I would have shattered—splintered into a million pieces on my kitchen floor. I turned around and looked at my family who were all staring at me, knowing that something was horribly wrong—my face had to have been white as snow. I was barely cognizant of the words buzzing in my ear as she continued to splatter me with this inexplicable anguish that I couldn't even begin to process in my mind.

"They've been calling over here all day, and I didn't answer because I saw her mother-in-law's name on the caller ID, but they wouldn't stop calling, so finally I answered and they said there was an accident—an accident with a gun—and now she's dead!"

The sleet in my veins made me bitterly cold and suddenly I was transported back to that dark, frozen parking lot at Kenny Roger's Roasters. I had no idea it would be the last time I would ever see my sister alive. Bile threatened to come up from my stomach as I remembered all too vividly the last words she would ever hear come out of my mouth: "You're throwing your life away! If you don't get your shit together, you're not going to have a life! Do you hear me? *You won't have a life!*"

You won't have a life… It was as if I'd said it a day ago.

She'd told me that night that she was pregnant with her third child. Everything around me faded, and I saw once again her thin, shivering form in the biting wind, trying to smoke her cigarette without shaking like a leaf. I felt sick. She would only be about seven months along now. "What about the baby?" I asked.

"The baby's dead too."

I closed my eyes in an effort to stop seeing my sister standing out there alone in the rear view mirror of my car, to block out the whole ugly scene. The phone beeped with another phone call. I looked at the caller ID.

It was my mother.

"Hold on…" I clicked over leaving her in the middle of an avalanche of words.

"Hello?" I muttered. Two monotone syllables. Lifeless.

I heard my mother's voice for the first time since I'd come home from that wretched trip.

"Your sister's dead." Her delivery was the polar opposite of Alicia's hysteria. It was eerily calm.

"I know, Mother."

"Does your brother know yet?"

My brother. Her first concern. Always.

"No."

"I'll tell him. I want to be the one to tell him."

I looked up at my brother who was standing beside me now with a look of dread on his face. Without a word, I handed him the receiver. He took it slowly. He knew. He knew his life was about to change forever with whatever words would meet him in just a few seconds. He stood for a time just staring at the phone in his hands, as if he wanted to prolong the inevitable for as long as he could. For him, our sister—his full-blooded sister—was still alive. In just four short words, she suddenly wouldn't be. Perhaps he was taking a mental inventory of whom it could be that was no longer with us. His father? One of our grandparents? A close family friend? One of the dogs?

Inch by inch, he lifted the phone to his ear. It took a decade. He didn't speak. I think our mother heard him breathe into the phone—I could barely hear her begin to talk. The rest of us stood helplessly as he was given the news. There was nothing we could do to brace him for it. The look on his face, I'll never forget. It wasn't shock. It wasn't horror. It was blank—a desolate, lifeless stare. He dropped to his knees without a sound, the phone still in his hand, which now hung flatly at his side. His expression, completely and utterly vacant. It's as if his spirit, for an instant, left his body in a panic to go find her—to see if he could coax her back to us. It seemed to us that he was gone forever, looking for her everywhere to no avail. Finally, and without warning, his stricken spirit returned to him and the emptiness on his face twisted into devastation as my mother's words began to tap his comprehension. He dropped the phone on the floor and began to scream, "No! No! No! No! No!" With each NO, he slammed his face against the kitchen table so violently that blood immediately began to spurt from his nose and mouth and drip down his chin onto his chest. The three of us raced to him, and the children began to cry out in fear. We could barely lift his dead weight off the floor as he sobbed.

He sobbed and he bled and he sobbed and he bled. The children cried and we cried; we wailed and held each other on our knees while my mother's voice became silent in the phone that lay ignored on the floor.

As if the relationship between Tabitha's two families wasn't bad enough, I felt compelled to lead a small entourage of people to the police station bright and early Tuesday morning to hear what their investigation uncovered. There was no way I was going to take the word of a family who had no use for ours as to what happened with my sister. Our imaginations and emotions were going a country mile a minute with all kinds of accusations flying around. The police assured us that her husband had been at work and the only people present at the time of her death were her little ones, so small they could not articulate what happened. Even though her death was ruled accidental, we left with more questions than we had going in. And the fact that we'd made those questions known to the police went over like a fart in church, I'll tell you what.

That right there put the pepper in the gumbo.

If we thought that family had hard feelings toward us before, they were fired up as hell now, with yours truly at the center of their storm. We weren't banking on the fact that they would even let us know where they laid that poor girl to rest. I called the funeral home and begged them to at least tell us where they'd buried her so that our family could come later and pay our respects after everything settled down. That was the most we expected.

All I wanted was to see her one last time, to hold her, and tell her that I was so sorry for what I said to her the last time I saw her. I was so sorry for driving away and leaving her there alone in the cold. I told the gentleman on the phone that I wasn't sure if our family would be welcome at the funeral.

"Would you like to come see her?" the man asked simply. Such is the kindness typical of the people in this town. The generosity of strangers has always been a constant from my earliest memories.

"Yes," I was sobbing. So guilty. So grateful.

He offered kindly, "Bring whoever you want, and I'll get her ready for you."

When we arrived, he led us into a small room and there she was. He had laid her on a gurney with a paper sheet wrapped tightly around her body up to her neck. I could only see her face. Her long, brown, wet hair was flowing over the top of the gurney. It was so long it almost touched the floor. Her face was pure white, like an angel. The life she'd had was so blaringly absent from her. In that moment, filled beyond capacity with regret, I wished. I wished that I'd known her. I wished I'd been kind to her—not just that bitter January night as cold as my heart, but our whole lives. I wished she'd been mine. I wished I'd raised her. I wished she'd been my baby, my child. My friend. I whispered to her, "*My baby, my baby…*" I couldn't even tell her what I wanted to tell her—that I was sorry—because we weren't alone and I was so ashamed that I couldn't bear to have another person hear my confessions. I'd had not one drop of compassion for her that night. But in my heart now, I was sorry, and I wept and wept and wept over her. Over us. And I'm sorry to this day. I am ashamed.

What solace is there for me? None. There is only shame and grief and regret. I don't know how not to feel guilty. If indeed I knew that she would not have a life, and maybe somewhere deep down I knew exactly that, then why couldn't I have simply told her that I loved her? Why didn't I just put my arms around her and her unborn child? *I love you.* Three words. Why could I not have used them?

This is the cross I carry. I pick it up daily.

Family began to trickle into town. All my cousins, my aunt from California and her new husband, and my grandparents. My parents, however, first said they were not coming. I believe they told one of the relatives, "She's dead. There nothing we can do about it." I am of the opinion that they couldn't afford the airline tickets to come out and bury their daughter. In the end, I'm sure someone from their church gave them the money for tickets to come to Vegas for their own daughter's funeral. My mother's husband has never been too proud to stand with his hand out for money in any amount, so they called and told me they were coming out after all. It just made sense to them since Jimmy and his family lived with me that we would all be together as a family during this difficult time so, of course, they would be staying with me.

Like hell.

How could I tell them all that I needed to say now that they'd just been devastated by the loss of one of their children? Could I be so cruel? Would they ever know that they lost me long before they ever lost Tab? At that point, I didn't know what I would tell them, but there was no way they were staying with me. After all this, I *still* wasn't strong enough to be honest with them. To say the timing on this thing was fucked-up is the understatement of the millennium. They were coming out for a week, and I had to try really hard not to go stark, raving mad and wind up in the psych ward by the time this was all over. I thought, *If they stay here, then I'm staying somewhere else!* And about two seconds later I thought, *Wait a minute. If I vacate my own house to accommodate them, I will have lost every bit of ground that I've gained over the last month since I've seen them. Not happening!*

I called my Uncle Gene.

He was absolutely heartbroken that his sweet Sugar Ding-a-Ling was gone. I told him, "Uncle Gene, I need you. My parents are coming to town, and they want to stay here. I can't handle that. I'll go crazy! Please come and stay here so that I can tell them there's no room for them." It was the best I could do. I was ready to crack. He promised me he'd drive straight through as soon as he could.

This uncle (the very man who had convinced this monster to marry my mother after he got her pregnant back in the day) and my aunt (this monster's sister) had divorced a couple years previous to this. Obviously, this was a jagged little pill for the whole family to swallow since he had pastored the church in Southern California. So, it was a double whammy to my parents—who supported my aunt wholeheartedly—that I would reach out to my uncle and offer my home for him and his new wife over them.

I shudder to think what would have happened had I let my parents stay with me. I'd probably be writing this from my 10 x 10 cell while I served out twenty years to life in prison. Since we couldn't assume we'd be included in her funeral services, we began to make plans for our own memorial service. I enlisted the help of Pastor Dean once again. The counseling sessions we'd had in regard to whether or not I could or would or should break ties with my parents no longer seemed relevant. Now he helped me navigate through the arrangements. Songs had to be compiled for the memorial service. Scriptures needed to be recited. A eulogy needed to be written. Spent, I sat in his office and muttered dryly what I thought would be nice.

He asked me, "Can you tell me about your sister's accomplishments? Things she'd achieved?"

I had to think. Truthfully, I felt like I barely knew her. I decided that her greatest tribute was her love for children.

"She was a wonderful mother," I whispered. The tears ran down both of my cheeks. I remembered fondly the times I'd been able to see her interact with her daughters. "She was always so kind to our children. She spoke to them so sweetly, and they were the light of her life. Geoffrey reminded me just yesterday of one time—just one time—that our family had all been together without my mother's husband. I don't even know where he was. Who cares?"

I smirked and shook my head at the thought.

"He was on some trip. He was gone. But everybody else was there—my grandma, my aunt and her son, Geoffrey and I... Tabitha and her children, my brother and his family. Everyone except for him. We made spaghetti and watched Jurassic Park. Geoffrey remembered how Tabitha sat on the floor and the kids all tried to run past her one at a time. As they ran past, she would reach out and try to grab them. They screamed and giggled and played that game..." My voice broke off, "...for a long time." I stared at the floor. Dean was quiet and let me have that moment to reminisce. Suddenly aware that I'd left the conversation, I looked back at him and reached for the tissues on his desk.

"You'll always have that memory, Daisy. It's a gift."

"It is," I agreed and held it fast to my heart. It was a measure of comfort.

In the end it turned out that our family worried for nothing over whether or not we'd be included in Tabitha's funeral service. We were given the details of her burial and assured that we were more than welcome to come and grieve her loss with them. That is, with one exception.

Me.

On the morning of the funeral, my Grandma Jean called me to relay a message that she'd received from Tabitha's husband who informed her that, because I had been the most vocal about all our questions, that it would not be a good idea for me to go to the funeral. In fact, if I tried to show up, I would be asked to leave. Period. She was calling me to let me know.

I thanked her.

I hung up.

I threw up.

I finished getting dressed.

I got in my car and drove to the church to attend my sister's funeral.

When I walked through the door, the pastor of that church immediately approached me and asked what my name was. I thought, *Holy sheep shit—I'm gonna have to punch a man of God right in the face.* And it didn't help that he was 157 years old.

I told him who I was.

He looked at me very kindly and said, "I'm the pastor here. I understand that there's been some hard feelings between the families." I clenched my fist and reared back slightly, ready to clock him one when the next words came out of his mouth. He continued, "I just want you to know that you are welcome in this place. I am a neutral party here, and I know you've had a particularly difficult time with all this. I'm here for you if you need me. You can come back and see me anytime if you just need to talk. In the meantime, let me show you where your sister is." He put his arm around my shoulder and led me to the sanctuary where my sister was lying in her casket.

Relief at not having to be arrested that day for assault and battery of a 206-year-old, 5'3", 80-pound preacher coursed its way through my system. My mind was no longer in charge. Logic was not present and could not be depended upon. All I could do was feel. I was at the mercy of my own pain.

Her casket was open at the end of a long, center aisle with pews on either side. Together we stood at the back until I was ready. Then I slogged down the aisle alone—my feet were cement blocks. I hadn't seen her since... January.

I had brought her unborn baby a toy. It seemed to me that every child conceived in this world needed to have a toy. And, by God, my little niece or nephew would have one. I set a stuffed Tigger in the casket; her baby would have something to sleep with. We brought pictures of our children, whom she loved. They were her favorite part of her time here on earth. She should at least have pictures of those children with her forever.

Our entire family swooped in and descended upon that church—all of the aunts, uncles, a cornucopia of cousins, grandparents, siblings, in-laws, nieces and nephews arrived. We were a formidable group, to say the least. My parents had not yet arrived leaving the event untainted; they would be attending our family's private memorial service for her. I was relieved that I only had to deal with one potentially volatile situation that day—the disdain of Tabitha's husband and his family.

My Grandpa Walker, who was quite elderly by that time, led our entire tribe down the aisle of that church and we all formed a circle around my sister's casket—a circle of love. We squeezed together to make room for everyone. I saw that my sister's husband was standing alone in a small room with a glass window looking into the sanctuary. It must have been the room where parents took their crying babies during the Sunday services. He stood and watched us as we gathered around her and held hands and started to pray, and I think maybe for the first time he was able to see that there were family members from his wife's past who loved her and cared about her, even if she didn't ever share that with him. My Grandpa Walker was a man who walked in the wisdom of God and in the compassion of Christ.

He prayed, "God, receive our loved one. Holy Spirit, please be with us and help us cope with this loss. Help us understand what happened here. We give her to You. We release her and entrust her into the care of her Creator." He prayed that prayer with such grace and dignity and, for the first time in my life, I was proud of our family. I realized in that moment that our family wasn't just a mess like I had always thought. Our family was beautiful. There was one person and one person alone who brought pain and devastation to our family, and that was my mother's husband. The rest of my family is wonderful. We love each other. We are there for each other. Many of my family members had traveled a long way to be a support for one another. I will always cherish that moment, and I will always be so proud of my grandfather. So profoundly broken and kind and formidable was he that my sister's husband respectfully left the room and gave us our time with her.

The dear, sweet pastor who had embraced me so lovingly, proceeded to perform the most boring service I had ever attended in all the years of my short life, God bless his 386-year-old heart. He didn't know my sister. What was he to do? My sister's husband knew she had come from a Christian background and, wanting to give her a proper service, he found this guy in the phone book, I believe.

When the service was over, we all poured back into the lobby. A voice behind me said, "Can I talk to you?"

It was him.

I turned slowly and looked at him. As we stood facing each other, it seemed like a scene from a western where two cowboys square off for a shootout in the middle of a dusty street. The crowd literally parted and moved to the sides, not blinking for even a second as we both ever-so-slowly put our hands out to our sides to see which one of us would draw first—and which one of us would draw quickest.

He said simply, "I don't want it to be like this," and he put his hands down.

I was stunned. I didn't know this man. I said nothing and made no attempt to move. He stepped forward and put his arms around me in a huge bear hug. I had to have disappeared in his embrace—the man is a brick house. The only other time I had spoken to him throughout this whole ordeal was when he introduced a few family members to his parents in an awkward moment before the service. His mother had about as much use for me as a trap door in a canoe. She wouldn't even look at me, barely touching my hand to shake it and recoiled as soon as she could rip her hand from mine as if I'd bitten her. His father made it a point to tell me, "We are a good family," to which I quickly retorted, "So are we!" That was the extent of our first and last conversation, which was enough for both parties, I'm sure. Now, here he was—this man I didn't know, couldn't know—hugging me and holding on for dear life. I didn't know what to make of it. He was holding out an olive branch, and I took it. My arms slowly reached up and around him.

The crowd sighed a collective breath around us.

Here was a man whose wife told him she'd been horribly abused by her parents, which was the God's honest truth. He, in the hastiness of his youth, lumped all of us together into one horrendous group that he felt he needed to protect her from—not understanding, really, that there were many victims in this story. I, in my fear of not knowing what on earth was happening in my sister's life for the past eight years, feared the unknown and the battle lines were clearly drawn.

My parents arrived very shortly thereafter and stayed with friends. My uncle and his wife had been driving half way across the country, but they would only be able to get here for her burial and would miss our family's memorial service. I spent as little time with my parents as I could and, again, my vigilance with Geoffrey was sharper than any Secret Service watching over any head of state. I did not sit with my parents and my brother in the first row of the church during our service for my sister. One of our long-time family friends came up to me and said, "Honey, I think you should go sit in the front pew with your family now. The service is about to start."

I answered numbly, "OK, I will."

When pork flies.

The service was lovely. Unlike the 538-year-old pastor who spoke at her funeral, Dean delivered an exquisite eulogy for my sister. I thought he should have gotten a Nobel for it. When he finished, the music rang out. I sat four rows back watching my parents as they lifted both hands toward Heaven with praise to the Lord in typical Pentecostal fashion.

Nuttier than squirrel shit.

Tons of childhood friends who knew and loved Tabitha from our youth group at Trinity also came to say goodbye. I'll tell you something about that youth group. We truly grew up together, all of us. We were our own family, and there was something very special about that community of kids and every leader who touched our lives and showed us by example how to live and how to be. I've seen so many churches whose youth grow up and no longer embrace the faith of their upbringing. I've read studies that claim that more than half of young people detach themselves from the religion of their childhoods. But the kids in the youth group I grew up in have largely maintained and nurtured our faith, and I think that's something special. The core of us who grew up together in that church still love God, we still serve Him, and we've raised our own children in Christian homes. Even I, who have had to sift through such hypocrisy and bullshit, still attest that I am, indeed, a Christian—even though many Christians would never accuse me of that! And there are often times that I don't follow many of the positions that have been adopted en masse by my "people." Like Anne Rice, "I refuse to be anti-gay. I refuse to be anti-feminist. I refuse to be anti-artificial birth control. I refuse to be anti-Democrat. I refuse to be anti-secular humanism. I refuse to be anti-science. I refuse to be anti-life." And, though the folks at Trinity might get sweaty underneath their armpits out of sheer anxiety for all they've heard come out of my mouth, I, to a great extent, have them to thank for keeping me on this path. It's been straight and narrow with a gazillion rabbit trails. But I'm still walking. I'm still walking. And, unlike Anne (whom I totally understand and applaud for her choice to abandon the church) I have chosen differently, to continue to wear the label in spite of the protests from others—as well as my own.

Speaking of rabbit trails... I'm on one.

My uncle arrived, and I fell into his care. The only thing left to do was to bury Tabitha. If you've ever been to Vegas in June, July, or August, you know how swelteringly hot it is. We all gathered out at the gravesite. We had everyone there but Tabitha. We waited. In the sun. And waited. My aunt who sat beside me commented that we all knew Tab would be late for her own funeral.

And she was.

Finally, she arrived. The most notable memory from that day was the empty expression on my brother's face when he helped to pull our sister's casket out of the back of the hearse. Losing her sucked the life from him and stole his spirit. Or maybe his spirit was out looking for her again. Uncle Gene gave the graveside eulogy—a beautiful tribute to his sweet Sugar Ding-a-Ling. He thanked God for her life and encouraged us that we will all be united again where no one will ever depart from another ever again.

When the service was over, everyone left. They just sort of walked away. I watched my parents saunter off together and was as perplexed as ever as to what I would do now in regard to my connection with them. I stood sweating in the heat of the high afternoon sun and found I couldn't leave. I looked to my right and to my left. The only two people who remained other than myself were my sister's husband and my brother. They, too, felt the need to stay and see this through to the very end. The men who worked at the cemetery came over to put her in the ground and asked us if we intended to stay. Apparently, this just isn't done—this hanging around.

With my brother on one side of me and Tab's husband on the other, arms around each other, we watched as my sister's casket was lowered into the ground. I started to drop to my knees, and all our tears flowed freely, although I couldn't have imagined that I had any left. The two men who stood on either side of me held me up as these strangers lowered my sister into the ground and covered her with dirt. So heavy, that dirt. It pounded like thunder into the hole on top of her. They set the plaque at the base of her grave that stated her name and beneath it, 1969-1996.

It was done. My brother left and the two individuals who'd been archenemies, for all intents and purposes, remained. I wondered if my sister was looking down on us expecting to see a fight, but I was too tired to fight. I said, "I think Tab would like it if we had one final bonding moment. I think we should have a cigarette." I don't even smoke, but I was just about ready to light one up after all I'd been through, and he certainly looked like he could use one. He put his hand over his chest, pretending to have a heart attack, and I managed a smile. He pulled out two cigarettes. Lit mine. Then his. And we stood there and sucked them down in silence, hand in hand.

In the years since, we've been able to kindle a loving and mutually respectful relationship. My nieces are exquisite and intelligent and full of laughter. I am excited to see where their ambition takes them in life. God provided them with a beautiful mother who loves them and has raised them as her own—they are every bit hers, and we are thankful. They also added two more children to their family, another girl and finally a BOY! I love them all and make no distinction between the older two and the younger two. They are *all* my nieces and nephew.

My brother-in-law and I have had some very intense conversations. We've broached subjects that would have sent lesser people back to the powder room. We've hung in there with each other. We've confessed our sins and asked each other's forgiveness. We've been gracious. We've let the past go. We've even joked around and enjoyed each other's company. He is *very* funny, as it turns out.

But all this resolution has been years in the making and was not initially available to either of us in those early years in the pandemonium of our pain. We didn't rely on each other but chose instead to wade through our own personal abyss of Hell alone. Looking back, I don't know that we could have done it any other way. I don't know if we'd have ended up friends if we had tried to hack out our collective shit together. In any case, we are both grateful that it turned out well for us. I am able to say without hesitation words that no one ever expected to hear in a million years: I love him. I love his wife. I'm glad they're in my life. I am proud of the job they have done in raising their children. They called last year on Mother's Day and passed the phone around. It is a blessing to be in their lives.

And I know Tabitha is pleased.

ஃ   ஃ   ஃ

I Will Fear No Evil, For Thou Art With Me

My uncle had come to be a support for me and to lay my sister to rest, but he wasn't even nearly done. They were staying one more night before he and his wife trekked back across the country. He was astute enough to realize that there was something more than just my grief for my sister's death. Something that had to do with why I didn't want to be within two feet of my mother and her husband—something that was only intensified in light of the recent tragedy.

"What are you not telling me, sis?" he asked. "There's more to your aversion to your parents than you're saying. What is it? What's going on?"

Without one second's hesitation, I looked him dead in the eye and broke his heart, "Your ex-brother-in-law is a pedophile. He molested all of us for years. It's the big 'family secret.'"

Here's the thing about telling someone something like this. You devastate them. You unravel them. You shatter them with all that honesty. And that's what you do to the people who actually *believe* you. The people you tell who do not or choose not to believe you, separate themselves from you and start believing bad things about you—that you are a liar. That you're crazy.

That's always a treat.

My Uncle Gene believed every word and I could see the sledgehammer in my hands crushing his heart, blow after blow.

You have to be really something to hurt a person like that.

"How long?" he asked. "How long did this go on?"

"Since we were very small until we all moved out. Tabitha was being molested while he worked for you at your church in Southern California if that's what you're asking."

Merciless.

Knowing that his niece, who was so especially dear to him, was being tortured right under his nose, right under his own steeple devastated him. He was undone.

"It explains so much…"

I told him of my wretched visit a few weeks before Tab died and my desire to be free of them forever.

"How can I sever ties with them after all this?"

We sat silent for a long time. No tears. No sound but the clock ticking on the wall.

The next few weeks seemed like eons of time to me. It seemed I'd lived centuries. I was at an impasse as to how to proceed with my life. Thankfully, my parents did not call to check on my welfare during this time. They most likely picked up on my reluctant dread of being near them, and they gave me my space. I went back to see Dean. So many people make decisions and say, "Well, after a lot of prayer," or "I just really feel God leading me to do this or that." You know what? I did pray about this. I did get counseling. But at the end of the day, I made the best decision I could and was ready to live with the repercussions.

I had to go through with this. I removed the banner of protection I'd always held over them and finally placed it above my *own* life.

I chose me.

I sent them this letter, pretty well word for brutal word. Knowing this was my 'swan song,' so to speak, and I would never speak to them ever again, I tried to include everything I wanted them to know.

6-23-96

I have thought long and hard about this letter and all that I have to say to you. You really have no idea what my life is like, what I think about, my problems. I have allowed you to continue in your belief that you know your own daughter when, in fact, that is not the case. Read this letter in its entirety, and you will have a better view of who I really am and what I live with.

The three days I spent with you in April were difficult for me, to say the least. I have made great strides forgiving the two of you for the abuse I suffered as a child. I still have some forgiving to do. One thing that is hard for me to come to grips with is the fact that I was taken away from the Loftons for twenty-three years. It's

not like you took away a car or a job—you took a
child. I've talked to Don about the fact that he
did not put forth a huge effort to fight for me—
that is something that we have had to work out
between us. But the fact that I now feel obligated
to try to replace those years is a tremendous
burden for me. It breaks my heart to watch my
grandmother tell me, "I wish you could spend more
time here," with tears in her eyes. They love me.
They have always loved me. It was wrong to take me
away. If I "chose" to have you as my lawful father
[when I was adopted by you] I don't remember it,
and I never had a true choice in the matter. While
I was there, I wanted to spend that Wednesday night
with the Loftons while you went to church, but you
thought the world would come to an end if I didn't
go with you to church. You wanted me to sing. I
told you I wasn't going to sing. I had a sore
throat. I hadn't prepared anything, and I really
didn't want to. But what I wanted was completely
irrelevant to you, as it has always been. I was
appalled that the pastor practically introduced me—
I was put on the spot because you told him I would
sing. You tried to tell me after the fact that I
didn't have to do it if I hadn't wanted to.
Bullshit. I got up—I sang. I didn't want to, but I
was being made to do what you wanted me to do. It
was like being molested all over again—my feelings
were not even considered. And all the while my
mother, sitting silently—like you've always done,
Mother. When I sat down I was nauseated. I wanted
to throw up. I wanted to leave. Then to top it off,
you gave a testimony at the end of service.

Remember? You said that when we were kids, you

and Mom were involved with Vegas Valley Christian
Church ministries to the youth and college groups.
You just didn't seem to be experiencing any joy in
your relationship with Jesus or the ministry. You
decided you'd been suffering from demonic
oppression. Did you ever stop to consider you
didn't have joy in your life because you were
molesting your children? How you can continually
redefine the past is sickening to me. Do you even
have a clue how it turned my stomach to listen to
you ask with all sincerity why [a particular woman
they knew] stayed with her husband? You asked,
"Doesn't she know he's abusive? Why does she put up
with it?" Yet, YOU were abusive!

When [my husband] and I drove to [location
unnamed] to confront you two about the childhood
I'd had, there are two things that I think are
pretty significant about the whole thing. First
when we went to your bedroom and [name withheld]
told you what he knew, your first response was to
lie to us and tell us that nothing had happened
since you'd been in the ministry for the last three
and a half years. You wanted us to believe that
being a minister had made a difference in your
life. But Tabitha had already told us that you were
still molesting her. I just have one question about
that. If being a minister didn't make a difference,
does being a police officer make any difference? Do
you understand that I have no obligation to believe
you have changed? Second, when we had our family
meeting, who was the person that was focused on?
Why, I believe it was the same person that was
ALWAYS focused on! YOU! You. We all had to go
around the table and give you our forgiveness. Once

that was done, I believe you had a meeting with Pastor Gebhart, and one men's retreat later, you were ready to go on with your life and put the past behind you. I sure wish all I had to do was go talk to Pastor Gebhart and attend a men's retreat, and then I wouldn't have to deal with this pain anymore. And I know that even now as you read this, you are not thinking about my pain. You are thinking about how painful this letter is to YOU. I have never had the opportunity to express to you my pain. I know what it's like to be raped. I know what it's like to be violated, to be completely degraded as a human being. What's ironic is, so do both of you. You were both molested. You'd think you would want your lives to be free from that pain, but instead you perpetuated it in the lives of your children. You did sexual things to me for your own pleasure, and told me you were educating me. That is sick. If I resisted, you would look at me and say, "Do you think I'm sick?! Do you?! Is that what you think?! If I ever knew you thought I was sick, I'd blow my brains out!" Then all of a sudden, I would be apologizing to you. I apologized for not wanting you to rape my little body. And you don't think that fucks a kid up? Believe me, I'm fucked-up. I'm fucked-up because one night when Mom was out, you couldn't ejaculate by just masturbating on me; you had to be "inside" something so you told me you were going to go get a prostitute. You even went so far as to get dressed and get in the car. Instead, you came back and sodomized me. It hurt so much that I cried the whole time you were doing it. I kept saying, "It hurts, Daddy! It hurts!" But you just kept pumping and kept pumping and kept pumping until you finally finished and ripped me to pieces. I bled for two days. But what did I matter? You got what you wanted. That's all that really mattered to you. It is a miracle that I'm sane. And without the therapy I've had, I doubt I would be sane. You say you love me, but you sodomize me, ignoring my crying, and tell me you're educating me? Go on with your life as a cop and a choir director. But I have no involvement with you anymore.

Mother, as for you, I love you will all of my heart. But you have chosen this man over your children our whole lives. My counselors have asked me if I could understand your situation as a victim in all this, and I just can't. [Your husband] would be lucky if all I did was divorce him if he'd hurt my children the way he's hurt yours. I will never understand why you did not tie him to the bed in his sleep and light that bed on fire. God help the man who even thinks of threatening my children. What's worse, Mother, is you truly believe you are lucky to have him. [Your husband] told me what that woman cop told you about him being lucky to have you. Your response was, "No, you have it backwards. I'm the one who is lucky to have him." If that is how you truly feel, after he has committed crimes against your children, after allowing us to wear hand-me-downs and living on peanut butter sandwiches, while he plays with his radios and music equipment and model airplanes, after having anniversaries and birthdays come and go without acknowledgment, then have him, Mother. That's your choice. But know that it is not my choice to continue our relationship. I can't. Maybe in years

to come, but not now. If I am going to be healthy,
I need to separate myself from both of you. I think
you've comfortably redefined the past, and
completely disregarded the pain in me. And I have
not, until now, expressed it. I'm going to
counseling again, and I'm thinking about going to
group therapy sessions for incest survivors. I
can't keep my feelings from you anymore, as was
pretty evident when you were here. When I am
involved with you, I don't have the strength to be
honest. I have no integrity. I sacrifice my
integrity for you because you couldn't handle my
honesty. My honesty puts your whole lives in
question. My integrity demands answers from you
that you can't or won't give. I can't continue to
support your view of life. You are taking this as
my rejection of you, I'm sure. You probably don't
even realize that I am only now embracing your
rejection of me, and making it a tangible reality
in my life. I don't expect that you will understand
me or this letter. I only ask that you respect my
space and the boundaries I have set. Don't try to
contact me or Geoffrey. Don't send gifts at
Christmas or birthdays. Let me get well. Let me do
it without your influence. I wish you no ill will—
only the best for you. Continue on however you
wish. Do what's best for yourselves. I can't be
affected in any way by your fate. You carry your
crosses. I'll carry my own and ONLY my own. And God
help me, because they're very heavy.

I do thank God for my life. I wouldn't change one
thing that has happened if it meant being different
from what I am. But I would sooner go to Hell
forever than to relive even one moment of my past.

I am asking God to help me regain the integrity
that I have lost and to heal my pain. I also ask
Him for the courage to live honestly and without
fear. I hope now that my nightmares will end. In
time, maybe I can have a healthy relationship with
someone special, but that is not something that I
expect or look for. I'm not without my scars.

So, I guess this is it. This is what you wanted
to know.

Now you know.

My mother called immediately after receiving the letter and left a message
on my answering machine for me to call them back. She was a sopping mess.

I did not return the call. I went and made myself a sandwich.

I have never once looked back.

෧ ෧ ෧

While I Wake and While I Sleep

I would love to report that I dropped that letter in the mailbox and walked away
a brand new person. That would be a news report from La La Land. Walking
away from that mailbox and putting up the flag to let the postman know to take
that shit several states away from me was monumental, absolutely, but there was
still so much to purge out of my life. When we detox our bodies, we're grossed
out by all the shit (literally) that comes out of us. But when we detoxify our
souls, what does that look like? For me, it was dreams and panic attacks.

Thoughts and memories and emotions did not just torment me while I
slept, but tortured me in broad daylight. My days were exhausting just putting
one foot in front of the other. Going to work. Seeing Tab in every chubby-
cheeked, brown-haired little girl. Seeing her in every drop-dead gorgeous
teenager with chocolate eyes. Seeing her suddenly with two little girls and
unexpectedly turning around to go the other direction just to follow them—
walking faster to catch up to these total strangers to see if I could catch a
glimpse of her in their faces.

I was losing my mind is what I was doing.

Maybe it was because I wasn't eating, I wasn't sleeping, and I was walking around like a zombie. Maybe it was because her death was so sudden—that her life was cut short while she was still so young, leaving babies behind and taking a baby with her. Most assuredly, I was agonizing over the fact that I could not wrap my head around what her life was like or the accident that took her.

I was driving down the road on a dark, hot rainy night when, without any warning whatsoever, I had a sudden and severe urge to turn my car around and race to the cemetery. My heart was hammering through my chest, and I became short of breath. It seemed to me that she was lying all by herself in the casket underneath all that dirt listening to the wind scream and whip the leaves around in the tree above her, and I was immediately panicked to go be with her. I knew she was afraid in that storm, and if I could just run out to her grave and lie down with her, with my arm across her plot and talk to her, that she would know I was there and not feel afraid. I wanted to lay my cheek across that tiny plaque that the men who lowered her down into that hole put down to let everyone know the name of the girl who's stuck down there all by herself. That plaque proved she was somebody. She was somebody to me. I wanted to bury my face in the warm dirt and cry until my tears seeped all the way down to where she lay.

And this was in the daytime—eyes wide open.

At night, dreams were vivid, recurrent, and incessant.

A beautiful meadow, teeming with life and buzzing with activity. Bees, trees, flowers. Beautiful sky. A river, wide and crystal clear flows gently between my meadow and the darkness that lay on the other side. My side of the river is vibrantly brilliant with every hue of pink, purple, blue, green; the other side looks as if it has been drawn in various shades of charcoal. In it stands one dead tree, looking like something out of Sleepy Hollow. Its branches stretch out toward a gray, dusty, moonless sky. It is night there. It is always night there. The windswept ground is nothing but black dust where nothing can be grown.

And there, standing alone and looking at me with forlorn eyes, stands my mother.

She does not speak. My mother never speaks in my dreams. But I know what she wants. She wants me to stay with her on her side of the river. Her eyes beckon me, implore me, not to go—not to leave her. The sadness in her, the desperation, the hopelessness is eternal. I see her in my dream as she is in real life.

Pathetic.

We look at each other for a long time. I don't speak to her with my voice—only with my eyes, the way she speaks to me. I break our gaze and watch the river meander between us. I know that crossing that river from death to life is life altering and irreversible. Not for a second do I ever consider leaving my meadow and crossing back over that river to the darkness from which I'd come.

Resolved as ever, I look back for a short moment before I shake my head and turn away. Forever.

Why I was holding court in the back of a dark semi-truck with members of my family sitting along a thin wooden bench is baffling to me. (Although, in the daytime when we're all awake, it could probably be psychoanalyzed in about three seconds or less.)

"You're a liar," I am told.

"Why are you bringing this shame on our family?"

"Just tell the TRUTH! Why are you making up these horrible stories?"

"He is a Godly man!"

The only witness for the defense is my sister, who sits by herself opposite the rest of them who are accusing me of trying to ruin the reputation of a good man while I plead with them to believe me.

"Why would I lie? Why would I bring this scandal on my own family? Where is your indignance for ME?"

Completely despondent, I turn to my sister and beg her, "Please, tell them! Tell them what we went through! Don't sit there and let them believe that I'm lying!"

"I can't," she replies calmly. "I'm dead, remember?"

Every night he slithers his way into my subconscious and into my dreams. This is where my most vicious and bloody battles are fought. If I believed in reincarnation, I would think that I must have been a fierce warrior in a former life because I look forward to these dreams almost with a wild sense of anticipation. I wait for him each night to sneak into my bedroom, to try to put his hands on me, to try to force me into some sexual tryst with him.

I wait for him anxiously because I have begun to fight.

One night I hit him. I hit him hard. The next night I hit him again. I hit him every single night in every single dream he dares to enter. He comes back every night with a vengeance. But I don't care. I want him to come. I want the fight. Every bit of anger I can muster is funneled through these nightly episodes, and I can't wait to get to sleep at the end of the day.

I dream that I am dreaming—having dreams of being touched and fondled—and I know that he is here again. I wake from the dream in my dream to find him crawling into my bed. My mother sits in the chair at my desk and watches silently from across the room. The initial burst of fear explodes in my stomach as it always does, yet I react with a fury of someone possessed. His left hand clutches my throat and pins me to the pillow, while his right hand rips into the t-shirt I'm wearing, leaving my breasts exposed and vulnerable. With all the strength I can conjure, I kick up as hard as I can and catch him in the ribs with my knee. He doesn't entirely let go, but it is enough that I can get out from underneath him. I try to run and manage to get off the bed, but his hand shoots out and yanks me back by my hair. He throws me to the floor. My mother now stands by the bed beside me, her eyes downcast, and waits patiently while the husband she can't live without pulverizes me. He beats me bloody, hammering me repeatedly in the face as he holds me up by my hair. His face shows nothing but bitter contempt and hatred for me, and he shows no mercy. I lay crumpled at the foot of the bed and feel myself slipping away into a dark unconsciousness. Still my mother says nothing, allowing him to do what he wants with me the way she always has.

From the corner of my eye, I see a book. It is lying on the bed just out of my reach. Slowly, I begin to reach up for it. My fingers brush the edge and with one more stretch, I grip it hard and swing it solidly around to the side of his head.

He reels from the blow. He stumbles back and catches himself on the dresser to keep from dropping to the floor. I take that opportunity to dig into him with a rage so savage that I am left without doubt that this is the nightmare I've been waiting for. He will not be back after tonight.

I take the book and cuff him upside the head as fast as my arms will fly. Power begins to surge up from somewhere deep within me and, suddenly, I am rejuvenated. Using every bit of momentum that I have stolen, I beat him to the ground and do not stop. I don't stop to look at my mother. I don't stop to think about what I am doing. I don't stop to think about whether or not I am killing him. I simply hit him as hard, as fast, and as long as I can. I don't stop even though he has had enough. He has long ago stopped resisting. I beat him long into the night and long after he loses consciousness. I am beating his cold, dead body for all I know, but I keep on. I stop when I can no longer lift my hand. Exhausted, I finally turn to my mother who hasn't changed her position in the God-only-knows-how-many-hours I have been whaling on him.

Finally, I stop and catch my breath enough to mutter without any emotion whatsoever, "Get the fuck out of my house." I drop the book back on the bed and move to the door of my bedroom and hold it open. I don't know how—it doesn't matter how—he is able to hoist himself up and stumble out the door. My mother follows him right out.

I walk around them to open the front door of my house and try to catch my mother's eye as she leaves to see if there is any acknowledgement in the windows of her soul. She refuses to look at me. Nothing else is said.

I shut the door behind them.

One more...

I spun, not only from the suddenness of my sister's death, but by the fact that my last words to her had been so harsh. We all want to live our lives without regret, but it's already too late for me. I will chew on the pungent acidity of those words forever. They taste like bile in my mouth. Still.

I was completely confounded. Her death seemed to generate more questions than there were answers for. The need to know what really happened haunted me continuously. My grief and guilt prevented me from being able to resolve this in my conscious mind so, because the mind always defends itself, I had to work it out in my subconscious mind—as if I hadn't already been busy enough at night, I had to "dream it out."

I must like meadows because I'm back in one. But this meadow is... something else. This meadow is not like anyplace any of us have ever been on this planet. I think of the most gorgeous place I've ever been: the rainforests of Alaska, the jungles of Hawaii, the ancient flower gardens of Japan. Recalling those places are like looking into a dark glass compared to this.

This meadow is alive. I remember that the beautiful places I've seen on earth teem with aliveness as well, but this is different. My blinders are removed in this place, and I know that this place is nowhere on earth. The grass and the flowers and the trees all have names. They are entities with purpose, and each blade of grass, every flower petal, every leaf carries out its design pristinely and perfectly. Every organism is connected and working together in unity for one single reason—to be glorious. I am connected. I share the heartbeat of this beauty. Every cell in my body is distinct and named also and is not only recognized for its contribution to the Divinity of this place, but it is celebrated as well. This is nothing I can describe if I write pages and pages. It is nothing I can ever put into words—any description is so flat. It is something simply to be felt. Being here—it erases all doubts, all confusion. I know that I have suffered—I know that I have experienced pain. I can remember it. But that pain is so far removed along with any and all discontent, sadness, grief.

Guilt.

It's gone. What's more is that, in this place, I am known. I am fully known. Fully embraced. Fully accepted. Fully loved. Breathing is sweet—to inhale the glory and blow it out again. The warmth is electric and hums throughout all of us as one essence. I can hold the breeze in my hand. I can throw it out and bring it back to me. I think, I could get used to this...

And there she is.

She comes to me smiling. Beautiful. Perfect, with all the aliveness of the meadow. She stands on the tree line for a few moments and then begins to make her way toward me. She doesn't hurry. No need to rush. Every step is deliberate and perfect. We don't touch. There is no need. We are already connected with everything that surrounds us.

She glows. Her hair shines. He skin radiates. Her smile glistens. Her eyes sparkle. She is flawless, and she knows as she is fully known. Growing up, I remember back in That Place From Before, I had been the one who knew more, made better choices. But not here. I know nothing here. She knows everything. I am no longer in a position to give advice or feel superior or tell her what she should do with her life.

We talk and laugh and whatever pain I remember melts away. Her mere presence is a cool compress on the burning grief and guilt that I recall from That Place From Before when I was awake.

But...I am awake now. I was clearly sleeping before. Is this a dream? Or was that a dream? Somehow I am aware that our time here is fleeting. I came here with a question.

"What happened, Tabitha? How did you die? Are the police reports..."

She interrupts me with the bells of her laughter. She shakes her head and flips a hand out as if to wave my concerns away like she was shooing a bee.

"I need to know," I try to protest.

"You know," she looks at me intently, although the laughter remains steady in her heartening smile, "things that seem so important where you are... just don't matter here."

I sat straight up in my bed in the darkness of my room, fully awake and still feeling the remnants of the peace and perfection of where I'd just been in my mind. The elation of that place seeped out of me slowly with each deep, cleansing breath I took. In seconds, the physical memories of being there in that meadow were gone forever, no matter how my heart and mind tried to hold on. With my blankets tangled around me, with my face and hands reaching out high in the air, I yelled out loud in the middle of the night, "WHY CAN'T YOU EVER JUST ANSWER A DAMN QUESTION?"

Whenever I tell people about this dream, I get varying reactions. Strangely, most people try to assure me that my sister actually came to me in my subconscious mind to bring me comfort. She was really there, they suggest.

I'm not as convinced. I think the mind is very powerful. I think my mind knew what to do to protect me. I think I was the architect of that whole scenario. Her answer did, in fact, soothe my grief, if not my guilt. Seeing her alive and well, beyond well, alleviated my torment and soothed my anguish, although not completely. Never completely. But it was what I needed. Note that she didn't answer the question. Why? Because I didn't know the answer to the question. My mind cannot give an answer it does not know. But my mind was able to create a comforting place and some dialogue that would preserve my mind against itself and all the emotions I was dealing with. It did its job. There is nothing miraculous about that.

Here's what *is* miraculous about that dream. I have tried intensely to get back to that place, both while I'm awake and while I'm asleep. I want to go back there, to feel that energy and oneness and aliveness. But I can't. I cannot replicate that meadow. It is gone to me. That place is a spot that Something outside myself provided for me, because it was that *place* that soothed and healed my mind, my thoughts, and my feelings. I can't replicate it because it did not originate with me. Its origin is from above. I was given a glimpse, a mere image, which is more than I believe most people get, so I am grateful. Although I can no longer "feel" the way I felt there, I know that I felt complete. I know that I felt an aliveness that can't compare with anything I've ever felt on this earth—"This Place From Before." I know that I was fully known—even if I did not yet fully know. I know that my sister is there, and that she's not worried one iota about her life or her death or my life or anything else because she is complete, she is whole, and she is perfection embodied. She knows as she is fully known.

It was an accident. The universe is random. This is Earth where sad things happen.

And God wastes none of it.

~p ~p ~p

Lies, Puking Dogs and Keeping My Dad Out of Jail

My parents must have gone into recovery mode after they got the letter. I know they shared at least part of it—I can't imagine them sharing it in its entirety—to relatives who have sympathized with them. I suppose there are few things more horrifying than finding out your close relative is a pedophile. Believing my parents over me was just easier for some of the people in the family. It's kind of crazy. I figured everyone would rally around me and stand firmly on my side. I mean, truly. What is there to be confused about? But my mother and her husband got to certain family members pretty quickly and told them that I lied about Tabitha being molested while they were in the ministry in Southern California. How very handy for them that she is no longer here to say otherwise. They claimed that the "indiscretion" that I called "abuse" was minimal and that I was making it out like we'd been horribly victimized. They also claimed that I was also trying to convince people that it had lasted years and years when the time frame was nominal. Plus, they added, these minor incidents had occurred nearly twenty years previously. They told family members that they just couldn't understand why I was bringing all this out now so many years later. They suggested it was because I'd had a breakdown of some sort when my sister died and had received some deplorable counsel from that Pastor Dean character, who clearly was misled by my lies. He was probably a good man, but he didn't have any other information to go on other than the scant and jaded information I was giving him. They were, in a word, baffled.

I was unaffected. The Bible says that *"...as a dog returns to its vomit, so a fool repeats his folly" (Proverbs 26:11)*. I'll be damned if I go back to my former life—I don't care who believes me or not.

One day, out of the blue and not long after I'd sent the letter to my parents, I received a phone call from a police officer from the county police department where Stepmonster had been employed as a court bailiff. They'd received an anonymous phone call informing them that one of their officers had molested his children and asked if they really wanted a person like that on the force. The gentleman who called me was conducting an investigation and wanted to know if I'd be willing to answer a few questions.

"I'll tell you anything you want to know," I answered without hesitation.

And I did. Boy, did I. I told him exactly who their court bailiff molested, how long it lasted, every gory detail I could remember, and that the abuse only ended when we moved out and away from him. He was not the one to end the abuse—we were. I could not think of any reason to believe he would be incapable of molesting someone again if given the opportunity. The officer was very interested to find out if he'd molested anyone in that state because then he'd actually be arrested if the statute of limitations had not expired, but the events in question occurred in Las Vegas and California out of his jurisdiction as far as I knew.

We talked for about thirty minutes. He thanked me, offered his condolences for the loss of my sister and for the injustices we'd been through. He also added that he "couldn't stand the guy" even before he knew of the abuse. Before we hung up, I asked for a favor. If this information got out and became a scandal, so to speak, I wanted to have officers follow my father in the next town over to make sure he didn't do anything stupid.

"My dad's a little bit of a redneck," I explained. "He doesn't know about any of this, because if he found out, I don't know what he'd do. Are you hearing me?"

The gentleman said, "Yes, loud and clear."

I gave him my dad's address and, in no uncertain terms, explained, "If this gets out, I want him brought in for I-don't-care-what! I don't care if you have to plant something on him. You guys put him in a cell and call me right away. I'll be on the next flight out. Don't LET him commit a crime."

He almost chuckled because what I was telling him to do was so shocking and blaringly not doable, but he stifled it because it wasn't, in fact, funny. He stammered, "Ma'am, I must assure you that no officer here would ever be involved in any kind of activity that is illegal in regard to planting evidence or bringing someone in on false charges or keeping someone detained unlawfully. We cannot infringe on a person's constitutional rights."

So we were being recorded. Good to know. I rolled my eyes.

"However," he continued, "there are some things we can do to prevent something potentially harmful from happening. We'll be aware of the fact that your father would be understandably upset if this blows up. The department is not looking to publicize this, but we were tipped off anonymously. There is nothing that says that person won't go to the media."

"If that happens," I warned, "I want officers on my dad immediately! His biggest regret in his life is that he didn't fight to keep me after he came back from Vietnam. If he knew that he gave me up and *this* is what happened to me? He'd freak out. He wouldn't be able to handle it. He can never know this. Look him up. You know him—he's in your computer, and he certainly isn't afraid of a little jail time, especially when, to him, it wouldn't matter how long he stayed in a jail cell. It would never be worse than the hell he would sentence himself to forever if he knew what happened to me."

"I hear you. I'll give you a call in the next couple of days to let you know what happens."

I wore myself out worrying about whether or not my dad would end up in the clink, but he never did. The shit never hit the fan. A few days later, though, I did get a hysterical voice mail from my mother that went something like this:

"This is your mother! You need to call me immediately! This has got to end! God has forgiven us—why can't you? Please! I need to talk to you! Please call me back!"

I deleted the message and went and made myself a sandwich. Ah, sweet detachment. As I have said, I don't wish them any harm. I truly don't. I wish them health, peace, and a million-dollar lottery ticket. But I just couldn't get all atwitter when it came time for them to pay the piper or lie in the bed that they've made either.

The very next day, that same officer called me back to let me know what had happened the day before. After he got off the phone with me, he got together with his people and pow-wowed over the information that he'd gathered. Then Stepmonster was brought in and made aware of the allegations.

"I was a little shocked that he didn't deny it," the officer explained. "He was quite up front about it. I guess he had a pretty bad alcohol problem?"

"What?"

"Uh… he told us he'd been quite a drinker, and the alcohol was what precipitated the abuse?"

I just laughed. I couldn't believe how nonchalant I was about everything. I said, "Honey, alcohol was never allowed in our home! It was a sin! Everything was a *sin*. Dancing was a sin. All music outside of church music was a sin. Cigarettes were a sin. The show *Bewitched* was a sin. Let me assure you, there was never a drop of booze in our house, and everything he did to us was done stone cold sober!"

"You've got to be kidding me," he was aghast.

"No. Don't tell me he duped you guys."

"Oh, my God, he had the most sincere look on his face—he told us he'd struggled for years with alcoholism, but he's since recovered and the abuse stopped when he stopped drinking."

"Yeah, I've seen the face. I'd appreciate it if you went back to the department and set them straight on that."

"I definitely will."

"So, I take it he's not a cop anymore?"

"Well, not for our county anyway. I know he volunteers there in the county where he lives, but he was definitely asked to resign immediately. We just can't have somebody like that on the force."

"I understand that."

I thanked him very much for his sensitivity. He was just a nice guy. Case closed.

So. Let the lies begin!

Stepmonster told my brother that the captain said he hated to lose him and offered to have him work for two more weeks.

Not according to the deputy I spoke to.

He said they told him he was an asset to the department.

Not according to the deputy I spoke to.

He said that he declined the invitation to continue working for two more weeks and, rather than risk embarrassment to the department (HA!) he volunteered to resign.

Not according to the deputy I spoke to.

He made it perfectly clear that he was not asked for his resignation—that he had done that of his own accord.

And finally, not according to the deputy I spoke to.

My Grandma Jean found out that her son-in-law had lost his job pretty quickly, and I remember her telling me that he and my mother just didn't know how they were going to explain to the rest of the family why he had lost his job.

I shrugged my shoulders and simply suggested, "Lie. Lie to them. Does that suddenly not work anymore or something? Why break from tradition when it's worked so well for them up to now?"

It was through this time that I knew I was really free from all this and that I'd forgiven and moved on. I dropped it. It wasn't mine anymore. I didn't have to spend one more ounce of energy on this. This man had stolen enough of my time and effort—he wasn't getting any more. That load had been laid down, and there was no way in Heaven or Hell I was ever going to pick it back up. It wasn't my responsibility that man was out of a job. It wasn't my problem that he was lying to anyone in the family who would listen. The burden was not mine to set everybody straight. Believe me or don't. The lines were drawn; people chose whichever side of the fence felt more comfortable to them. I didn't need anyone to stand with me to make the truth any more true. It was what it was. I had better things to do than to stay and wallow in all that smudge. I experienced freedom at a new and deeper level.

I had pretended to be something I wasn't—I pretended my family was something it wasn't—for the first nineteen years of my life. That ship has sailed and sunk. I've continued my life with a renewed sense of honesty. Brazen honesty. I-don't-give-a-shit-anymore, honestly. Sometimes I think I even have some form of "Honesty Tourette's."

All I know is, as long as I'm being authentic, I'm free. Secrets hurt people, and I do my damnedest to have none. I am never going back to my old life.

ॐ   ॐ   ॐ

Bat Shit Crazy

Whenever my kids have to do research papers, I tell them that using primary sources of information is the best place to glean the information that they're looking for. If they're doing a report about slavery, they might want to include some quotes from Frederick Douglass' autobiography. If they're doing a report about civil rights, they might want to go straight to the Constitution. Look for diaries, letters, photographs. Fascinating stuff! With these tools, my kids can use the "experts" to really enhance and validate the project.

I could sit here and tell you all day that my stepmonster is bat shit crazy, but why don't we let him convince you himself? It just so happened that he sent a letter to my Uncle Gene after he lost his job with the police department. Now, he could deny that he ever sent this letter. But gosh darn it, he did send it certified mail, and I have the letter with the envelope in my hot little hand.

I must edit names and certain paragraphs that contain sensitive information that could potentially hurt innocent people. These portions will be left out. The capitalization, punctuation, and other grammatical errors will be left intact.

So, in his own words:

Gene;

In Sept. 1996 I was called to Sheriff [name withheld]'s office in regards to some allegations of misconduct that had happened 15 to 20 years previously and that the call had come in anonymously. However, after receiving your letter and reading your famous lines, I prayed about it, you always used that as a excuse to do what you wanted! Two to three weeks prier to your actions,

God revealed to me exactly what you were going to
do, which I shared with [name withheld] our Pastor.
I put a fleece before the Lord and He again
confirmed what your actions were going to be. You
called your brother [name withheld] and had him
call the Sheriff's office with the allegations.

I have a letter from [me] from several years ago
where She said she forgave me and that Satan would
try to destroy our family, and that She loved me
and we cannot let that happen, and you and [her]
councilor in Las Vegas played right into his hands.
Before Tabitha's death, I knew that [she] was in
serious spiritual trouble by the way she talked and
the job she had and the company she was keeping. I
also know that after Tabitha's death, you caught
[her] at a very vulnerable time and badgered her
into talking to you.

When I received your letter, requesting an
answer, I thought "based on your past track record"
I don't owe you a response. What you tried to do in
secret by calling your brother and having him call
the Sheriff's office is slander and makes you
liable!

[My wife] quit as church secretary in
[California], because she was tired of hearing
about all of your counseling sessions that should
have been kept in confidence. Trust is a terrible
thing to lose!

You have a great responsibility as a councilor
and even more as a Christian and a lot to answer
for on judgment day, you can redirect peoples lives
or destroy them as a councilor.

One Sunday in [California] a friend of ours [name
withheld], a Missionary with Youth with A Mission

in Hong Kong, visited us, and He was going to speak
at services that Sunday night. Tabitha had told him
she wanted to go to Hong Kong with He and His wife
and become a missionary, Do you remember that? When
[he] and I talked to you about that you said that
you would not help her in anyway, and even became
angry and didn't even let [our friend] speak that
night at church. Consequently, Tabitha ran off to
Las Vegas, and married an old boyfriend that was an
Atheist...

I am not surprised you tried to get me in
trouble, you must think we are all stupid! By the
way the Sheriff stated that I had been an asset to
the department, and the man I was years ago I am
not today. Sheriff [name withheld] is a fine
Christian man, but he was afraid you would cause
more trouble so I resigned, He did not ask for my
resignation, So indirectly you caused me to lose my
job. Gene I want you to know that I forgive you for
what you have done, don't you know that if I wanted
to cause you problems I could have?

[Some paragraphs left out here...]

Who is the greatest sinner? You or Me? All have
sinned and come short of the glory of God! In Gods
eyes sin is sin, one who lies is as wrong as one
who kills. God forgives and then it's forgotten, it
is man who keeps bring up the past!

Gene I forgive you and I'm not going to bring up
the past again. There comes a time in a persons
life that you have to take responsibility for what
you have done, as I have had to do, ask forgiveness
and forget about it and serve God the best way you
know how. Don't let Satan keep bringing your past
up, you can't change the past, only the future!

I have seen no change of heart, or remorse for
what you have done. I saw the same hard shell in
Las Vegas in June as I did in [California]. In my
opinion, until you have a real conversion you don't
belong in the ministry, the Spirit of God is not
one of destruction but of forgiveness and grace,
your spiritually dangerous! I'm sure that you won't
accept these words as true.

I don't want a response to my letter, I have
wanted to write you for a long time, but God didn't
give me the freedom to do so until now.

I don't want you to be hurt any longer, as I
don't want to hurt any more. I have lost two
daughters and four grandchildren… Isn't that
enough?

Suffice it to say it only took him a mere 21 words for the first lie to emerge. That's darn quick, wouldn't you say? I don't recall a letter ever telling him that Satan would try to destroy our family, but that's not to say I never wrote them any letters. I'm pretty sure I never sent them certified. My uncle never badgered me into anything, although I can recall plenty of times Stepmonster badgered me into doing more than just talking.

My uncle responded that he did not recall sharing any details about his counseling sessions with people, although he did tell her that she, as the church secretary, might "…hear or have knowledge of things that should not go out of the office." He added, quite appropriately, I believe, "To the best of my knowledge [she] always kept that confidence, but if she now tells you things, then I guess that speaks for itself."

Stepmonster still believes I'm in serious spiritual trouble. So I went ahead and wrote a whole book about it.

I'm not sure a man can be slandered and another held liable by telling the truth, but whatever. Perhaps Tabitha wanted to go to Hong Kong because it was on the other side of the earth from her own personal Hell? I'm a little perplexed at how that one got spun, but hey… Whatever helps some people sleep at night. My Uncle Gene responded simply, "As to helping Tab go to

Hong Kong, [we] agreed Tab had some problems she needed to deal with (I had no idea how big these problems were or that they involved you) before taking on a task in a foreign country."

And, finally, I must say what a victory and a testimony that Stepmonster has found forgiveness, has taken responsibility for his actions, and can now assess when another person does or does not belong in ministry and conclude who is or is not spiritually dangerous.

As I said. Bat. Shit. Crazy.

≈ ≈ ≈

Cleaning House

Some people have told me that they wish they had my bold and brazen sense of honesty. But I have had to hone my powers and learn to use them only for good and not for evil.

Of course, I had to work out a few kinks.

After my sister died and I severed ties with my parents, I decided for some reason that I needed to rid myself of anyone who didn't belong in my life. I apparently felt subconsciously compelled to start with the people I worked with at Applebee's where I tended bar.

One of our new waiters (who sucked) was complaining that he'd gotten three tables all at the same time. It happens. You just greet all three, get their orders, bring their drinks back, and don't panic. I've literally had my station fill up in about 60 seconds. No big deal. If you need help, ask for it. This dipstick totally dropped the ball—one of these typical people who screws everything up and blames everyone else. Blah. Those people bore me. How honest is that? Anyway, he came up to my bar, mistakenly thinking that I would validate him, and started telling me how they can't seat three tables at once, and he guessed those people would just have to wait. I explained to him that there would be no customers waiting for anything in this restaurant. I told him how he was to handle the situation, and he started to argue with me. I flatly said, "Well, sweetie, perhaps a lower-volume store would be more suited for you." The next day, he was a no-show. I didn't think it had anything to do with me until another little waitress (who also sucked) had about ten tables in the bar area, and she wanted to pick up all of them. As the bartender, I could step out from behind the bar and grab a few of those tables to help out. "Oh no," she said. "I can handle it." As I sat and watched her crash and burn miserably to the ground, her customers came up to me wanting things like silverware, refills on their drinks, more napkins… A few of those tables wanted to give me the money to pay their bills. I gave the customers what I could, but if someone came to me wanting to pay with a credit or debit card, I had to send them back to her—that was not a transaction I could take care of. One gentleman, however, came up to the bar and slapped down about $80 in cash. He said, "Can YOU take this?"

I smiled and said, "Why, yes. Yes, I can."

I waited for her to realize that those guests didn't pay her and come ask me if, by chance, they'd paid me; but she was so far down what we servers call "in the weeds" that she didn't even realize they'd left, let alone whether or not they'd paid their bill. She never came to question where that money was. She thought she must have taken it, so she cashed that table out on her computer screen. I said nothing but did my side work and cleaned and stocked my bar for the night shift. I was waiting for her to do her own side work, count her money, and realize she was about $80 short. She would probably have just enough money to pay the house, with nothing left over to take home. Since she sucked as a waitress, she may not have even cleared $80 in tips that day, and may have even come up short, owing money out of her pocket. I kept waiting for this to occur to her, but before long, I was done with everything I needed to do and was ready to go home before she'd even counted her bank. Having no intention of keeping her money, I finally approached her as she was cleaning something, slower than snot, smiling to her smug little self. Clueless.

I went up to her and said, "How do you think you did today?"

"Oh, I did great! I made a lot of money today." Still smug. I smiled and nodded.

"How much do you think you made?"

"Probably between $90 and $100."

In her dreams! I was walking with a little over $100 myself—there was no way in hell she was walking out with that much money. She wanted to inflate the amount anyway, knowing that she'd hogged all those tables and fell on her face. I was setting her up, bless her heart.

"I'll bet you don't have enough to cover what you owe the house," I said matter-of-factly. She just stared at me. "Do you know what this is?" I pulled her $80 out of my pocket.

"What?"

"It's eighty bucks. From a table you cashed out, but they never paid you."

"What are YOU doing with it?" She was getting pissed.

"Well, funny you should ask. You were so far in the weeds between ketchup and running food and ignoring your customers that they finally got tired of waiting for you and came up to the bar and paid me. I don't keep money I don't earn, but you know what? I could have, and you'd never be the wiser. I could have walked out with almost $200 today, and you could have walked out with none after all that sweating you did. That would have been a shame." I handed her the money. "Honey, let somebody pick up a few tables for you in the future. You get greedy, and you end up working twice as hard for half the money. See you tomorrow."

She didn't say anything to me. I stayed and talked with some of the cooks and servers after the shift. She went into the office where my manager, Brent, was. In a few minutes she came out and walked past us without saying anything. I knew she was miffed. She'd get over it. I'd take her under my wing. Brent leaned out the office door.

"DAISY, GET IN HERE!"

Hmmmm. Mr. Grumpy today! I went into his office.

"What did you say to her?" he wanted to know.

"To who?"

"To Shelley?"

"Nothing! What's the matter with you?"

"Nothing's the matter with me, but something's obviously the matter with Shelley. She just quit on me."

"What?"

"What did you say to her, Daisy?"

"Nothing, Brent! One of her customers paid me for their bill, and I kept waiting for her to panic. She never did. I gave it back to her, we had a talk about working hard and working smart and she was fine!"

"Obviously not, Daisy. She's outta here. That's the second person who's quit on me after talking to you. In three days."

"I am not responsible for these people quitting!"

"Well, you seem to be the common denominator."

"Oh, give me a break! Two people! And if I did have anything to do with it, I did you a favor—they weren't worth a bucket of warm spit!"

"Girl, I'm telling you—you'd better stay the hell away from my cooks! I'm short on the line, and I need every damn one I got!"

"Brent! I'm not doing anything!" I turned to leave.

"Hey, Daisy?" he said as I was walking out the door. "You know that day hostess, Kaitlyn?"

"Yeah."

"She sucks. I want her gone by Wednesday."

"SHUT UP!" I walked out and slammed the door behind me.

"I'M NOT KIDDING!" he yelled from behind the closed door.

As fate would have it, the very next day was Friday. I worked a busy day at the bar, and we were anticipating an even busier night with two hostesses short. Brent begged me to stay through dinner and hostess for him. Now, if I don't get to go to Heaven, I'm sure the job I'll have in Hell will be standing at the front door asking people, "Smoking or non?" Hostessing bites great big furry ones! I hate hostessing. But before I would endure this grown man suffering a panic attack, I agreed to endure being a hostess through this Friday night dinner. Brent was leaving for the day, the mid-shift manager had been on since 11:00, and the night manager was already, as we say in the restaurant business, rockin' and rollin'. I'm glad Brent was not there for what transpired on what turned out to be a phenomenally busy night.

We had a row of round tables in the bar area—hell, you've all been to Applebee's—that we call "Death Row." It's a station nobody wants because those are the last tables in the restaurant to get people into, and they are the first tables to clear out. They are in the bar area right by the front door. Funny thing, I was at the front door. We usually put slow (or new) servers in that station to break them in. As the night progressed, the guy on Death Row was nowhere to be found. His customers kept asking me for drinks, silverware, napkins, mayonnaise, sides of this and sides of that and whatever the hell else he wasn't bringing them. Finally, after his customers started to believe I was their server, I went into the kitchen to find him.

"My love, why am I waiting on your tables?" I asked him.

"You're not."

"Oh, really? Then why do I have two bottles of ketchup, a side of ranch, four silverware rolls, and three diet cokes in my hands? They're all for you, baby! What the hell? Are you friggin' Haley's Comet or something? You only visit your tables once every eighty years? What?"

"My tables are fine."

"Yeah, because I'm taking care of them, while you're back here getting your nails done or whatever it is you do. Get out here!" I walked out to appease his tables, thinking he'd be right behind me.

Now, you have to understand the restaurant business. We're funny like that. Everybody loves each other, and there's a lot of camaraderie. But you'll definitely sink or swim. The veterans will take the new guys under their wings, but we'll also bust your chops if you're screwing up. And we'll all be best friends again after the shift. I don't think this guy understood the restaurant business. Somebody came out and said, "Daisy, I think you'd better get back in the office."

"Why?"

"Jack's quitting."

"Get the hell away from me!"

"No, I'm serious. He's blaming it on you."

"He's quitting?"

"Yes."

"He's quitting."

"YES, Daisy!"

"He's quitting RIGHT NOW!"

"YES!" The server pulled me by the arm and dragged me away from the hostess stand. *Oh, my Lord!* I thought. *Brent's gonna shit a Twinkie!* I walked back into the prep area just as this guy was walking out of the office—sans his apron.

I said, "What are you doing?"

"Get out of my face, Daisy," he warned and didn't miss a step as he walked right past me.

"You're walking out?"

"Yep."

"You're walking out on a Friday night in the middle of a shift?"

"Yep."

"What the HELL?" But he just ignored me. Everyone seemed to stop what they were doing and watched us as I followed him through the kitchen completely incredulous. With all my questions pelting off of him, he kept walking and never said another word. He made his way steadily toward the door, past all the cooks, the servers and the bartenders. The eyes of his own customers were fixed on us, and he ignored their stares as he walked silently past them, while I protested as loudly as I could the entire way like a yippy dog, biting at his heels. He left me at the hostess stand as he walked right out the front door, never to return. The place seemed silent as I turned around slowly to face all the customers on Death Row. Every one of them had their eyes fixed on me. The place stood still. No noise. No movement.

"Did our waiter quit?" one of them asked meekly.

"Yes," I nodded. "Yes, he did."

No one seemed quite sure what to do.

"Does that mean our dinner is free?" another asked softly. Everyone started laughing, including me. The place exploded once again in the normal business of a Friday night at Applebee's. Movement and noise and the hustle and bustle returned.

"No," I answered. "No, that is not what that means." I laughed as I got everyone taken care of. They were all really good about it. It never occurred to any of them that I'd had a part in the night's adventures, but certainly every person on the staff knew it. And they were a buzz! In twelve short hours, Brent and I would be sitting down for another little talk.

Oh, joy.

As sure as the sun rises in the morning, Brent came out of the office the next day and sat down at one of my bar tables with a cup of coffee. The restaurant hadn't opened yet, and I was setting up my bar.

"Good morning, Daisy," he greeted me. Very cheery this morning. This was good.

"Good morning." Maybe he didn't know? I smiled at him sweetly. Innocently.

"Why don't you stop what you're doing and come have a talk with me."

Shit.

He knew. Reluctantly, I came from around the bar and sat down beside him. He didn't even acknowledge the previous night. He simply asked, "Are you okay?" Now, usually he would ask that in a teasing way, insinuating that I was obviously losing my mind or having some other crisis. But when I looked at him, I knew he was dead serious and genuinely concerned.

"I'm fine, " I answered him.

He was quiet for a while, but he continued to stare at me. He didn't even blink.

"I'm fine, Brent," I repeated.

Still silent, he nodded his head but said nothing. He continued to look at me very intently.

"Daisy," he finally said, "I'm going to tell you what I think is going on."

"Okay."

"You've just been through the most difficult thing you've ever gone through with the death of your sister. Not a lot of time has passed. You've told me about some issues with your parents, and I know you've had to set some pretty serious boundaries with them. You don't speak with them anymore, correct?"

"Correct."

"My dear, I think your sister's passing has brought you to a place of screw-it-all honesty. I'm not saying that's a bad thing. I'm just saying that it seems like your sister's death has made you take a good, hard look at your life, and you're cleaning out everything and everyone that doesn't need to be there. If someone's not healthy for you, you have such an aversion to that individual that you'll cut him off, get him out of your life. You've had to do it with your parents. That's probably a good choice for you. If your life is better off without them in it, fine. I'm glad. You had a 'moment of honesty' with them. But you're having these 'moments of honesty' with everybody. Do you understand what I'm saying?"

"I think so."

"The thing is... now you're cleaning out my restaurant."

I started laughing. He was right. He nailed it—it was exactly what I was doing. "It's part of my life," I explained. "I'm getting rid of people who don't need to be here!"

He laughed too, thank God. His seriousness had been killing me. "Daisy, I want two things to happen here. Number one, I want you to be okay. I don't think this will last forever—I think you're going through a phase. But I just want to have some semblance of a staff left by the time you get over this thing. I have a business to run."

"I hear you."

He continued to stare at me silently. The man knew when to talk and when to stop. Maddening for the rest of us.

"I hear you!" I said again.

"Okay. That's all I can ask." I got up to go back to the bar. "Hey, Dais..."

"Yeah?"

"You're still gonna get that hostess out of here, right?"

"SHUT UP!"

We both laughed, and I went back to work...a little more gently.

Chapter 5

Sean-Martin With a Hyphen

BALANCING GRIEF AND life is no small task. I dropped fifteen easy pounds in about four weeks. This is how I handle grief. I don't eat. You know, you lose someone you love and what are you supposed to do? Go make yourself a sandwich? I plummeted to a waiflike ninety-four pounds. At 5'7", maybe a smidge above, I needed to run around in the shower just to get wet.

These days I'm always one tragedy away from my ideal weight.

Having such a great boss in Brent, who was so supportive of my situation, was a blessing. Even still, returning to my day to day was just plain hard. On one particular day, I showed up to open my bar with not one stitch of makeup on. What was the point? I would just cry it all off anyway. I dropped into a chair as soon as I arrived and stared off into space. I'd been crying all morning. There was still more crying to do. I was oblivious to the new waiter who was taking chairs off tables and wiping them down, getting the restaurant ready for the lunch crowd, until I heard him say, "Are you okay?"

I hadn't even realized he'd stopped working and was standing a mere two feet away. He knew who I was and what had happened to my sister. Everybody knew.

I barely responded and continued to stare off into nothing. I didn't even really look at him.

"I don't know if I can cry anymore. Maybe I just want to hit somebody."

Undaunted, he offered, "How about a hug?"

I looked at him for the first time. Numbly, I shrugged and muttered, "Okay." He bent down and put his arms around me. It was only a brief moment, but the gesture gave me comfort.

"Thank you," I managed to whisper in his ear.

"Anytime," he whispered back.

I had no idea in that moment that these were the arms that would hold me forever.

Enter Sean Martin.

He'd recently moved from Pennsylvania and was waiting for his teaching credential to transfer over to Nevada so he could get a "real" job. In the meantime, he was stumbling and bumbling through lunches at Applebee's with us. I wish I could say he was a good waiter. I can't. He asked customers continually how they wanted their veggie burgers cooked: Medium rare? Medium? Medium well? Bless his heart. How many times did he forget to bring the salads and soups out before the meals and blame it on the cooks in the back? How many times did Brent bring him into the back office for a little "encouragement?"

"Now, Sean," he'd say. "This number *here* tells us what your sales are for the day. This number here is what I have to comp off people's bills when you screw up. Your *sales* need to be *higher* than your *comps*! That's how I stay in business. That's how I get to keep my job. Got it, buddy?" You gotta love Brent.

I kept my eye on this new waiter from my bar and helped make sure his ducks were all flying in V-formation. He kept his eye on me too, apparently, although he'll tell you to this day that I did nothing but scare the hell out of him.

Silly boy. I'd never hurt *him*.

Sean-Martin—for some unknown reason I had already begun to address him by his first *and* last name which I have continued to do every day for the last several years—stood on the other side of my service bar while he waited for me to pour his customer a 32 oz. Coors Light and flirted with me shamelessly. Pretty much everything Sean-Martin does is shameless. He doesn't believe in shame and tries his hardy best to avoid it always. And I flirted right back. My bar was full—my Nevada Power guys were there along with John Bear and all the rest of my regulars. Salacious, nosy devils—they hung on our every word.

"So," Sean-Martin turned on the charm as I handed him his beer, pulled his ticket and tossed it down in front of him. "You like baseball? I'm going to a Las Vegas Stars game tonight with my sister and her family. We have an extra ticket. You wanna go with us?"

"I love baseball."

The gentleman at the end of the bar beside us suddenly threw his napkin down on his plate, put his hands on his hips, and looked back and forth at us from one to the other.

"You wanna go then?"

"Sure."

"It's a date."

"I hope so," I smiled.

Sure enough, the man who had been eating his lunch beside us got up in a huff, threw ten bucks on the bar, and stormed out the door.

"What's his deal?" Sean-Martin asked.

"Oh, crap," it occurred to me as Brent walked up to us wanting to know if there was a problem. "He's got season tickets to all the Stars' games. He's been asking me all season long to go see a game with him, and I've always turned him down."

"And?" Brent prompted as Sean-Martin laughed and stabbed his ticket through the metal spire.

"And Sean-Martin just asked me to go to a game with him tonight, and I said yes."

"Dammit, Daisy..." Brent shook his head and walked disgustedly into the kitchen as one of our regulars walked out the door forever.

Sean-Martin looked just like the canary who just outsmarted the cat.

"Brent hates when I date the customers... He hates when I don't date the customers... It's really a lose-lose for me."

"I'd rather you not date the customers either," Sean-Martin smirked and took the beer out to his table.

Well, well.

And so it began.

The next months were filled with affection and laughter and smooching and, of course, Sean-Martin having to convince our little Geoffrey that his intentions were completely upright. It wasn't easy.

Geoff would wiggle his tiny buns in between us whenever we'd be on the couch watching a movie and glare menacingly at Sean-Martin for having his arm around me. Geoff had never been anything but the man of the house, and he had no intention of giving up his rank or station.

But it sure was hard for Geoffrey to maintain his disapproval when he found himself sailing down the sidewalk on his bike without training wheels with Sean-Martin running alongside. Or when he was biting into a gourmet burger that Sean-Martin barbequed up for him—one that was bigger than his own head. Or when he was pulling a fish out of a little pond somewhere with Sean-Martin standing right beside him, a right-handed fly-fisherman teaching a left-handed boy how to cast and mend and set the hook.

Life was almost perfect.

Almost.

I'd been on my own for almost five years, and I'd had a lot of time to get used to the idea of being divorced. Sean-Martin had been married before as well, but he'd barely had a year since the demise of his first marriage to acclimate to being single for a second time. The thought of settling down again so soon was slightly more unsettling in his mind than it was in mine. Can't fault him for it. A lifetime commitment is certainly not anything to rush into. He seemed to be content to compartmentalize his life: Our relationship was in one tidy box. His career was safely in another. His "guy time" was in another. He liked to party once in a while—another slice of his life. He was Danish, after all. Danes can whoop it up, I'm not gonna lie.

I'm not saying this man didn't have a genuine affection for me because he most certainly did. But our relationship was out of balance. It became clear that I was more committed to our relationship than he was. This meant that he held the lion's share of the power in the relationship, and that doesn't work for this girl. Some girls like to wait around for some guy to pull his head out. Not I.

I had to break up with him.

And Lord knows I tried. I really and truly tried, but he hung in there like a hair on a biscuit. He'd argue and be sweet and talk me out of it every time, and I'll be darned if I could make it stick.

"Okay," he'd say, "you're breaking up with me."

"Yes."

"And you're telling me that you're breaking up with me because you love me. More than I love you. Is that right?"

"Yes."

He got it. I was relieved.

"You love me," he'd establish one more time.

"Yes."

"And you know that I love you."

"Yes."

"So you're breaking up with me."

"Yes."

"I don't get it."

So much for that.

"You hold more power in the relationship," I explained. "I can't be in that kind of relationship. I'm more committed to us than you are. That sucks for me. It's not balanced. My life is not in balance. I need balance."

"You need balance."

"Yes."

"Uh-huh. Can we go eat and talk about this?"

It took me a month to break up with him. But in the end, he accepted the fact that he couldn't give me the kind of commitment needed to justify my love, simple as that. And I understood him completely. Believe me, I didn't try to change him. I didn't want to change him. But I wasn't going to be that hair on that biscuit just waiting until he finally woke up one morning and thought to himself, "Geez, I've not made that girl a priority. She deserves better, and I have to give it to her—starting now!" I tell women all the time, "Honey, he's either enough or he's not enough. Right now. As we speak. Which is it? If he's not enough right now, then what are you doing? What are you waiting for?"

"But I *love* him!" they always complain. I'll tell you what they're waiting for. They're waiting for him to…*change*. Yeah, and I'm waiting for the fairy godmother of liposuction to take ten pounds off my ass.

I don't have time to stand around and wait for someone else to change his stripes into spots. And I didn't have time for Sean-Martin to want to be with me unless his loser friends called to go put a drink on and then he'd "catch me later."

Please believe me when I say that I had no problem with him partying with his friends. Live and let live. Go be a dumbass. What I have a problem with is waiting by the phone for the one I'm vesting my heart in to make me a priority and dial my number. I do that for about twenty seconds, and then I'm a mile down the road and I'm no longer sure I recall your name. I make sure everybody stays in a blame-free zone. No harm, no foul. I don't have any intention for apologizing for what I need, and I would never expect a man to apologize for his. Sean-Martin didn't owe me explanation one.

Go.

Do.

Your.

Thing.

Just don't expect me to sit on the sidelines and watch you play whatever game you're playing or be waiting until you decide you miss me. It's only fair.

I.

Love.

Me.

For the next few months, I busied myself with work, mothering, and an enjoyable social life. My friends were invaluable, Sean-Martin had gotten a first grade teaching position and was no longer blaming our cooks for long-forgotten salads, so I was able to continue on at Applebee's without having to see him.

I just had to remember seeing him.

And wouldn't you know, after about five months the phone rang?

Hearing his voice again made me smile. The very next night, which was Good Friday, he was kissing my hand in a Tony Roma's over a St. Louis Rib Sampler. He kissed me and said he missed me and asked if he could go to church with me on Sunday for Easter services.

Church? Good Lord, if he was volunteering to go to church, the man was serious. And Easter Sunday of all days—my favorite holiday. It had to be a sign. I love Easter more than Thanksgiving or Christmas or the 4th of July.

I asked him if he wanted to drive out to the cemetery before the service to put flowers on Tab's grave.

"Absolutely," he kissed me so sweetly. He took me home and stood with his arms around me in my kitchen.

"I've missed you," he told me. In Sean-Martin-Guyspeak that means, "I'd really love to…" Hell, y'all know what it means. I have to admit, part of me definitely wanted him to stay the night with me, but I wasn't about to make this a walk in the park for him.

I sent him packing.

He left. Saturday came and went. I certainly wasn't going to be the one to call. Sunday came, and if we were going out to the cemetery before church, we needed to get going. Still, I hadn't heard from him. Well?

This was a big phone call right here.

I dialed. He answered. I said, "Hey, it's me. I'm going to be leaving in about a half hour."

"Oh, baby," he sounded like he'd been ate by a dog and shit off a cliff. That would be because he was—by a dog named Rolling Rock. "Yeah, church. Yeah… wow. Would you mind if I took a rain-check?"

Click.

See, the last thing I do when I decide I'm never speaking to someone again is to continue speaking to him—even if it's to say that I'm never speaking to him again. *Especially* if it's to say that I'm never speaking to him again. The last sound he heard was my phone slamming back into its cradle.

The next day I gathered up every memento, every card, every letter, every ticket stub, every picture and every scrap of memory I could find in my house regarding this man and sat down to write him a little note. It simply said, *"You are wasting my time. Do not EVER write me, call me, talk to me, find me, look at me, or come to my house again. We are done. I'd better never lay my eyes on you or ever hear again the sound of your voice. Daisy."*

I drove to the school where he worked with this bulging envelope and stuck it on the windshield of his truck. When I'm done with somebody, I'm scary-done. I drove away and refused to give him one more ounce of my thoughts or tears or energy.

Eleven months later, I was his wife.

ﻬ   ﻬ   ﻬ

The Poopie Bridge and Other Stories From a Lonely Boy

Boobies.

In Vegas you see them everywhere, pairs and pairs of them. You see them on billboards and taxis, magazines and flyers. You see them in shows and walking down the street barely covered in the sweltering heat of summer and in the beautiful sunny days in spring and fall. You get to see them in the chilly winters with *nippilus erectus*. You can't get away from them.

So, at thirty years of age, when I looked down my chest and found that my boobies, which should have been akin to two ripe honeydew melons (the natural born right and privilege of anyone native to Las Vegas) were really more the size of bing cherries, I went and did what any good Vegan would do: I bought me a pair. And threw in a rhinoplasty just for good measure.

Plastic surgery is big business in Vegas, and my surgeon was also Mike Tyson's plastic surgeon, so I was told. I know Mike isn't the prettiest walking advertisement for plastic surgery, but I knew this guy had augmented half the city. My surgeon—not Mike Tyson. When your city is filled to the brim with dancers and who show their boobies six night a week, it's good to go with the best.

I set a date.

These surgeries are nothing to take lightly. My nose was demolished, shaved down, and literally rebuilt. My chest muscles were cut into a matching set of filets. My nipples had smiley faces on them for a good amount of time, and my skin was stretched right out of my 32A's and into my new 36C's—300 CC's of saline weighing 2 ½ pounds a piece. Times two, that's an extra five pounds that I always shave off the scale when I step onto it, bring me down to a nice 145 instead of 150. Yeah. My ideal weight was thirty pounds ago. What about it?

I had to orchestrate who would be taking care of me. My friend, Jeana, and her boyfriend-who-eventually-became-her-husband agreed to come out and keep me doped up on Percocet and Valium every four hours and make sure I didn't run with scissors or something crazy like that while I was in my drug-induced state. My doctor wasn't about me being in any kind of pain and, as a result, I can't recall about a week of my life.

They tell me I hugged everybody. My doctor. The nurses. My neighbor's cat. The guy at the car wash. What I was doing at a car wash is anybody's good guess.

Sean-Martin, meanwhile and unbeknownst to me, was driving the gamut of the Pacific Northwest and fishing some of the best trout streams in North America on a soul-searching excursion.

One night while in Wisdom, Montana, he decided to mosey on into an old cowboy bar one early afternoon smelling like a river and thirsty as hell. He bellied up and ordered a brew. And another. And…another. A whole caboodle of construction workers were apparently stuck there waiting for the right set of roof tiles to be delivered. The wrong ones were sitting in boxes in the corner. Since this was the middle of nowhere, everybody had a little while to drink— you know—just to pass the time away.

The tiles arrived in time, and I think it's safe to say that no one was feeling any pain. Why anyone allowed a bunch of drunken construction workers to get up onto a roof with hammers and nails is outside my own capacity for logic, but somebody must have decided it was a good idea. Sean-Martin, who was now best friends with these guys, somehow dragged himself up a ladder with them and was keeping right up, throwing tiles and pounding nails.

When they got done? It was BEER TIME! To say he'd tied one on is understating the obvious. He flat stuck a tourniquet around his head and twisted it with a long neck bottle of Coors. By midnight the boy was six sheets to the wind.

He asked the bartender, "Ish there uhhh…. sumphlace a guy kin… camp ferthuh night 'round… 'round… (hiccup) 'round here?"

"Yeah," she told him and pointed out the back window of the bar. "Right out back. Showers. Shitters. Three bucks. Just pitch your tent."

Near as he can figure, he stumbled out to the back past some cabins. In one, a light was on and the windows were wide open. He thought he might have been hallucinating when he looked and saw some couple doing it—doggie style—right there in front of God and everybody.

"I'm goin' shtraight ta Hell…" He put his hands on his head and shook it to try to clear the image out of his mind to save himself from eternal damnation, but he got dizzy and ended up face down in the grass where he stayed, stone still, until morning.

No one knows what time the bar opened up the next day, but by noon, the barkeep stood staring at the window at him wondering if she should go out and see if he was still alive. (I'm wondering if it's still three bucks if a person doesn't get the tent up and sort of just sprawls out on the grass like that.) Luckily, he twitched. Then he rolled over. Another half hour and his head lobbed to the side, straining futilely away from the hot, mid-day sun. He sat up. Then he stood up. Then he took one step.

He stumbled back into the bar and ordered a great, big, greasy bacon and egg croissant with extra cheese and a coffee in the biggest canister they had—straight after he put a dip in his mouth. Isn't that what everybody does when they're hung over?

When he polished off his breakfast, he paid his tab, thanked everybody for a great time, and headed off toward the Wise River. Ironic, isn't it? From Wisdom to Wise? I love the cosmic poetry in all this. But hanging out in places like Wisdom and Wise doesn't make you a scholar any more than being in an outhouse makes you a roll of toilet paper.

And speaking of toilet paper, the first intestinal twitch hit him about a half hour outside of Wisdom. One twitch turned into another, which turned into rolling cramps. These turned into a full-blown-not-even-remotely-kidding-you shit attack that any person sitting in the truck could have audibly heard. His sphincter-factor was at a twelve on a ten-point Richter scale. You know the symptoms:

The glean of sweat on the forehead.

The contortion of facial muscles.

The crazed, squinting of the eyes.

The haggard breathing in through the nose and out through the mouth.

The desperate rocking back and forth.

And, yes. The whimpering. A grown man, whimpering and praying to Jesus. Have you ever promised Jesus that you would go to church every Sunday, volunteer at the old folks' home, and read your Bible every day—all right, once a week at church—if He would only help you keep your underwear clean?

I might mention here that Sean-Martin hasn't worn underwear since he was twelve, making the situation all the more dire.

Not a damn place to pull over and go poo poo! Not a bush, not a ditch, nothing. So make sure you take note of that the next time *you* wolf down a slick, big-ass, lubricated breakfast sandwich with coffee and Copenhagen in the aftermath of a drunken stupor and decide to drive down through the middle of nowhere.

Jesus, in His mercy (or more likely because He was looking down upon this man and laughing hysterically) provided a bridge under which Sean-Martin could relieve himself. He was already going about 90 miles an hour, so when he slammed on the brakes, his truck naturally carved donuts in the dirt.

Unfortunately, as he came around the bend, he shat his pants.

That's right. *Shat.* The past tense of shit. It's a word that Sean-Martin is positive that he has coined, so if you hear it somewhere else, just know that the origin of this word came from this whole event which Sean-Martin refers to as one big Charlie Foxtrot.

The truck came to a screeching halt. Sean-Martin threw it in park, slid out the door quite literally, and did the crab-walk to the back where he pulled out a clean pair of pants and some toilet paper so he could make a run for the underside of that bridge and finish what that gargantuan, mondo-sized-wannabe Egg McMuffin had started.

It took two seconds for him to assume the position underneath that bridge. The explosion that came out the back of that man's ass put permanent dents in the concrete. I know this. I was an eye witness two years later when he took Geoffrey and me back to that same spot to show us the evidence—as if either one of us doubted his mad skills.

"BRING THE CAMERA!" he called over his shoulder as he scampered back down the hill on Memory Lane.

Yes, I brought the camera.

Yes, I have the proof.

The attestation remains—a testament to the power of poop and the human body. Somebody should've called Guinness.

The story does not end there.

Sean-Martin fell to his knees in sheer relief. But then, a haunting feeling began to creep into his head—as if he were not alone. As if he was being watched. Slowly, he lifted his head and, to his horror, he realized that thousands of pairs of stupefied, beady little eyes were watching him.

Swallows.

Swallows who had made their nests underneath that bridge to keep themselves safe from the winds, the torrents, and the storms—and the occasional hungover fishermen who randomly felt the need to use their safe haven for a restroom. They huddled together, frozen with mortification that this intruder had just defiled their sanctuary, their tiny beaks agape with astonishment and outrage.

Instinct told Sean-Martin not to make a move. Rooted stock-still with his pants around his ankles, he stared them all down. Those eyes, those thousands of eyes which were previously wide in shock, slowly began to narrow their glares in acidic indignation.

The frenzy began with a battle cry. One lone screech turned into a chorus of shrieks, and the attack began.

If you can picture…

…a man running for his life out from underneath a bridge with his pants down around his ankles, trying to pull them up while concurrently waving off thousands of angry birds—foul fowl, if you will—being pecked half to death. Pecked on his head and face. Pecked on his shoulders and arms. Pecked on his ass. Pecked on his legs. He was suddenly in a scene from Alfred Hitchcock's, *The Birds*. He barely made it back to the truck with his life.

I guess you could truly say he was having a shitty day.

The day got better, though. He escaped from the nightmare and heard a little "bloop." Looking at the stream that ran underneath the bridge, he saw the rings getting bigger in the water where a grayling had popped up.

Graylings. He hadn't caught any graylings on his trip thus far. He went back to the truck, pulled out his fishing gear, and had the time of his life pulling those little guys out of the river for the rest of the afternoon.

He has talked about bringing me with him on that trip—not in person, of course, but in his mind. In his heart. He thought about me every day. He contemplated his life and tried to prioritize all that was truly important to him. Somehow I ended up on the very top of his list, and he was determined to win me back. He knew and took very seriously the fact that my last correspondence to him was final. But how final was final? The man would never consider staying in a motel during a camping adventure, but motels have phones—private ones that don't require coins to be plugged into it every three minutes. (For those readers who have no idea why he didn't just pull out his cell phone, he didn't have one. Hard to believe. I know. Also, if you are wondering how on earth or why you would ever stuff coins into a telephone, ask someone who is old enough to describe to you what is called a *payphone*. You might find one in a museum somewhere.)

Somehow the stars aligned such that the evening he decided to get a motel room to call me was the same evening I was recovering from all the plastic surgery I'd had that day. Jeana was pumping me full of meds. I wasn't even conscious—laid flat out on the bed looking like a Klingon off of *Star Trek*. With boobies. She was the last person Sean-Martin expected to answer the phone and probably the last person he would have wanted to answer the phone. Sean-Martin never got the warm fuzzies from Jeana. He was a drinker and a chewer. He cussed like a sailor. He broke my heart, he didn't love Jesus (even though he *claimed* to be a *Lutheran*), and he could just keep on walking as far as she was concerned—right off a bridge. In fact, he could get pecked to death by a thousand swallows with his pants down as far as she cared.

"She can't talk to you right now," she told him on the phone. "She's just had a major surgery! She's not even aware of her surroundings." Then for good measure, she added, "And she's moving to California!"

Well, truthfully, I was thinking about it.

Sean-Martin sat slumped over on the edge of the bed staring at the phone in his hand, hardly believing what he'd just heard. Surgery? Was she in an accident? Is she sick? Did her appendix explode? What the hell?

There was no sleep for him that night. He got up the next morning and had a choice to make. He was supposed to drive up to Bellingham, Washington, and take the ferry up to see his buddies in Sitka, Alaska, and do some serious fishing up there.

Or he could come home and try to win me back.

When I awakened from my drug-induced fog, Jeana did happen to mention that "that guy" called.

"Can you believe that?"

Well. The idea of talking to Sean-Martin again didn't seem nearly as infuriating when I was half-crocked on pain meds. And as I continued to recover, that not-so-negative feeling stayed with me. It was hard to forget how funny he was and dismiss how very enjoyable it is to be near him. He fills a person up. He warms a heart, a room, a home.

A life.

The memories began to take purchase in my heart, and, pretty soon, Sean-Martin was on my mind.

I told Jeana that I was going to call his apartment and talk to his roommate to see when he would be home from his trip. She thought I was nuts, however, being the good and supportive friend she is, she wasn't going to interfere in my relationship with this drunken Lutheran heathen who was clearly beneath me on his slick-as-snot path straight to Hell and eternal damnation.

Maintaining a balance of power in the relationship was still a central issue for me, so I knew I had to tip toe around this whole endeavor. I wanted the power pendulum to swing my way, and I knew I had to find out what kind of time frame I was dealing with. I had to find out when he was coming home so I could be prepared for it when he tried to reconnect with me.

I called his apartment.

"Hello?"

Shit! It was *his* voice! He was *home!* So much for the power struggle. I was clearly at a disadvantage now. Jeana had said he was supposed to be on this fly fishing excursion for almost the entire summer. I never expected this.

"Hello?" he repeated.

Shit.

"Umm… Hi. It's… Daisy."

"Daisy…"

Uncomfortable silence. At least he was as taken aback as I was—but I could *hear* him smiling.

"I heard you called."

"You had a surgery?"

"I did."

"Are you all right? What's going on?"

"I'm fine. I am. It was no big deal."

"Well… do you mind if I ask what happened? Did you get sick? Were you in an accident?"

"No, no. Nothing like that. I got a nose job."

"What?"

"And... I got my boobs done."

Another stunned silence. Sometimes it's best to move the conversation along without acknowledging what another person just said, so he changed gears.

"I talked to Jean."

"I heard. You recovered from that?"

"Yeah, she's... it's... You're moving to California?"

"I'm thinking about it."

"Wow. Lots of changes."

"Lots."

Tick tock. Silent again. Since I had been blindsided with the fact that he was home and had answered the phone, I was totally befuddled.

He stated the obvious, "You called me."

Shit. Damn. Hell.

"Yes, I...yes. I did. Jeana told me you had called. I was just calling your roommate to see when you were planning on coming home."

"I came home a little earlier than I expected to."

"How was your trip?"

"It was amazing. I fished nearly every trout stream in the Northwest—lots of streams I'd never fished before. I took a lot of pictures..." he paused. "I'd love to show you where I went."

And here we were. The fork in the road. Which way to go?

"Why don't you give me a call when you get those pictures developed?"

He let go of a short breath of air, which gave away his relief.

"I could do that."

I didn't need a video-phone to know that he was grinning from ear to ear.

"I'll see you soon, then."

"I'll see you soon..."

I hung up the phone and thought, *What the hell just happened?*

He might have had the upper hand on that telephone call, but I would regroup and be ready for picture night. I made sure I had the tightest, most low-cut, hoochie-Vegas top I could find. No reason to make this night any easier than it should be, right?

To his credit, his eyes never ventured below my chin. I knew he wasn't looking. And he knew I knew that he wasn't looking. Nor did he comment about any of my enhancements. He's quite the photographer; his pictures were incredible. But the night itself was slightly excruciating. He was so apprehensive and nervous. Every attempt at humor didn't just land like a fart in church. It floated around like a Babe Ruth in a public swimming pool. We cut the evening short, and he ended up going home quite early.

I was a little sad, actually, as I closed the door behind him. The nicest guy in the world was walking across my lawn to his truck and would be driving away, gone forever, in about thirty seconds. *It wasn't meant to be…*

Except nobody told *him* that.

Leo Kottke, a world-renowned guitarist—a musical genius, really—was performing outdoors at one of our libraries nearby. One night only. I'd never heard of him, but Sean-Martin said he was fantastic and wanted to take me. Maybe he could take Geoffrey and me to dinner and then drop Geoff off at the sitter? Persistence. Now that's a handy little quality in a man.

He showed up at my house wound tighter than a drum. If this man had been jittery at my house just looking at pictures, his anxiety about quadrupled that night. This was his last shot. We both knew it.

It didn't take long for Sean-Martin to put on a good story and get us both tickled. Thankfully, the ice began to break up a bit. We had some time before having to drop Geoff off with his friends, so Sean-Martin suggested we go on down to the bookstore and have a listen to some Leo before the concert. Borders was featuring his CD's to help promote the concert that night, and Sean-Martin wanted me to get a taste of what I was in for later in the evening.

I watched the way Geoff and Sean-Martin seemed to talk conspiratorially with each other while my head was between a pair of headphones listening to a preview of Leo. I had to wonder what they were up to. When I got done, Sean-Martin said, "Daisy, come listen to this for a minute." I set my headphones down and took the ones he offered. "This is a cool song. It's by a guy named John Prine. Every hear of him?"

"Nope."

"He's cool. Listen."

As I began to listen to the words, I knew it wasn't just a cool song that Sean-Martin had by chance run across and wanted me to hear. Sean-Martin was letting John Prine tell me exactly what he wanted me to know but couldn't say himself:

If you loved me
Tell you what I would do

Wrap the world in silver foil
Bring it home to you.
Do you remember
When you were my friend?
That's the way I'd like things
Just like way back then.

The boys disappeared while I listened. I believe it's safe to say I got the message. Sean-Martin and Geoffrey were peeking at me from behind a bookshelf in the kids' section. I looked around just in time to see them both duck their heads back down behind the shelf. Neither one is too great at being sneaky. When the song was over, they came back looking like they'd both been caught with their hands in the cookie jar.

"Did you like that?" Sean-Martin asked meaningfully.

"I liked it a lot," I smiled. He'd been planning to bring us to that Borders all along. He later told me that he'd been there for hours that day trying to find something romantic that would schmooze me and win me back. He'd even been in the poetry section, for the love of Lord Byron. For a man who embodies Grizzly Adams and Archie Bunker, that is one desperate move.

He only tripped over himself about fifty-hundred more times getting us to the concert and settling in with our blanket on the grassy knoll. I lay in his arms beneath the stars, which, if you get far enough away from the Strip, you can actually see. Vegas nights are fabulously warm. We don't have mosquitoes. Sean-Martin stroked my arm while Leo's guitar serenaded us. Everyone around us faded into the periphery until it was just the two of us. Three, if you count Leo. The night was perfect.

Sean-Martin turned over to his side to face me. "Daisy," he said as he brushed his thumb across my cheek. "I want you to know that I'm sorry for how things were when we were together before. I know exactly what was wrong with our relationship. I didn't make you a priority."

He paused for a second while he tried to gather his thoughts. These next words would make all the difference. "On this trip I did a lot of thinking. In a lot of ways you were right there with me. I thought about you—about us—a lot out there." He looked out to the surrounding mountains as if he were remembering those solitary nights out by his campfires. "I want to make you a promise right now," he looked me right in the eyes. His own had tears—he denies that to this day, but he was definitely what he calls *misty*. "Daisy, if you would just take me back, I promise you, I would never make you feel like you weren't the most important thing in my life—you and Geoffrey both. I would spend the rest of my life with you. I'll even move to California with you if that's where you're going. I love you. I want to be together. I'm talking forever."

And I said it because it was true and it had always been true, "I love you too." The relief that swept over him was palpable, and he rubbed his hand down his face in that manly way to prevent those tears he says he never had from falling down his cheeks. A couple of grunts and the man was back—with his woman. And he was one happy camper.

"I have relinquishing issues," I warned.

"You don't say."

"I only need fifty-one percent of the power in the relationship."

"Hell, woman," he laughed and wrapped me up in his arms. "Take eighty-five!"

Engaged by Christmas, married by spring. Eleven months.

Pastor Honey, I'd Have Poisoned Your Banana Bread a Long Time Ago and Other Confessions from the First Church of the Bermuda Triangle

Sean-Martin is great in a crisis. He'll survive any catastrophe and rescue all the women and children as he breaks through walls of fire, jumps out of falling airplanes, and makes his escape from whatever foe or fiasco he encounters. He never panics. He never falters. He's never uncertain.

He's Captain America.

So when the lady who was standing and singing right next to him at church got "slain in the spirit" (aka dropped to the floor, laid flat on her back, eyes closed, arms extended into a crucifixion pose) I could tell that Sean-Martin was on it! I was barely able to intercede on his behalf before he leaped into action.

"Sean-Martin! Leave her be!"

"Why? What's she doing?"

"She's… She's… Well, she's praying."

"Down there?"

"Yes. Down there."

"Why?"

"She wants to."

"Why does she want to?"

"Umm... Because she really loves Jesus."

He shifted uncomfortably and tilted his head to the side in deep thought. "You really love Jesus."

"Yes, I do."

"Are you gonna do that?"

"No." I put my arm in the crook of his arm to reassure him.

"Why not?"

"Because I like to pray standing up."

We skipped verse three of the hymn. After a few more stanzas, he stated flatly, "I think she's dead."

"She's not dead! For the love of Sam Pete, Sean-Martin!"

"I just gotta check on her."

Before I could stop him, he removed my hand from his arm, grabbed one of those dull golf pencils out of the seat in front of him and started toward her. I am here to testify that the Holy Spirit was, indeed, moving that day because He revealed to me in that moment precisely what my hero husband was about to do: he was about to take that pencil, lift her eyelid, and poke her in the eyeball with it the way he does his critters when he's out hunting in the forest somewhere. He says it's not a bad idea to give an animal a little poke in the peepers as to avoid getting an antler through the ribcage or a hoof in the family jewels before you try to haul the beast off to the truck.

Frantic, I lifted both arms toward Heaven and screamed, "HALLELUJAH! THANK YOU, JESUS!" He turned around dead in his tracks and glared at me. I had his strict, horrified attention. With eyes wide with warning, I spat through clenched teeth, "Get *back* here, before I start dancing in the spirit and run right down this aisle!"

He came back and put the pencil in its place. I could tell he was not happy.

"If she's dead, it's not on me."

"She's *not* dead, you crazy Lutheran!"

"Somebody does that in *my* church, it means they're dead," he muttered under his breath.

God bless him, Sean-Martin went to church with these peppy Pentecostals who fell out under the power of God and spoke in tongues and all that brouhaha for two years without really ever understanding or embracing the movement. You know why? He wanted to marry me, plainly and simply. So, he went to this…well, should I reveal the denomination? No. That would be bad form. I shan't.

Sean-Martin always has a plan. And he has the patience of Job, which he pronounces, "job" as in, "He does a great job!" Not Job, which rhymes with "lobe" or "globe" or "strobe" like it's supposed to be, bless his heart.

He had read about this dude in the Bible who had to work for some chick's dad for seven years before he got to marry the woman he loved, so several months didn't seem like that much of a sacrifice compared to that. Only *that* poor schmuck must have gotten so wasted on his wedding day or some such thing that he didn't realize that the girl's dad pulled the ol' 'bait and switch' and hooked him up with his older daughter instead of the younger one that he'd wanted in the first place. That poor bastard had to work another seven years. In any case, my sweet guy quietly and enduringly walked into the church of my childhood with me every single Sunday and finally the day came when he got what he was after and we were wed.

Two very important things changed on our wedding night. We got married up at the lodge at Mt. Charleston (Vegas' best kept secret!) in the snow. I was cold. My feet are ice cubes even in the middle of July. The man is his own heat source—another handy survival technique. I curled up behind him under the blankets and stuck my feet in their usual place, right up under his butt cheeks between his thighs—the warmest place (a sexy-toasty-double-bun oven packaged especially for me) on the man's body.

He did a back flip and sprang out of the bed like a jujitsu master.

"You know what?" he announced. "You are not putting your cold feet in the crack of my ass anymore!"

"I'm not what?" The side of my mouth curled up in a sassy smirk as I curled into a ball for warmth, my extremities turning blue—as were his.

"I mean it, woman! We're *married* now! I don't have to put up with that anymore!" His hands moved protectively around to his backside as he stood there like General George Custer taking his last stand. I turned on the sweet, puckered my lips, and did that thing with my eyelashes that he likes. You know. *That* thing.

"I can't warm my feet in your butt anymore?"

"No! You are no longer allowed to put your ice-cold feet in my buttcrack! I'm setting a…what do you call that…a *boundary*, right? That's what that Oprah woman calls that? I'm setting a boundary around the perimeter!"

My amusement dissipated. He was serious. I gaped at him completely horrified. A *boundary around the perimeter*? What? Was he back in the 82nd Airborne or something? Out on some Ranger mission? The crack of his ass has a *perimeter*? Then, as if to add insult to injury, he stood there beside the bed buck-naked and pointed a finger in the air adding, "Oh, and by the way? We're *Lutherans*!"

"We're *Lutherans*?"

"You heard me."

"We're *Lutherans*?" I repeated just to be sure I'd heard him correctly. How many surprises could a woman handle on her wedding night?

"That's right."

"Why are we Lutherans?"

"Because Lutherans go to church for 59 minutes flat and we get to the Olive Garden before everybody else. Nobody's jumpin' up and down, nobody's dancing in the aisles, nobody's throwing their arms around my neck. I'm not kidding. We're finding a new church—one where people speak one language and no one has seizures during the singing."

"Who *are* you?" I screeched as I sent a pillow flying his direction.

"I'm your husband who loves you." He deftly caught the pillow I'd launched and tossed it nonchalantly toward the headboard. One quick leap up on the bed brought us face to face, his hands suddenly on my hips, our knees slightly touching on the mattress. He leaned in to steal a kiss from my pouting lips and informed me, "I'm buying you a heating pad."

After having been officially married for a whopping four and a half hours, I looked him square in the eye and said, "You've changed. We need counseling." This only resulted in his explosive laughter, prompting him to envelop me in his arms and take me to the mattress for a roll in the hay so amazing that it warmed my heart *and* my feet and absolutely unequivocally made a Lutheran out of *me*!

When it came to putting some clothes on deciding on a church, however, it wasn't as easy as we'd first believed. Now, I love me some Lutherans. Those people love Jesus. They really do! And the great thing about Lutherans is that their services really are 59 minutes and 59 seconds from beginning to end. Sean-Martin could not have felt more at home. And we did, in fact, get to the Olive Garden before the Baptists.

I, however, was bored out of my mind. We agreed to find a church that landed somewhere between "Jumping for Jesus" and "Snoozing in the Spirit." Maybe something along the lines of simply "Hanging with His Holiness."

Enter: Pastor Honey and the First Church of the Bermuda Triangle. Of course, the names have been changed to protect the…innocent.

A friendly looking gentleman knocked on our door one afternoon and told me that he was starting up a small non-denominational church in our neighborhood. No labels. No swinging from the chandeliers. No poking anybody in the eyeballs. I told him we'd try it out.

In the time it takes to poach an egg, we became enmeshed in many of the church tasks that needed to be done. Sean-Martin suddenly found himself setting up the folding chairs in the little elementary school we were renting. I was playing the keyboard and singing on the worship team. When new Sunday School teachers were needed for Children's Church, we were recruited because, being teachers, we were obviously "gifted" in that department and expected to teach Sunday School in addition to everything else. Sean-Martin flat out said he wasn't doing it (I couldn't blame him) so I was the one who took on that job as well. It turned out that between the rehearsals and the prep time and the setting up and tearing down, we were devoting hours and hours of our week putting together what amounted to 90 minutes for making Sunday mornings happen.

To make matters worse, we were expected to participate in every event the church put on. I showed up one Sunday morning, and was almost waylaid into a women's retreat. One of the more visible and vocal women of the church commanded, "Come over here, Daisy! You need to sign up for our next women's retreat. It's $75. You can write a check to the church." Thus saith Sister Susie.

I looked at her, and then I looked down at the clipboard she carried with a bunch of names and phone numbers on it. I looked up at her once more.

"I don't go to those."

"I'm sorry?" she seemed confused.

"I don't go to those." I repeated for her. "Unless I'm the keynote speaker, of course."

Her eyebrows came together and her lips puckered down in the corners. "Why is that?"

"Because, honestly, the last thing I need is to be stuck in a room full of enthusiastically conservative women without some kind of an exit strategy. Plus, I tend to break out in a rash whenever somebody has entire Bible studies about a woman's place in this patriarchal pecking order everybody around here seems so obsessed with, and I've got a sneaking suspicion that just might be what's in the works here. And, frankly, I'm just tired. I am plumb worn out. I cannot do another thing."

"Well, if you're weary, you should come be refreshed with your sisters in the Lord!"

"Honey, if I want to do something womanly, I'll go get a pap-smear. But thanks."

I thought I was fairly safe in assuming that at least part of the focus of a woman's retreat might be reminding the ladies of our divine responsibility to find fulfillment in our roles beneath the penis-clad lads of the church. After all, hadn't I been asked by the pastor, "Daisy, will you get up and go help the ladies in the kitchen bring out the pot luck dishes? I'm sure you would be willing to serve."

Sure.

You know how you think about what you should've said way after the fact? Why didn't I say, "I could surely do that. I can also bring the message next Sunday if you need a break. I can exegete scripture, I can lay hands on the sick, I can organize a valley-wide food drive for the people of this city who are suffering and marginalized in some way, I can prophecy as God reveals Himself, I can discern, I can baptize the saints, I can counsel, I can balance the church budget, I can partner with other churches in the area to promote unity in the body of Christ, all working together to usher in the Kingdom of God, *and* I can walk and chew gum at the same time! You don't look too busy—so as long as you haven't come down with a bad case of polio, why don't *you* bring out the tuna casserole?"

The roles of women in the church were clear and the roles of women in their families were made clear as well. Sean-Martin and I hosted a small group Bible study for married couples. This pastor's wife had a beautiful metaphor for how God Himself set up the correct structure of a marriage. The wife sits beside her husband on the front bench of a wagon as his equal as they blaze a trail on the journey of their life together. *I'm with you so far.* The husband is the one who God has entrusted to take the reins. *You jussst lost me.*

"And what if he's an idiot?" I asked point blank. Everyone looked right at Sean-Martin.

"Uhhh… she's not talking about us," he explained quickly. The group laughed, and the question was almost dismissed as a joke.

I wasn't, in fact, talking about us. Sean-Martin is a great partner. We are equals in every way. No one is above—no one is beneath. I was talking about the family I was raised in as a little girl. Before she could soldier on with the lesson, I opened up this Pandora's box.

"No, I'm serious. What if the man of the house—who is holding the reins—what if he is leading that family straight into who knows what? The woman has to what? Endure it?"

"This is the way God has ordered families, Daisy. It's His perfect plan. We need to be obedient to Him."

"And if he runs that wagon over the side of a cliff?"

"It's the word of God."

"And if there are children in the back? What is to become of them? I mean, it's one thing for a woman to decide to follow blindly if she wants to. But for her to make that decision for her children as well? When there's no one to advocate for them?"

"I don't make up the rules. I obey the rules. And, by faith, I believe God will bless me for it. And my children."

"Hmph." I'm sure that what I *didn't* say for the rest of the evening was louder than what I did.

I was burning out quick.

Sean-Martin wasn't burning out because Sean-Martin apparently learned from Oprah and the United States Army how to set decent boundaries around his *perimeter* and, honestly, he could take or leave the whole church scene that, more often than not, interfered with some sporting event he wanted to see. He had only been going to church because he knew it made me a happy girl, and he's convinced his mission in life is to make sure I'm happy. "Happy wife, happy life," he always says. But I wasn't happy. I was frustrated. He was getting frustrated watching me get fatigued with all that I was doing. It didn't take much convincing on his part before I told the pastor I needed to step back and relinquish some of the responsibilities.

He responded flatly, "Well, Daisy, if you're burning out, that is usually an indication that you're not in right relationship with God."

My heart hit the mat like Mike Tyson knocking out… anybody.

Not in right relationship with God.

"I don't even know how to respond to that," I stuttered. "I don't even know what to say."

"Well? Why don't you pray about it? Seek God."

And she's down for the count. ONE! TWO! THREE… Ten chopping claps to the ground and the big guy wins by TKO!

I came to the conclusion shortly thereafter that church work is like getting stuck in the Bermuda Triangle. You can find your way into it, but you can never find your way out. To relinquish responsibility is often a personal affront to the pastor and then accusations start getting hurled around and people start getting their shorts in a twist. This is why I, Daisy Rain Martin, will never, *ever* again become involved in church work.

Ever.

One night during a worship team rehearsal, he made a comment to his wife that…let's just say that addressing me in such a manner wouldn't fly in the Martin home. Let's just say that Sean-Martin speaks differently to me. And the way that pastor spoke to his wife was none of my business. Should not have said a word. I admit it. But I looked at him and said, "Honey, I would have poisoned your banana bread a long time ago."

"Daisy, you need to call me Pastor."

"Okay," I replied. "Pastor Honey, I would have poisoned your banana bread a long time ago."

The proverbial fly in the butter.

The next Sunday morning before service, I was told out of the blue that I needed to be "discipled"—Christianese for being "mentored in the faith." This can be really amazing, or this can be really frightening depending on who is doing the discipling and whether or not anybody's passing out poison Kool-aid.

"I need to be discipled?" I asked.

"Yes, Daisy. You need to go through our discipleship program."

There was always a freaking program. A program for everything. A formula for everything. An answer for everything. There was no *wonder* in his world. It seemed to me there was no question that anyone could pose to him that would leave him stumped and scratching his head. He could always reply quickly, as if he'd already canvassed the expanse of the universe and gathered up all the mysteries of humanity and put them in his pocket: "Well, it's *simply a matter of…*" and he'd fill in the blank with some pat and tired answer.

"You haven't been discipled as far as I can tell. I have the gift of discernment."

Of course, you do.

"I can see that you have unforgiveness in your heart. You struggle with bitterness. My wife has confirmed this. She has a real gift of discernment too."

Of course, she does. Strange how it always seems to mirror yours.

"Tell me, Pastor. What does a 'godly' woman look like? Your wife? Sister Susie over there? Tapping her full potential for the Kingdom of God by arranging cookies on a plate?" I looked him straight in his accusing eyes and promised him most assuredly, "…because I'm *never* gonna look like that."

"My advice to you is to get into our discipleship class as soon as possible."

Needless to say, we were once again soon after, church-homeless. No one kicked me out. No one asked me to leave. I, of my own volition, cut myself from the herd. Frankly, for the second time in my life, I needed to take a powder from the whole church scene for a while.

There were a few women who slipped over to my house with secrets to tell or met me for a cup of chai across town—certainly not near our own digs. They'd been "cautioned" about me, after all, and admonished to be careful. One in particular, who was extremely immersed in church work there, told me one day, "I want to leave my husband. He's horrible, Daisy."

He showed up with her every Sunday and talked a good game, but I had suspected as much. Tears rolled down her cheeks as she said, "I have tried to think about how I could get away from him, but I can't. I'm stuck."

"The church will support you. You do so much there. Surely they would…"

"No," she interrupted and put her face in her hands, hunching over in complete despair. "There's no one at church I can tell."

So, let it be noted. I may cuss. I may question authority. I may be the worst Christian in the world. The church has called me rebellious, unforgiving, and bitter. But perhaps the church should know that its women are still sneaking over to my house in the night like Nicodemus, falling apart in my arms and smearing their tears across my cheek.

When I emerged once again about six months later from my church hiatus, Trinity Life Center beckoned me back like a magnet. It wasn't even a Sunday. I got in the car and made my way to the freeway. I took the 95 to the 15 and got off at the Sahara exit. I took it down, crossed the Strip, steering my Ford Explorer between the towers of the hotels, underneath the skywalks, past "The Platters and The Coasters" billboard—I didn't even know who those people were. They weren't part of my grandmother's group. Lord knows who they were. I drove past the World's Largest Gift Shop on down the street, cut across 6th Street and hung a right. I pulled into the parking lot, not even a block down, and felt like I was home for the first time in two years.

I didn't care if those crazy people jumped up and down and screamed 'Hallelujah." I simply wanted someone to put his or her hand on my head and pray to the Father on my behalf. I wasn't even that particular about what they prayed for. I could sing, *"Just As I Am Without One Plea"* for the gazillionth time. It didn't matter. I was tired and beat down, but I was home. Everything was going to be all right.

Pastor Dean was there to welcome me back with open arms and an open heart.

"What brings you back to us, Daisy?"

"I'm tired. We're coming back, but there's something I want you to know. I'm not helping out with anything. I'm not meeting, I'm not greeting, I'm not bringing the donuts. I'm not singing, I'm not playing an instrument, I'm not cooking, I'm not folding the bulletins, I'm not teaching Sunday School, I'm not setting up anything, I'm not tearing anything down. I'm not working in the nursery, I'm not on the prayer chain. I'm not calling people, I'm not organizing any events, I'm not handing out communion, I'm not taking up the offering, and I'm not going to *discipleship* classes! And if you have a problem with that, don't you even talk to me about how it's *simply a matter of* a girl who has obviously fallen away from the Lord! I'm not interested in 'ministering' inside the four walls of this or any church. My mission is outside this place. My ministry is to be a light to my kids, my students. They are my heart. They are my calling. I don't need to spend hours upon hours during the week making sure you fine folks have a good show on Sunday morning. I need to be *out there!* I need to focus on my kids. I need to come here and *just be here!*"

And with one word and a shrug of his shoulder, he validated every frustration: "Okay."

We both sat across from each other with stupid little grins on our faces. He knew exactly where I'd been. I came home beat up, and he and Randy were absolutely thrilled to open their arms and receive us back into the fold.

"Daisy, you just need sanctuary. You need a place you can come and be ministered *to*. There's nothing you need to do. We'll take care of you. Just come home."

Home.

And those guys did take care of us. They loved us. They laughed with us. They walked with us on our spiritual journey and provided wisdom and grace and sanctuary. Even though Sean-Martin still insisted we were Lutherans, he readily traded the brow-beating of the First Church of the Bermuda Triangle for the love that had always been there for us at Trinity Life Center.

❧   ❧   ❧

Of Mice and Men

As the sun peaked over Sunrise Mountain, the usual morning hustle and bustle ensued upon the Martin household one fine day. Alarms screaming. People stumbling. Showers running. Pets stirring. Mommy peeing. Daddy shaving. Boy still sleeping. Parents threatening. Boy awaking. Cereal pouring. Radios blasting. Teeth brushing. Family rushing. Books gathered. Hair slathered. Routine steady. Family ready.

Being the last one downstairs can be interesting since the insanity is new every morning. On this one particular, particularly fine day, I descended with my keys, sunglasses, and purse to find my son straining to hold up one end of our couch; our dog barking frantically, running in circles; and my husband with the stick part off of the Swiffer wildly pounding and poking the carpet underneath where the couch had just been.

"What's goin' on?"

The frenzy froze. Even the dog froze. All three of them snapped their heads in my direction and said nothing, my husband stalled in midswing.

"What's goin' on?" I repeated.

"Nothing."

"So you're just whacking the shit out of that carpet because you didn't have anything better to do?"

They just stood there with these goofy looks plastered on their faces. Even the dog. Especially the dog.

Just then a little brown mouse, traveling at the speed of light, burned a path in the carpet right by my feet.

Now, I'm not a very athletic person. I've never run a race. I don't play sports. Until very recently, my definition of "working out" has had to be disguised with words like "dancing" or "sex." I've never been accused of being exceptionally talented kinesthetically. In fact, I've been called "challenged" in that area. But in that moment, the spirit of Asafa Powell possessed my body, and I tore back up those steps with shutter speed. A deafening sonic boom pounded our living room, and the G-force on my face pulled my cheeks clear back behind my ears. Concurrently, I peeled the paint clean off the walls with the most earsplitting, unintelligible screech I've ever produced. And the hang-time on this scream was impressive. My lungs must have supernaturally expanded in my ribcage, affording me the ability to expel air and sound out of my body for several minutes without taking a breath. I stopped at the landing and jumped in a circle while screaming one, continuous, deafening, six-minute holler. I'm not sure, but I may have been speaking in tongues. I, literally, was blind. Darkness is all I remember. When the light returned and I was able to form a thought, I stood on the landing and announced hysterically, "I AM NOT COMING BACK TO THIS HOUSE!" I was serious as somebody's *second* heart attack.

I flew back down the stairs and out the front door I went, my husband chasing not far behind.

Pardon me for a brief moment while I set this scene for you. This event occurred when my husband decided one day to grow his hair out longer than mine. He had long, black and gray, wavy hair down past the middle of his shoulders. Sometimes he wore it in a ponytail or a cork-braid. But today, he wore it down and had the whole "Do I look like Jesus or Charles Manson?" look going on. Along with his hippie hair, he had a very cool, very sexy Fu Manchu. He kind of looked like a drug dealer, let's be honest.

A house was being built right across the street from us. In fact, that piece of desert had probably been the poor little mouse's home. He thought he'd move in with us because it was quieter than his former location. The construction workers started pounding and sawing away at the butt-crack of dawn, and they were all taking a coffee break when I came tearing out of the house screaming at the top of my lungs, "I am never coming back to this house!" That got everybody's strict attention across the street. They were bowled over when my husband came running out after me—big, long stick in hand still raised high into the air—hair a-flapping in the wind and yelling, "Baby! Come back! Don't leave!"

You know what they were thinking, right? "Holy shit, he's beating the hell out of her!" I mean, what would you think?

I screamed, "NO! I'M NOT COMING BACK!"

I got into my car and sped away, leaving him there alone to explain to those surly construction workers all giving him the evil eye, that he would never in a gazillion years lay a hand to his sweet wife and that this wasn't even close to what it looked like. Surly construction workers, might I add, with heavy tools and machinery.

I went through my day recovering from the traumatic events of the morning and began crafting contingency plans for where I would now live. My grandparents' door was always open, but they lived in a single-wide trailer across town. Not too convenient. Of course, Las Vegas has some of the most amazing hotels in the world. I worked in the inner city, not too far from the Strip. It would shorten my commute quite a bit. I might just saunter on down to the Mirage or the Venetian or the Paris. Hell, maybe I'd just get a two-room suite in the Bellagio. I could live in a hotel and do just fine, believe me. Sean-Martin would have to contribute financially, obviously. The Bellagio is a five-star hotel, after all. And I would most certainly let him stay with me whenever he wanted. I do love him. Geoff would come to live with me. Thus, the need for the two-room suite. The dog would stay at the house with Sean-Martin. All settled. If, and only if the mouse were caught and released somewhere far, far away would I ever consider going home. When my day was over, I called home to find out the status. He'd been home for probably a half hour. Plenty of time to save your marriage, right?

"Is the mouse gone?" I asked.

"Honey, I just got home. I did not catch the mouse," he admitted reluctantly.

"I'm going to the Bellagio."

Now, Sean-Martin only had a split second to decide on an effective strategy as to how he was going to get me home. He usually either goes on the offensive or the defensive. And if one looks like it's not going to work, he immediately switches gears and tries the other. He initially chose to go on the offensive on this one.

"Woman! You're being ridiculous! Now just get home! I mean it!"

"I need you to give me some money for the hotel."

Cha-ching! That's the sound of Sean-Martin switching gears.

"Baby, C'mon. Geoffrey needs you to come home."

"Geoffrey's coming to live with me."

"I need you to come home."

"You can have conjugal visits at the hotel. I'm hanging up now."

"Baby, listen! Don't hang up! Just… listen to me! All you have to do is come home and go straight upstairs. I'll make dinner, I'll bring it up with a glass of wine, and all you have to do is sit on the bed like Queen Sheba and eat your dinner and watch Oprah. Just come home, baby. C'mon."

"Why would I go straight upstairs?"

"What, you don't know?"

"Know what?"

"Honey, mice can't climb stairs. You didn't know that?"

"No."

"Oh my God, everybody knows that. Just come home, go straight upstairs, and I'll bring you dinner."

"Are you lying?"

"No, baby! C'mon home."

After a brief pause, I conceded and hung up the phone. When I pulled into the driveway, Sean-Martin was there to greet me with a smile and a nice glass of Zinfandel. He scooted me through the front door and right up the stairs where I parked myself on pillows and enjoyed dinner in bed with Oprah Winfrey.

He's a good man.

Chapter 6

Making an Impression

I DIDN'T KNOW how small Geoffrey was until I signed him up for preschool. It turns out he was only in the 10th percentile for his height and weight. Looking around at the other little tanks, I thought, *Good God, what are they feeding these kids?*

So, it is with a certain amount of pride that I recount the time Geoffrey took a certain situation in hand. I'm not sure if I've ever mentioned the fact that Geoffrey is slower than frozen snot. No sense of urgency. No get-up-and-go. The fire alarm went off in our apartment once while we were waiting for our house to be built. My husband ran buck-ass naked into his room where he found Geoffrey barely awake trying to put on a sock instead of running out the door in a respectable panic. If a kid won't hurry when he believes his *home* is on fire, I don't hold out much hope of motivating him to come in from the playground with any sort of dispatch.

The teachers were corralling all the sweet darlings in for their daily dose of Barney. Tempting though it was, Geoffrey sauntered lazily toward the door. The last one to come inside. The *littlest* last one to come inside.

A big boy stood between Geoffrey and Barney at his own peril. He blocked the door and would not let Geoff through.

"Move," Geoffrey stated simply.

"NO!"

"Move."

"NO!"

So Geoffrey popped him one and left him sitting on the ground bawling like a… well, a baby.

Of course, there's no hitting in preschool! The director, a wonderful lady whom I loved tremendously, told Geoffrey he had to sit in her office in time out. This did not compute in Geoffrey's head. At three years old, he could not eloquently say, "Look, here's the way it went down. Nobody's gonna stand between me and my favorite purple dinosaur. Anybody who tries is going to get about two opportunities to get out of the way. I think that's fair, don't you? I mean, maybe he didn't hear me the first time I told him to move it or lose it. So, being the nice guy that I am, I gave him the benefit of the doubt and told him one more time. I don't know if that kid's too skippy, but you know, that's not really my problem, is it? He didn't move, so I moved him. I'm not sure what the problem is. Now, if you don't mind, I think I hear *Barney and Friends* calling my name."

Instead, he just threw a fit.

A few attempts were made to explain to Geoffrey why it was highly inappropriate to sock that boy in the eyeball. He wasn't hearing it. He just became more and more incensed at the injustice. Plus, he was missing Barney. There was no reasoning with him.

"Come on," Miss Debbie instructed. "We're going to go sit in time out."

Yeah, right after he pinched her leg and screamed, "FUCKERRR!" at the top of his lungs.

When this story was related to me that afternoon, I thought I was going to fall out in a dead faint. All the teachers came and stood around me. This was a good one, after all. Grins covered their faces in the retelling. They were all very animated and *very* entertained.

I wanted to crawl under a rock.

"Dear God…" My hands covered my face for a full minute. "What did you do?"

Miss Debbie said, "Oh, I just picked him up, looked him right in the face and said, 'You have lost your mind!' I put him in my office, closed the door and let him scream. No big deal."

No big deal. I love that woman to this day.

I wish I could say that is the only time Geoffrey got in trouble at school. He didn't get in trouble too often, but when he did, it was usually entertaining.

In fourth grade, there was a little girl who'd had a kidney infection. She went to the office twice a day to take antibiotics. During a kickball game, this little girl got bonked in the head with the ball. Geoff immediately held his head in his hands, started doing the silly dance in the outfield, screaming, "My kidney! My kidney!"

She cried, went home and told her parents, and they called the teacher to complain she was being teased.

Now, many parents would defend their son's behavior, saying, "Oh, boys will be boys," or "It's no big deal. She's being hyper-sensitive—she needs to get a grip."

Nope.

Having taught school for years and becoming quite knowledgeable with the social dynamics of children, I gotta file this under "being a pillbox!" If the recipient of the teasing is affected, stop the teasing. Period. Every child deserves to come to school and get a stress-free education. Isn't that the way it should be?

It's not that I didn't chuckle when I heard the story. I mean, 'Oh my kidney! Oh my kidney!' It has some comedic merit. I'm still not putting up with it.

I told his teacher, "I'll be right there."

God bless Mr. Campbell's heart. He patiently sat between us as I addressed this issue with my son.

"Geoffrey," I began. "I want you to explain to me why you are under the impression that teasing and making fun of another person is an option you have?"

Because of how I took the time to explain the wonders of the world to this boy since the time he could barely open his eyes, he decided he could turn the tables and explain a few things to me. This kid looked me straight in the eye and explained in all earnestness, "Well, I believe it's because I'm an only child. I never had any brothers or sisters, so I never really learned how to relate to other little children."

Bravo!

Impressed though I was, my expression didn't crack one iota. I moved my chair closer for dramatic effect, leaned in, and said in my lowest, most monotone voice, "Bullshit. Try again."

Mr. Campbell backed up slightly.

Geoffrey's entire demeanor deflated. He might be quick, but he'll never be quicker than his mother. I'm sure the teacher's lounge was burning up THAT day. As well it should have.

A Geoffrey Halloween

When I was writing this book, I had a talk with Geoff about some of the horrid events it contained. He was slightly more interested in his bowl of Cocoa Puffs he'd talked me into buying for him against my better judgment.

"Honey, there are some rough places in this book."

"Mmm-hmm," he mumbled with his mouth full.

"I don't want to put anything in your head that you don't want in there. In fact, I totally invite the readers to skip an entire chapter."

"Uh-huh…"

"So, if you don't want to read that chapter, you certainly don't have to."

He swallowed. "I probably won't read any of it, Mom."

Which might actually come in handy since he would possibly rather be dragged behind a truck naked—nipples down—than to know that the whole world knows that he was once a hard core fan of Barney, the big purple dinosaur.

He even had a Barney sleeping mat as a toddler. After growing up a little bit and after much deliberation, Geoff finally included the little mat in a collection of treasures he'd sell at a garage sale one Saturday when he was about four.

He wanted sixty-five dollars for it.

When a kind-hearted gentleman, about 70 years old, asked him if he wouldn't consider coming down on the price just a bit, Geoffrey was happy to negotiate. My four-year-old thought about it for a second and decided, "How about nineteen cents?" The old man had been stooping slightly, but suddenly stood upright, threw his head back surprisingly far for his age, and expelled short, quick bursts of wheezing sounds that we took for laughter. Taking his hat from his head, he bent down low so he could look Geoffrey in the eye. After some intense bartering by both sides, the two businessmen settled on exactly one dollar.

Sean-Martin, who Geoffrey calls Fa, and I were sad to see Barney replaced by the Power Rangers just before kindergarten. After all, Geoff had been wholly devoted to his purple buddy since he was about a year old. While many one-year-olds have the attention span of a tzetze fly, Geoff could lock in for one whole blessed half-hour episode of his blithering, purple friend. Needless-to-say, this was my escape route to a sane corner far from said toddler, like the bathroom. As a result, I wasn't all that familiar with the show myself. Can anyone blame me?

On Geoffrey's second Halloween, we fully embraced the next monumental rite of passage in a child's life. I went and got him a Barney costume. Like most store bought costumes, this one was cheesy, but adorable. I held it up in Wal-Mart imagining it's pokey dinosaur tail swinging out behind my son's tiny butt, his round face peeking out the other side. My son, the dinosaur. I smiled all the way home.

Turns out it was Baby Bop.

If you are not in the *Barney and Friends* loop, you are reading this unaffected. If you are privy to this enthusiastic happy cast of characters, you know what is coming. I failed to notice the obvious green hue of the material, never thinking for a moment that the primary color should have been p-u-r-r-p-l-e.

Little did I know the merciless chastisement that awaited an exhausted working mom who had grossly missed these cues. I thought the debate as to whether or not children should watch the damn show was bad. But, *nooo!* Not only did I get an earful from every two-year-old on the block, mothers everywhere had their lipstick smudged about this till Ground Hog's Day.

"BABY BOP IS A GIRL!" they chided.

Really. Who knew?

"How can you make him wear that, Daisy?"

"Listen," I stuck to my guns. "This is Vegas. If a kid could pull it off anywhere, it's here. Look at him! He loves it!"

"This kid's gonna have problems!"

"Oh, hooey! He's fine!"

Panties, panties everywhere, still in uptight wads.

Whatever! It's not like it's *Christmas*!

Even though Halloween is far from my favorite holiday, I would never rob a child of the sheer and utter joy of dressing up and going door to door for free candy. At first our little Baby Bop was leery about walking up to a door and knocking, especially if there might be anything spooky jumping out. But once he heard that first, big, handful of candy cascade to the bottom of his plastic bucket, he was *running* to the next door. His little pumpkin soon runneth'd over with the sweet stuff.

When I tried to empty some of his candy into a plastic grocery bag so he could get a refill, the kid just about had a come-apart. Try to reason with a two-year-old in dinosaur drag about candy on a strange, dark, romp around the neighborhood. That night goes down in history for the biggest tantrum of Geoffrey's toddler career. Spooked out of their wits, ghosts and fairies and goblins crept past us gaping at the little green dinosaur screaming, flailing arms, legs and tail all over the sidewalk.

Ah, the memories.

As the years passed, Geoff rivaled the biggest and best at collecting Halloween candy. He gave the Baby Bop costume to his cousin, Amanda, and she was absolutely adorable in it the following year. Funny, how I never noticed that bright pink bow on the head before. Geoff left his cross-dressing dinosaur days behind and, as he grew to be a big boy of 6 and 7 and 8, he ventured out into the neighborhood as a Power Ranger, a ninja, a cowboy, a soldier—much more manly costumes, which made up for his rough start due to the fact that his mother didn't pay attention to the oversized, purple blob on TV.

Now, as I stated, I'm no huge fan of Halloween, but if there ever was an opportune moment to throw on a pair of Jimmy Choos, a fat feather boa, false eyelashes and a tiara and walk the streets without having to be afraid you're going to get arrested for solicitation, it's Halloween, my friend. For that we must all be grateful. Let us give thanks.

Vegas has plenty of costume shops, and believe you me, baby, you can be *anything* around here. Given so many choices, a bit of guidance is a good idea especially when children are involved. They don't always make the best choices due to their lack of reasoning skills, let alone any and all fashion sense. I always steered Geoff away from bloody, gory, messy, mauled things. Why? Because I said so, that's why. And don't even talk to me about going as the devil himself or one of his spooky minions.

The year *The Matrix* came out, Geoff wanted to be the Matrix Dude. I'm not sure he has a name—I thought Keanu Reeves had come a mighty long way from his *Big Adventures with Bill*. Or Ted. Whichever. I've not gotten any better at clueing in on these things than I did in the days of *Barney and Friends*. If the Matrix Dude has a name I surely don't know what it is. All I can tell you is that Matrix Dude wears a long, slick, black trench coat with black boots and black sunglasses. Shouldn't cost too much, right?

Forty bucks. Had it included the boots, I might've considered, especially if they were thigh-high.

For a costume he was only going to wear for about two hours, minus the boots, I was not going to pay forty bucks, *plus* tax! Even when my son promised me he'd wear it to school every day, I was not swayed.

"Geoff, this is a bad week, honey. I just got a root canal that cost me $200. Let's see what else there is."

We looked and looked. Of course, nothing was as cool as the Matrix dude. With Barney and Baby Bop a distant memory, the kid was all about cool.

"What about this?" I offered up a pirate.

"No."

"Why not?"

"It's stupid."

Okay.

"I could be *this* guy!" he offered up a bug-eyed ghoul with an axe hanging out of his bloody forehead.

"No."

"Why not?"

"It's stupid."

Two could play at this game.

"It's not stupid! It's cool. I want to be something bloody this year."

"Here's a hockey player," I suggested. "He's bloody."

And he's $14.95!

"I don't know. Maybe." His hands retreated into his pockets and his shoulders got that attitude. You know the one. He got that look on his face that told me plainly I was currently blowing chunks with all the lame suggestions.

"Son, we don't have to get a costume today. We can come back later and see what else comes in or we can go to another party store."

"No, let's just get the hockey guy."

"If you don't want to be the hockey guy, we'll come back. Do you want to wait?"

"No, I'll be the hockey guy."

"Wonderful!" I put it in the basket and let Geoff pick out some silly string and a candy bag. Halloween was done, and one Andrew Jackson took care of the whole thing.

I like those days when I can brag about being such a good mom. Those are good days. I had a lilt in my step as we scuttled out to the car. The radio played a great song. October, the nicest month in Vegas, had brought us another glorious day and my son was hooked up for Halloween. I buzzed out of the parking lot and happily headed home humming along to the song on the radio. It might have even been an Indigo Girls' song, and they hardly get the airplay they deserve. Life was good.

Has it ever happened to you that, not only were you barking up the wrong tree, you were standing in the entirely wrong forest? As far as Geoffrey was concerned, the song on the radio sucked, October sucked, and he was *not* hooked up for Halloween. This I realized when I glanced over and saw him scowling. Seething, even.

"What?!" I exclaimed. "What? Are you kidding me? What's the matter?"

I couldn't believe what exploded out of that kid's mouth.

"You never let me be what I want! You never let me be anything bloody! You don't let me be anything creepy! I wanted to be the Matrix guy! I don't know why you don't like Halloween anyway!"

Don't like Halloween? I bought him silly string, for crying out loud.

Since I was still wearing my "I'm the Best Mother in the Whole World" hat, I calmly explained, "Geoff, you didn't *have* to be the hockey guy. We could have waited. We could have gone somewhere else. I think we talked about this."

"I either want to be the Matrix guy or something gross and bloody!"

"A hockey player IS bloody!"

"He's not scary!"

"Ever been in an ice rink with one?"

"He's not Halloweenie!"

Halloweenie? *Hallowfrigginweenie!*

"He's not evil!"

"You're not being anything evil."

"You're just like all those CHURCH PEOPLE!"

I sucked in a sharp, horrified gasp and almost wrecked the car. Good God. Why didn't he just stab me through the heart with a bloody pitchfork personally autographed by Satan himself? That was a low blow. The lowest. My "I'm the Best Mom in the Whole World" hat was tilting ever-so-slightly. Hell, that hat came clean off. I was pissed.

"Geoffrey..."

"I didn't *want* to be the hockey player! You MADE me be the hockey player!"

"You're not happy with the hockey player costume?"

"No!"

"You're not happy?"

"No."

"You don't want the hockey player costume?"

"No."

So I did what any good mother would do. I chucked it out the window. We were going about 55 miles an hour, in case you were wondering.

"MOM!" he was stupefied.

I leaned over to him and looked him squarely in the eye. "You owe ME twenty bucks!"

"You threw my costume out the window!"

"You didn't want it! You weren't happy!" My tone softened sweetly. Too sweetly. "See, my job as a mom is to make sure that *you* are *always* happy! You weren't happy; so I got *rid* of it." Suddenly, once again the wretched and horrible Mommy Dearest returned and something otherworldly clearly took over my vocal cords as I glared at him with eyes that he was sure burned yellow: "Are you happy now?"

Yeah, don't tell *me* I don't have this Halloween thing dialed in. Geoff did not have a response, so what else could I do but assume he was happy? Problem solved. I *did* my due diligence as a mother!

I assure you, some kid walking down the street was, no doubt, scuffing his Converse, untied, along the cement gutter lamenting that he had nothing to wear for Halloween. No bag to put his candy in. No silly string to spray on his friends. Nothing. Was probably praying to Jesus our Lord and Savior about it when, suddenly, a bag miraculously hurtled out of the sky and landed gloriously at his feet! Yes, the clouds parted, the sun shone brightly, and he unmistakably heard a Heavenly choir belt out a C-major chord for a full two measures.

Geoffrey didn't hear shit, only the sounds of silence as we drove the rest of the way home without another word.

The child recovered brilliantly, as we all knew he would. He commandeered a white gorilla mask from one of his cousins, took my pink robe and slippers out of my closet and trick-or-treated that year as, "Mom-Before-Breakfast."

Educating Geoffrey

My two favorite food groups: wine and pasta. A smooth glass of Zinfandel sat half full on the counter. My glasses are always half full. I stirred the spaghetti noodles in my big, deep, black pot to make sure it wasn't sticking.

Geoffrey stomped through the back door in a huff, interrupting my peace and quiet.

"Will you take the trash out, honey?"

In frustration, he shot back, "I'm going to learn to sever relationships with people like you!"

I lifted my head from the rising steam and looked at the air straight ahead wondering if I'd heard that right. Geoff grabbed the garbage out of the trash can and walked out the door without another word, slamming it behind him.

Sipping calmly on my wine, I pondered his words for a moment. Tilting my head slightly, lifting an intrigued eyebrow, I responded placidly, "Hmm. Well. I suppose if you're going to sever your relationship with someone like me, then I guess you don't live in *my* damn house."

Carrying my wineglass in my left hand, I locked the back door with my right. Sipping nonchalantly, I walked through the house locking all the doors and all the windows. Having arrived back at the stove from my mission, the banging commenced. I turned up the Dixie Chicks and put the bread in the oven.

Geoff made his way around to the sliding glass door.

"MOM!" I could hear him yelling.

I ignored him while Natalie Maines rode the Sin Wagon.

"MOM! OPEN THE DOOR!"

Humming, sipping, and stirring continued. The doors remained locked.

About twenty minutes later, a different knock rapped on the sliding glass door. I turned around to find my husband standing in the back yard perplexed as all hell. For him, I unlocked the door.

"Honey," he asked cautiously. "Is there any reason you've locked us out of the house?" For all he knew, there could have been a reason they both were locked out.

"You're not locked out. Geoffrey is."

"And why is that?"

"Because I asked him to take out the trash, and he said he was going to learn to sever relationships with people like me. So I figured he didn't need to live here anymore."

"He said *what?*"

I started to repeat myself, but he shut the door sharply and went to find our child.

It was unfortunate that Geoff wasn't going to live with us anymore because dinner was turning out superbly.

In a few moments, the sliding glass door opened and my husband walked through and closed it behind him.

"Honey?"

"Yes, my love?"

"You need to hear what Geoffrey has to say."

"I did."

"No, you need to listen again."

"Why?"

"When he came in from outside, he was in a tiff with Joey across the street. Joey was being a shit, I guess, and pissed Geoffrey off. He came in and said he was going to learn to sever relationships with people—like *you* do!"

"Like *I* do?"

"Yes. Sever relationships with people the same way *you* do! He wasn't talking about severing a relationship with you. The trash was just bad timing."

"Oh my God!" I burst into tears. "I'm the world's WORST MOTHER!"

Here I stood, Mommy Dearest. I wouldn't be getting the Coolest Parent Award that year!

"Go get him!"

My sweet baby boy came in just a little miffed, bless his heart. I smothered him with kisses (a punishment all its own) and contemplated just how sobering it is that for all the time and energy we spend making sure their homework is done and that they use their manners and speak as eloquently as possible and wash behind their ears, the biggest lessons they learn are often the ones that we don't even realize we are teaching them.

∽   ∽   ∽

Thelma: Louise?

Louise: Yes, Thelma?

Thelma: You're not gonna give up on me, are ya?

Louise: What do you mean?

Thelma: You're not gonna make some deal with that guy, are you? I mean, I just wanna know.

Louise: No, Thelma. I'm not gonna make any deals.

Thelma: I can understand if you're thinkin' about it. I mean, in a way, you've got something to go back for. I mean Jimmy and everything.

Louise: Thelma, that is not an option.

Thelma: But I don't know...something's crossed over in me and I can't go back. I mean, I just couldn't live...

~Thelma and Louise

Chapter 7

Give Me Liberty or Give Me Death – I'm Not Kidding

YOU CAN GIVE a pig a bath and take it to Sunday School, but when you get it home, it's just gonna strip down and go right back to root in the mud and its own crap. A dog will puke up that beef ravioli it mooched out of the trash and think it looks just as scrumptious as it did the first round. It doesn't even hesitate to go for another round.

Little girls who come from abuse the way I have, often grow up and find someone who will keep them in the lifestyle that is familiar to them—even if it's nothing but mud and crap and puke—even if they've known better at some point in their lives.

Not this girl. Something's crossed over in me. I can't go back.

I just couldn't live.

Know this: It does not suck to be Daisy Rain Martin. I enjoy a life of abundance and hope and freedom beyond anything I could have ever thought or imagined because I have let go of my past. Literally. That includes people.

My choices have mortified and offended other people. As I have said, members of my own family and close family friends are deeply frustrated by my refusal to open the doors I have closed, never to go near them again. They are praying for a miracle—for reconciliation.

They don't see my miracle. They don't see that I have reconciled my life to God. The very freedom that I consider to be my lifeblood—the sustaining air I breathe—is, to them, my certain undoing, a malignance that poisons my relationship with Christ and threatens my eternal security. I am lost in the fog of my own unforgiveness and have fallen into the hands of Satan.

And it *really* doesn't help when I say the f-word. In fact, that is unbelievably counterproductive. But what can I do? After all these years, I have found my voice. I have found joy in my life: my husband and the son we've raised together, the life we continue to build together, our home, my inner circle of friends and confidants, my writing and my teaching. If I haven't yet found all my answers, I have still found peace and love and hope and laughter.

And life is not over for me yet. There may yet be answers for me on this earth. I might not have to wait for eternity for all of them.

As for my family who continue to pray for the haze to be lifted, for my eyes to be opened and for me to come back into the fold? I love them. I understand why they cannot accept my choices. They love me immeasurably, and I know I have hurt them. A lack of love has never been a problem with our family. It's plentiful and abundant. But so is the pain. The collateral damage from one man's perversions and his wife's condoning and participation of his actions has reached far into the fabric of this family. The butterfly effect has upheaved our very foundation. If there are those who need it to be my fault because they cannot face the truth, so be it, but the truth has set me free. And I am free indeed.

I'm moving on. I'm not going to loiter around this issue waiting for people to believe me, waiting for people to understand. And I'm never going back to the life I had.

Something has crossed over in me. I can't go back.

I couldn't *live*.

Only Hope

So many people think the church is that building on the corner with the cross on it. Really, the church is the people in the community who are meeting the needs of the people in the community. If those people are Christians, they're very likely doing it because that's what they believe Christ would want them to do. Randy has a pretty keen awareness of this, and he calls the community, the "marketplace." He preaches about it all the time.

Funny, like many preachers, Randy's "marketplace" is that building on the corner with the cross on it. I mean, I'm sure he gets "out there," but his job requires him to show up to that cross-clad building pretty regularly and provide that gathering place everybody goes to on Sundays and Wednesday nights. One day after church I found him and said, "You need to come hang out in *my* marketplace."

My marketplace is a concrete building older than I am surrounded by more concrete and beyond that, some asphalt and then more concrete. It's filled with kids of every race, religion, and background. Some are sweet. Some are hoodlums. And some are sweet hoodlums. Walk around in my marketplace, and you will see an accurate, to-scale cross-section of the world. Vegas is like a pint-sized planet Earth.

Now, I would never engage in peddling Jesus at my school, that is, to try to sway my students to my religious or political beliefs in an effort to "recruit" them, so to speak. It's against the law, as it *should* be! These kids have parents who are in charge of raising them in the faith (or not) that they decide is best. Obviously, Randy wasn't going to be reading from the Bible and, frankly, I told my vice principal that he was somewhat of a social worker, a community advocate, who helped people who needed second chances. And third chances. And fourth and fifth and sixth chances. He was a hope-giver. She approved it.

When I introduced him to my kids, I simply said, "This is Randy. He's my pastor, and he's gonna read you guys a story."

Immediately, just about every hand in the room shot up. Every one of them sat on the edge of their seats, shaking their hands eagerly in the air, frantically trying to be called on. Randy looked at me a little baffled and then called on one of them.

"Yes, how about you there in the green shirt?"

"Umm, we just want you to know that, after 2:36? Mrs. Martin says cuss words."

My eyes popped out of my head as I watched all forty-three of them put their hands back on their desks and nod their heads in agreement, busting me out like dawgs! After 2:36. This, because whenever I caught one of my little darlings using foul language, I would say, "Lovie, if I'm not allowed to cuss until 2:36, neither are you!"

Incidentally, these are the same kids who would never say a word about a colossal fight after school or somebody who was hiding a knife or a bag of weed in their pocket or who boosted the tires off some car—but they'd rat *me* out to my own pastor for a little potty mouth!

Randy, of course, did what any good shepherd would do—he stifled his laughter and assured them all, "I know, I know. I'm working on it." And he proceeded to pony up a little hope for everybody.

One of the best things about being a teacher is watching what hope can do in the lives of such amazing young people—even if they did hang me out to dry that day. I've met very young people who have never known hope or abundance or freedom. But they sure know where their boundaries are and what colors should not be worn outside of those invisible, yet well-established lines. I met them Monday through Friday in the inner city, full of my own faith, hope, and love. Initially, my kids had no faith in me, no hope for anything else in their lives except for what currently was, and even though I told them the first day of school that I loved them, they didn't believe me until the end of October. Two months it took me to convince them that I wasn't just some white chick who drove in from the burbs every day. I was, in fact, a white chick who drove in from the burbs every day, but they discovered I was so much more than they expected. And, delightfully, so were they. Rough, but delightful.

I mourned the lost time between the first day of school and the last days of October. By November, however, they began to believe me when I told them they mattered to me. Their faith in me grew and so did our genuine love for each other. But, sadly, hope remained elusive. After all, people can only walk in the light that they know. Determined to shine brighter, I began to talk about hope, believing that these kids of mine would be compelled by it and hold it close to their hearts, allowing it to be a catalyst for their dreams.

I talked about college. Travel. Success. Safety. Freedom. Destiny.

They thought I was smokin' crack.

They weren't compelled by all this talk about a bright future. They were repelled by it. They resented these discussions. It seemed a cruel joke to them. Undaunted, I became more determined than ever to shove this life-giving gift into their hands and hearts and minds and spirits. So I dug in!

Here's the thing. You don't ever want to get into a pissing contest with some kids. They could win. These very savvy individuals believe they know their place in their world, and they expect you to know yours. If you don't know your place in their world, don't bother coming in. You won't last. I was told, "Miss, we love you. We respect you. We know you are trying your best with us. But the bottom line is, you just don't know. You don't know what it's like to be in our place. You live in a nice house. You live in a nice neighborhood. Your kid can go where he wants. You love us, but you're just not us."

How freaking patronizing is that? From fourteen-year-olds, no less. I'm talking about kids who've never seen a cow, and they're telling *me* that I don't know? Well, that just pissed me off.

I decided to bring them Alaska. I put our last vacation video together with the sound track to *"The Mission,"* the most beautiful music ever composed.

Whales. Waterfalls. Trees. Bald Eagles. The open ocean. Tlingit Indians. Our friends who still live there over-nighted two chum salmon packed in dry ice, a male and a female full of eggs.

When the package got there, the kids thought Christmas had come. We ripped the tape off and opened the top. The packed dry ice covered the fish; when I took it off, the screams erupted!

They got to hold the fish in their hands and touch the scales and poke the eyeballs. Eggs fell out of the female when they picked her up. "NEMO!" they screamed. Two kids puked. It was fabulous. My room stank for days. They wanted to go to Alaska.

They *wanted.*

I took that golden opportunity to remind them of our previous conversations about "Little Miss White Girl From the Burbs" and how I didn't know anything about their world. I told them, "You know what? *Your* world consists of about a five-block radius. Do you think the world just might be slightly larger than five city blocks? You say I don't know what it's like in your world, and you know what? You're probably right. I don't know. But maybe there are some things that *you* don't know. Like what the rest of the world might be like. Or where you can go. And what you can do. And what you can have."

Crickets.

I continued, "I can't be the only one who has hope for your lives. It's too heavy for me to carry around all the time, so I'll tell you what I'm gonna do. Everybody hold out your hands like this...Like a little cup. I'm gonna come around and put some of my hope in your hands. Just hold it for a while and see how it feels."

Groans. Rotten, pre-pubescent children. They're too cool for anything. I was trying to have a moment there. Okay, it was the corniest thing I'd done to date, but I was desperate. And so were they—they just didn't know it.

"DO IT! I'm coming around!"

Chica Blanca was now *Chica Blanca LOCA!*

The rolling of their eyes did not deter me, and I went around and spilled a little measure of hope from my cupped hands into theirs. They couldn't leave the room without their hope.

"How's that feel?" I asked exuberantly.

"Great," their flat response. So, at that point they were patronizing *and* blowing smoke up my shorts. I didn't care. I was doling out the hope!

I brought hope every day. My mercies were new every morning. Love and affection abounded. I introduced them to Monet and a *real* nut job, Van Gogh. They loved those guys. And loved their work. We met Abraham Lincoln and John Kennedy and figured out all the things they had in common with each other and with us. We took on the sixties, made commercials and a music video, and filled out applications for anything a person could think of. And somewhere in all that, we learned how to become better writers and I had a record number of students pass the writing proficiency exam. When someone would make a negative comment about themselves or another person, I would "STOP THE PRESSES!" That student would have to walk up to me at the front of the room, put out his hands, and ask for a little bit of hope in a loud, clear voice. In both English and Spanish or whatever else their native language might have been. Yep, in front of the entire class. Soon, they'd catch each *other* not having enough hope for themselves or one another and yell out, "Miss! Javier needs some hope!" Poor Javier would smack his forehead and come up to the front and hold out his hands in that infamous cup and ask in two different languages if he could please get some hope—which sprang eternal, hallelujah. Sometimes my kids would come to me in private and tell me about some of the things that threatened to steal their hope away, and eventually they would say, "I guess I just need a little hope."

Yeah. I knew that's why they were there. I had plenty to give. The more I gave, the more I had left in my heart to give. I gave away as much as I could. I couldn't possibly guess how much hope I gave away.

I was moved to see my kids—yes, you remember the cool ones whose eyes can roll back so far in their heads with disgust you'd think their sassy little pupils will never come back around—actually scooping hope into each others' hands on occasion while working together in groups or standing out in the hallway between classes when they didn't know I was watching. But there were days that I also had to endure watching some of my kids drop that hope. Or lose it. Or throw it back in my face. As time passed, though, the majority of them got used to how it felt in their hands. They started to like the feeling of carrying it around. They started carrying it around a little longer, a little more carefully. Some started to become protective of it and hold it closer to themselves. Some kids would literally scoop their hands up to their hearts when they got another little dose of hope and turn the key to lock it in tight.

I thought we were all making pretty good progress until one day, when all the magnet high schools came to our middle school to give out applications to study at their schools. I knew my kids had just as good a chance as any to go to magnet schools and specialize in any one of the various programs available: technology, performing arts, leadership training, teaching academies, international studies, aviation, medicine, architecture, engineering, computer animation, veterinary services, culinary hospitality, tourism, business, media arts, emergency and fire management services, computer forensics, or even learn how to become a CSI, just like on television (although that show came out years later).

And what did my kids do? They dropped their hope right on the floor and couldn't seem to find it. Oh, we had a little "Comin' to Jesus" meeting over *that*, believe me! They'd come so far! There was *no way* I was letting them begin to doubt and define themselves according to their old ways. I got out the Hope bucket! There was no more scooping out a little hope here and a little hope there. I literally stood on a chair, poured my imaginary (but very real) bucket out over their heads, and drenched the little Cretans! I slapped those magnet school applications onto those desks and made an assignment out of it!

I told them, "You have to fill these out for a grade! I will be looking over every single one! You'll get extra credit for filling out applications to more than one school. You'll get extra points for every application you fill out! By God, you're doing this!"

I ignored the groans.

"But here's the deal," I continued. "I will not turn them in for you. You decide whether or not you're going to turn these applications into these schools. I've given you all the hope you will ever need to do anything you will ever want with your lives. I keep giving you hope whenever you need it, whenever you ask for it. But you know what? You don't need me to do that for you anymore. You've got to come to the place where you can find hope by yourselves. Inside yourselves. And you've got to be able to do it in the next month because this school year is almost over. I'm not going to be able to go any further with you in this life. You've got to show me what you're taking with you. This is the biggest test you've had all year long, but you're not going to get a grade for it—at least not with me. It's pass/fail. I hope...that you have enough hope."

I don't know how many of my kids actually turned in their applications. But I did count the number of kids who were accepted into magnet schools, and I found out that 84% of my kids were accepted into different schools all around the city. Some of my students applied to all seven magnet schools and three were accepted by all seven. Many of my students had to decide which magnet school they would attend. They created something for themselves that they'd never had before—options. It hadn't occurred to them that they had the *option* of creating options! Some of my kids who were accepted to magnet schools opted not to attend a magnet school at all, but went instead across the street to the high school they were all zoned for. The following year at that particular high school, guess whose former student the freshman class president was? Mine. The freshman class vice president? Mine. The freshman class secretary? Mine. The freshman class treasurer? Mine. The freshman class historian? Mine. Three freshman class representatives? All mine. My students dominated that high school for the next four years.

I guess a little hope goes a long way.

As I walk out into America every day, I see people who are not so very different from how my kids were when I first met them. Yes, the darling little gangstas. It makes me think there's a little ghetto in all of us. There's a lot of beauty in the ghetto, after all, and I don't think people really consider that fact. There's a lot of beauty in this country and in people. I try to remember this when my own hope is diminished by one thing or another, and it seems there's always something to complain about and someone to blame. I can't lie. Little Miss Hope Scooper, and owner of a very large Hope bucket, gets discouraged when she considers the war, those displaced from natural disasters, or, hey, maybe just some guy who is flipping another guy off on the highway. We are diminished by our division and intolerance. We are manipulated and pitted against each other by forces we choose to ignore. We align ourselves, draw lines through the flag, and rally the supporters for this cause or that to see whether we'll stand on the stars or the stripes, trampling each other in the whole messy process. Hmm? My kids, too, were diminished by division and intolerance. Manipulated and pitted against each other by forces they chose to ignore. They aligned themselves, drew lines through their own colors, and rallied their supporters, trampling each other in the whole messy process. Yep! *Mismo!* The same.

We are all, accept it or not, the same.

We need some hope in this country. We need some hope in this world. And who would have guessed that a little Vegas baby, who quite literally had no chance of ever becoming anything in this world, would be doling out the hope every day?

Hope is a great thing. Let me tell you how great it feels when it comes back to bless you.

From the aforementioned group of students, my Rachel came back to see me two years after that class had gone on. She'd been one who had kept me up plenty a night, worried because of her gang affiliations and her propensity for hostility and violence. I almost didn't recognize her when she walked back into my classroom that day, because she was—this is the I best way I can describe it—calm. Her whole demeanor was different. She hugged me and told me that her grades were all A's and B's and one C. She hadn't been in trouble in over a year with the dean or with the police. She didn't have a boyfriend—she had a *job*, of all things. No, she wasn't running drugs or jacking cars. She worked at a shoe store in the mall. She was going to go to beauty school after graduation.

Graduation. She just expected it. It was a given in her mind.

Hope-overload surged in my heart, and I was elated. After all, this was why I did what I did for all the years that I did it. I held my baby girl in my arms and told her how proud of her I was. We visited for the rest of my break, and then the bell rang. My current little hope scoopers would be strolling through the door any second. She turned to go, and the tears I'd barely held back for the last fifteen minutes with her finally started to surface. I turned back to my desk as she turned to go so she wouldn't see.

From behind me she called out, "Miss?"

I turned to look at her one last time.

She scooped her hands out in front of her and said, "I still have my hope." And she was gone.

Such is my life now.

I sow seeds of hope, and every once in a while I get to reap the harvest. More often than not, though, I sow seeds that I do not reap. And I reap where I have not sown. God made and established this Daisy flower and poured His Rain of hope on me, faithfully and meticulously tending to me throughout the seasons of my life.

I've often wondered what keeps me on this path of Christianity when it is so often fraught with such inanity and incongruity. I stand here in the abyss between what the church should be and what the church sometimes *is* and share every criticism of all those who rail against organized religion. I get it. Believe me, I smack my forehead and look exasperatedly toward Heaven because I get it. But at the end of the day, how else can I explain my loyalty to Christ except to simply say, "Once I was blind, but now I can see," even though there are those who are also on this path of Christianity who doubt that very seriously.

Still, I am grateful, eternally, and I can't for the life of me abandon this journey no matter how much I struggle with it sometimes. I'm like Peter whom Jesus asked, "Are you going to leave me too?" who shrugged his shoulder and said, "Pssh…and where else am I gonna go?"

What keeps me pursuing God? I don't know. Perhaps the better question is, What keeps God pursuing me? For, as Francis Thompson wrote in *The Hound of Heaven*, "*I fled Him, down the nights and down the days; I fled Him, down the labyrinthine ways of my own mind; and in the midst of tears I hid from Him…*" The Hound of Heaven has chased me down and sunk His teeth so tenderly into my heart.

I am my Beloved's. And He is mine. His banner over me… is love.

Epilogue

An Adaptation of Francis Thompson's "The Hound of Heaven"
by Daisy Rain Martin

I fled from Him every night, every day.
I'd been running from Him my whole life.
I ran from Him in the twisted maze of my own mind.
Through tears, I hid from Him.
Wedged between the walls of hope, its narrowing pathway closing in
around me,
I hurled myself, impulsively and prematurely,
Down to the depths of despair, into an abyss of fear
From those strong feet that followed, followed after me.
Those feet didn't hurry or rush in their pursuit.
No acceleration in His pace.
His speed—composed, deliberate, serene.
Dignified. Majestic.
His feet—immediate in their proximity.
He was upon me. And His voice...
His voice was even closer than His footsteps,
His breath upon my cheek:
"All that you trust will betray you the way it betrayed Me."
"Nothing you find will shelter you. Nothing ever sheltered Me."
"Nothing you hold will make you happy; Hold Me."

Cornered, naked and afraid, I flinched beneath Your love's raised hand,
That strapping, terrifying hand suspended high above my head, and I
braced myself
For the blows that I knew were coming.
Faithfully, You struck the manacles that bound me

Time and time again.
Again
And again
And again
With cutting force.
My shackles, piece by piece, hammered away.
I was smitten to my knees.
Smitten.
(I was smitten by You—
Are you smitten with me?)
I am defenseless—utterly.
It's as if I'm waking from a dream.
I am stripped of my chains.
Nothing remains.
Nothing is left.
I am completely bare.
I cannot remain this vulnerable, this exposed.
Recklessly, in my impetuous distrust, with what little strength remains,
I rummage through the debris that was my life to find a covering for myself.
I try to pull it back upon me, grimed with smears..
There is nothing left.
It's rubble.
It's dust.
I stand in the middle of all these wasted years
And find my mangled youth beneath the heap.
Those days are gone, crackled and gone up in smoke
Like the beams of light that disappear in an instant
As the sun flashes on a stream.
And from this long pursuit
Comes again the clamor of His Voice,
This time pounding in my ears like the bursting sea:
"And is your world so damaged?
Shattered all around you like shards of glass?
Listen to Me! All that you long for escapes you simply
Because you struggle to escape from ME!
All that I 'took' from you?
Was NOT to bring you harm!

But only so that you would look for it in MY arms!
All that you had childishly mistaken as lost,
I have kept safe for you at home!
Rise! Take My hand! And Come!"
His words hold me fast.
I am suspended in them.
Did I confuse my ever-hovering shadow for darkness?
When really it was just the shade of His hand upon me?
Outstretched lovingly?
"Ah, fondest, blind and weak,
I am He whom you seek.
You drive Me to love
... to chase
... to keep."

≈ The End ≈

About the Author

Having overcome an abusive childhood, Daisy now lives a rich and peaceful life with her husband, Sean-Martin, and son, Geoff, writing in the Northwest. The juxtaposition that is Daisy Rain Martin stems from being born and raised in a show business family in the bright lights of Las Vegas and simultaneously attempting to navigate her way out of an abusive, ultra-conservative, religious home. She answers the question so many ask: If I were to get in touch with my spiritual side and embark on a path with God, would I have to look like all those... church people? Her fervent wish is that her writing will help others facing similar trials in life find hope and know that they are not alone.

CPSIA information can be obtained at www.ICGtesting.com
Printed in the USA
BVOW010603150612

292766BV00003B/3/P